Indiana NEGRO REGISTER

1852–1865

Compiled by

Coy D. Robbins

HERITAGE BOOKS
2012

HERITAGE BOOKS
AN IMPRINT OF HERITAGE BOOKS, INC.

Books, CDs, and more—Worldwide

For our listing of thousands of titles see our website
at
www.HeritageBooks.com

Published 2012 by
HERITAGE BOOKS, INC.
Publishing Division
100 Railroad Ave. #104
Westminster, Maryland 21157

Copyright © 1994 Coy D. Robbins

Other Heritage Books by the author:
Forgotten Hoosiers: African Heritage in Orange County, Indiana
Indiana Negro Register, 1852–1865
Reclaiming African Heritage at Salem, Indiana
CD: Indiana African Heritage

All rights reserved. No part of this book may be reproduced or transmitted in any form or by any means, electronic or mechanical, including photocopying, recording or by any information storage and retrieval system without written permission from the author, except for the inclusion of brief quotations in a review.

International Standard Book Numbers
Paperbound: 978-1-55613-940-6
Clothbound: 978-0-7884-9198-6

CONTENTS

INTRODUCTION v-xv

MAP OF LOCATIONS xvi

BARTHOLOMEW COUNTY 1

FLOYD COUNTY 9

FRANKLIN COUNTY 47

GIBSON COUNTY 50

HARRISON COUNTY 67

HENDRICKS COUNTY 75

JACKSON COUNTY 77

JEFFERSON COUNTY 88

JENNINGS COUNTY 107

KNOX COUNTY 117

MARTIN COUNTY 149

OHIO COUNTY 151

ORANGE COUNTY 153

SWITZERLAND COUNTY 161

WASHINGTON COUNTY 163

NAMES INDEX 171

INTRODUCTION

This study involves a compilation of fifteen "Registers of Negroes and Mulattoes" maintained by the Clerk of County Circuit Courts between 1852 and 1865. These registers were mandated by a state law, "An Act to enforce the thirteenth article of the constitution approved in 1852."

Important public documents today, they are significant contributions to the history of African Americans in Indiana and also contain a wealth of genealogical information. Over two thousand registrants are identified as free people of color, Hoosier citizens, and residents of fifteen different counties located primarily in the southern region of the state. These registers provide incontrovertible evidence that Africans, as well as Euramericans, dwelled here throughout the antebellum era.

Background

Whites never wanted persons of African descent in Indiana. At best, they were merely tolerated in the subservient role, either as slaves and indentured servants or as "disabled citizens" having few human rights.

For those of African ancestry who did establish homes in Indiana, it became a day-by-day existence. They lived constantly on the edge of life, never knowing when yesterday's peace might be suddenly broken by whites who would threatened them with physical harm, imprisonment, banishment or death for just being "uppity" in their presence.

From the time the United States of America was created, Africans were declared as "non-citizens." Even those with a history of free ancestors extending over several generations on this continent were excluded from participating in the new democratic government "for all the people." Consequently, Africans became the ghostly Americans on the national, territorial, and state levels, invisible except when they were needed to protect the Nation. As a minority, they were forced to yield to the rule of the majority, no matter how unjust the laws.

Indiana, upon achieving statehood in 1816, declared the guiding principles of its newly formed society as:

> ...all men are born equally free and independent, and have certain natural, inherent, and inalienable rights; among which are the enjoying and defending life and liberty, and of acquiring, possessing, and protecting property, and pursuing and obtaining happiness and safety...[Art. I].[1]

However, at the same time, the founding fathers made certain that some citizens were excluded by putting several "Black Laws" into the first constitution:

> (1) Every white male citizen of the United States, of the age of twenty-one years, who has resided in the State, one year immediately preceeding such election, shall be entitled to vote in the County where he resides [Art. VI].

> (2) The Militia of the State of Indiana shall consist of all free able bodied male persons, Negroes, Mulattoes and Indians excepted [Art. VII].

> (3) There shall be neither slavery nor involuntary servitude in this state, otherwise than for the punishment of crimes, whereof the party shall have been duly convicted [Art. XI:7].

Over the next thirty-four years, Hoosiers busied themselves, vanquishing the Native Americans, overcoming the rugged and harsh aspects of pioneering, supporting an agriculture economy, expanding the white population with rapid increases of immigrants directly from Europe, and organizing all but one of the ninety-two counties as they exist today.

In October, 1850, a constitutional convention assembled in Indianapolis. It resulted from mounting agitation over the past five years for changes in the first constitution. Citizens complained of the legislature's irresponsibility as evidenced by the corruption, inefficiency, and the high public debt which followed the failure of the 1836 internal (transportation) improvements system. Other major proposed revisions included extending suffrage to foreigners who had declared their intention to become citizens and had met a minimum residence requirement, the establishment of a statewide system of common schools, the introduction of free banking, and objections to any further African immigration into the state.[2]

Racial Exclusion

White male delegates who advocated keeping all Negroes out of the state gave speeches covering the gamut of arguments in defense of racial supremacy. It was emphasized repeatedly during debates that the white race must take immediate action to preserve itself. One supporter declared: "We ought not to have in our midst a race, daily increasing, who must, of necessity, remain disenfranchised; a class of people to be taxed, without being represented; on whom burdens are imposed, and who have no voice in deciding what these burdens shall be. . ." [Robert Dale Owen, Posey Co.][3]

Some spoke fervently of the need for Indiana to protect itself against any flood of Black immigration as the Southern states enacted more and more stringent laws regarding free Negroes and emancipated slaves. They cited the recent legislation in neighboring states trying to cope with the same concerns. Illinois held a constitutional convention in 1847 and mandated the state to legislate a law banning Negroes from coming into the state. Ohio was considering passage of a similar statue. What alarmed many Hoosiers, however, was knowledge that Kentucky recently passed legislation making it a felony subject to five years in the penitentiary for any free Negro to come into the state or for any emancipated slave to remain in Kentucky. Advocates for exclusion believed that "this worthless and degraded population" would soon inundate Indiana.[4]

Introduction

One delegate succinctly summarized the alternatives as he saw them on the issue of the two races in Indiana: "It appears to me, sir, that there are but three courses left open for the people of Indiana to pursue with regard to the negro population of the State. The first is, amalgamation--aye, sir, I repeat it, amalgamation. The second is, to give up the State to the possession and rule of the black population. The third is, to prohibit the immigration of negroes to the State, to give no encouragement to those that are here that they can ever enjoy equal social or political privileges, and keep the State for ourselves and our descendants. Mr. President, I do not hesitate to say that I am for the latter course as a choice of the three. . ." [James G. Read, Clark Co.][5]

Another speaker warned that the anticipated racial influx would create bitterness and tension: "I would say--and I say it in all sincerity, and without any hard feelings toward them--that it would be better to kill them off at once, if there is no other way to get rid of them. We have not come to that point yet with the blacks, but we know how the Puritans did with the Indians, who were infinitely more magnanimous and less impudent than this colored race. . ." [James Rariden, Wayne Co.][6]

Several delegates denounced the proposals for Negro exclusion and colonization. Their arguments, nonetheless, were unavailing and the convention adopted an article barring Negroes from the state and the voluntary colonization of its colored citizens in Africa. As incorporated into the 1850 Constitution, Article XIII, the primary provision was that "No negro or mulatto shall come into or settle in the State, after the adoption of this Constitution."

On August 4, 1851 the article was submitted to the electors (only white male citizens) as a separate issue from the rest of the Constitution. It was ratified by a larger vote than that given to the Constitution itself [113,230 for Constitution; 113,828 for Negro Exclusion]. The majority of voters in only four counties cast their ballots against Negro exclusion: Elkhart, Lagrange, Randolph and Steuben. Of these, only Randolph County had a sizeable population of persons of color.

By this democratic feat African Americans became the only racial or ethnic minority ever prohibited to enter or settle in the state. Thirty years later and long after the Civil War ended Indiana voters finally repealed this article in a special election held on March 14, 1881.[7]

Registers Decreed

At the first session of the General Assembly after adoption of the new Constitution the legislature passed a statute to enforce Article XIII.[8] As approved on June 18, 1852, the regulations outlawed Negroes from coming into the state, instructed the county clerks to notify all Negroes who were residents before November 1, 1851 to register, ordered the creation of the register of negroes and mulattoes, and empowered the clerks to subpoena witnesses and to issue certificates attesting to the registration of legal residents.

In addition, the law voided all contracts made with Negroes who came into the state after that date, and persons who employed Negroes violating the act could be penalized with fines between ten and five hundred dollars. Negro offenders could receive the same penalties.[9]

This enforcement edict remained in effect until the Civil War ended and the 13th, 14th and 15th amendments were ratified. By that time its stipulations were in conflict with those of the United

Introduction

States Constitution. A legislative act repealing the 1852 law was approved on February 22, 1867.[10] The revocation, however, never altered Article XIII in the 1852 constitution.

Earlier Negro Registers in Indiana

Requiring persons of African ancestry to be accounted for or cataloged as property was a fairly common practice in early America. So it is not surprising to discover that "Negro Registers" were used in Indiana before 1852.

More accurately, these earlier ones were called "Registers of Slaves or Indentured Servants" and were created prior to statehood by the Indiana Territorial government. Their need resulted from a measure entitled "An Act concerning the Introduction of Negroes and Mulattoes into This Territory" passed in 1805. Challenging the anti-slavery provisions of the 1787 Northwest Ordinance, legislators authorized any person owning or purchasing slaves outside the Territory to bring them into Indiana and to bind them for service over an extended period.

This new system of "involuntary servitude" was equivalent to slavery. If the slaves were over fifteen years of age, the owner or possessor could make a contract with them for any term of service. Male slaves under fifteen years had to serve until the age of thirty-five, and females until age thirty-two years. All children born to indentured servants were also slaves and remained so until they reached the age of thirty for males, or twenty-eight for females.[11]

While the territorial government repealed this law in 1810, it still failed to end completely the practice of bringing Africans into the state and binding them to long terms of service. Slaves continued to be counted during the federal population censuses in Indiana until 1840 when there were only three listed in the state: a girl in Putnam County, and a man and a girl in Rush County.[12]

The contracts of indentured servants had to be recorded with the county clerk within thirty days after the arrival of the slave within the Territory. Two surviving books of these indentures are in southern Indiana. The Knox County "Register of Negro Slaves, 1805-07" holds indentures for fifty persons, and the Clark County "Register of Negroes, 1805-10" contains documents for a total of thirty-six persons. Listings in both books indicate that the largest number of slaves came from Kentucky (60 in all), and others were from South Carolina, Tennessee, Virginia, North Carolina, Georgia, and Maryland.[13]

These slave lists are the only "Negro Registers" many Hoosiers ever knew to exist in Indiana.

Negro Registers 1853-1865

Unlike the earlier ones intended for use with slaves, these registers mandated by the 1852 law were planned for Indiana citizens who happened to be of African ancestry. No one seems to know today how many of the registers were created nor how many are still available for research purposes. Every county clerk was required to establish a register, therefore it is reasonable to presume that a sizeable number of them, perhaps more than fifty, once existed.

What follows in this publication is a compilation of the "Registers of Negroes and Mulattoes"

Introduction

located to date. Entries in the originals books were all in handscript, and several presented some deciphering difficulties. The bound books had cloth covers in varying shades of blue fading to gray with brown leather trim on the spine and right-hand corners. Overall dimensions were approximately fifteen inches in length and ten and one-half inches wide.

Except in one book, all pages were printed in either of two distinctive styles and apparently designed by commercial print shops. One set of registers for five counties (Bartholomew, Knox, Martin, Switzerland, and Washington) had pale blue colored pages containing two printed certificates with blank spaces. The back section consisted of lined pages with alphabetical tags for indexing. These certificates read:

STATE OF INDIANA,..............COUNTY S. S.

I, ... Clerk of the .... Circuit Court, within and for the county of .... aforesaid, hereby certify that ...., a...............................has been duly Registered in my office, in pursuance of an "Act entitled an act to enforce the 13th Article of the Constitution, approved June 18th, 1852; that he is ....years of age, that he is..that he was born in..and that he now resides in ....county, Indiana..................and that the said ....was a resident of the State of Indiana prior to the first day of November, A. D., 1851, and that the same was proven by examination under oath of...

In Witness of which, I hereunto affix the seal of said Court, and subscribe

{SEAL}   my name, at........................this...................

                day of............................A. D., 185.....

[written signature placed at bottom]

A second set of registers for nine counties (Franklin, Gibson, Harrison, Hendricks, Jackson, Jefferson, Jennings, Ohio and Washington) applied a different format design. Across the top of two sheets was a printed heading, "Register of Negroes and Mulattoes." Each double-page held six columns with the following printed headers: (1) Name, (2) Age, (3) Description, (4) Place of Birth, (5) Place of Residence, and (6) Names of Witnesses. Blank pages with alphabetical tags for indexing were placed in the back section. This second page design turned out to be the most practical one

Introduction

for reproducing the registration entries in this compilation.

Handwritten notes which appeared to be the originals were found inside the register for Washington County. They contained hastily scribbled data, and probably written while the person talked with registrants. Later the notes were transcribed at leisure into the official book. Undoubtedly, a similar routine was followed by clerks in other offices using several staff members and would account for possible duplicating errors in the official registers.

According to the enforcing act each registrant was to receive a copy of a certifying document confirming the legal residence status. Nothing has yet been located to confirm that this procedure was ever followed. Perhaps the pages using the certificate format style described above were planned to serve this purpose, but neither the forms nor the actual registers held any notations to the effect that the registrant obtained a copy of the filled-in certificate.

Floyd County did not use a register with pre-printed pages. Instead, the book is of the standard ledger-type volume with lined blank pages ruled by hand into six columns and the same headers for the prescribed data to be collected. On the initial pages all columns were placed on a single page, but soon they were expanded across double-pages. There was no indexing of entries.

Other counties in addition to these already identified are known to have kept Negro Registers. This information comes from some published inventories of Indiana county archives completed by the Works Progress Administration (W.P.A.) personnel in the 1930s. Examination of several volumes reveals that at least thirteen more counties had a "negro register" listed in their inventories.[14] These were: (1) Allen County (Fort Wayne), (2) Clay County (Brazil), (3) Delaware County (Muncie), (4) Fulton County (Rochester), (5) Jay County (Portland), (6) Marshall County (Plymouth), (7) Monroe County (Bloomington), (8) Morgan County (Martinsville), (9) Posey County (Mount Vernon), (10) Shelby County (Shelbyville), (11) Tippecanoe County (Lafayette), (12) Warrick County (Boonville), and (13) Wells County (Bluffton). So far not one of these registers has been located.[15]

Three more registers were mentioned in Indiana histories but they also are missing today. One was called a "Negro Registry" by Ebenezer Tucker in his 1882 history of Randolph County. He pointed out that although there were two large "colored settlements" (Cabin Creek and Greenville) in the county, only twelve persons ever registered: one in 1853, and eleven as a group with the Peelle surname. The group included the elderly "Cesar Peelle," of near Spartansburg, Indiana who died in 1880.[16] Emma Lou Thornbrough cited the other two registers in her 1957 publication, *The Negro in Indiana* (page 70) which mentioned one for Clark County (Jeffersonville) and another for Marion County (Indianapolis).

In summary, the current research shows that at least thirty-one counties kept a Negro Register for varying periods between 1852 and 1865. This publication contains fifteen books, the 1930s WPA inventories lists thirteen more books which are still missing, and historical writers mentioned three books not yet located today (see map on page xii). Persons aware of the whereabouts of any Negro Registers not printed in this compilation are requested to notify me or local public officials, librarians, archivists, historical and genealogical societies.

Introduction

Listed below are the locations for fifteen Negro Registers. Coding: *ISL* = Indiana State Library, 140 North Senate Avenue, Indianapolis, IN 46204. *ISA* = Indiana State Archives, Commission on Public Records, Room 117, State Library Building, 140 North Senate Avenue, Indianapolis, IN 46204.

1. Bartholomew County. Original in courthouse. On microfilm and in *The Hoosier Genealogist*, 17-2, June 1977. *ISL*
2. Floyd County. Original in courthouse. On microfilm in the New Albany-Floyd County Public Library and Church of the Latter Day Saints, Salt Lake City, Utah.
3. Franklin County. Original in *ISA*. On microfilm and in *The Hoosier Genealogist*, 17-2, June 1977.
4. Gibson County. Original in courthouse, county commissioner. Microcopy in Indiana Room, Princeton Public Library.
5. Harrison County. Original in courthouse.
6. Hendricks County. Location of original unknown. Contents published in the *History of Hendricks County*, 1885, pp. 292-3.
7. Jackson County. Original in courthouse. On microfilm. *ISL*
8. Jefferson County. Original in courthouse. On microfilm. *ISL*
9. Jennings County. Original in courthouse. Published in *The Hoosier Genealogist*, 17-2, June 1977. *ISL*
10. Knox County. Original in Knox County Records Library, Vincennes.
11. Martin County. On microfilm. ISL
12. Ohio County. Original in Indiana State Archives. *ISA*
13. Orange County. Original in courthouse. On microfilm. Contents published in *The Journal of Afro-American Historical and Genealogical Society*, 7-2, (1986).
14. Switzerland County. Original in Indiana State Archives. *ISA*
15. Washington County. Original in Washington County Historical Society Library, Salem.

Enrollment Period

Although not required by the 1852 law, many county clerks included the date of registration in their registers. Often the date was inserted in the first left-hand column above or below the name, or in the space of the far right-hand column on the opposite page reserved for the names of witnesses. This recorded date was useful to the clerk when tabulating the daily office activities or compiling periodic reports for the County Commissioners.

For research purposes these recorded dates of registrations show the overall period of enrollments in each county except Gibson which did not provide any dates. The earliest date of registration was in Jennings County on April 25, 1853. The last date of registration date was in Floyd County on February 20, 1865, just weeks before the Confederate Army surrendered and President Abraham Lincoln was assassinated. Most registers began in the spring and summer of 1853 (12), although the first entry in Ohio County came in 1854 and the first dated registration for Harrison County was in 1857. Registers for Floyd, Franklin and Harrison contained several undated entries at the beginning of their books.

Introduction

Calculations based upon these registration dates show that the average enrollmment period for these fourteen counties lasted almost five years, or roughly between the years of 1853 and 1858.

Number of Registrations

The fifteen counties together had a total of 2,138 registrations. The largest number was in Floyd County (New Albany), situated on the Ohio River across from Louisville, Kentucky, and the three counties of Hendricks, Martin, and Switzerland had the smallest registrations. Total number by counties was: (1) Bartholomew 57, (2) Floyd 668, (3) Franklin 27, (4) Gibson 238, (5) Harrison 60, (6) Hendricks 14, (7) Jackson 123, (8) Jefferson 165, (9) Jennings 100, (10) Knox 412, (11) Martin 19, (12) Ohio 23, (13) Orange 137, (14) Switzerland 17, and (15) Washington 78.

Duplicate registrations which might have resulted when persons enrolled in more than one county register were ignored. Such practice was possible because once citizens established themselves as legal residents of Indiana within the provisions of the 1852 law they were then free to change residences at will. Individuals and families who registered initially in adjoining counties such as Clark, Floyd and Harrison probably shifted their residences often in search of gainful employment.

Percentage of Population Registered

It is difficult to say with certainty what percent of the Africans living in the state actually enrolled in the 1852 registers. A reliable answer is not possible although it would seem reasonable today to assume that many did not comply with the law. First, the statute failed to specify the legal cut-off date for registration, and second, it contained no penalties for those legal residents who remained in the state but did not register.

Population data for Indiana counties was never compiled annually as the cost would far exceed their usefulness. Nevertheless, it is possible to obtain some rough percentages by comparing the number of African Americans counted in the 1850 decennial U. S. population census with the total number who enrolled in the county Negro Registers found so far. Percentages from these calculations were: (1) Bartholomew 70%, (2) Floyd 114%, (3) Franklin 13%, (4) Gibson 107%, (5) Harrison 66%, (6) Hendricks 39%, (7) Jackson 57%, (8) Jefferson 29%, (9) Jennings 31%, (10) Knox 78%, (11) Martin 20%, (12) Ohio 62%, (13) Orange 55%, (14) Switzerland 26%, and (15) Washington 31%.[17]

In other words it might be estimated that overall about sixty percent of the number of African Americans enumerated in the 1850 census were enrolled in these Negro Registers. The range was from only 13% in Franklin County to 78% in Knox County. For two counties, Floyd and Gibson, there were actually more registrants than there were living in the counties during the 1850 census.

Indiana's exclusion law was just one of several historical events in the 1850s which impacted gravely upon the daily lives of African Americans. Intersectional strife mounted nationally over the slavery issue. Waves of newly arrived European immigrants augumented the white population. And the hostility of whites toward racial minorities intensified as they competed for farm land and available jobs.

Introduction

A devastating blow came when the United States Congress passed the 1850 Fugitive Slave Act. Enacted while the Indiana delegates were considering constitutional changes, the law had provisions which severely curbed the liberty of those African Americans not enslaved. This single piece of legislation stripped away at once any legal protections African citizens had under state laws to prevent them from being kidnapped and sold into slavery. As a result, those free Americans of color who were financially able fled immediately for safety in Canada.[18]

Definition of Racial Terms

Neither the new Indiana Constitution nor the 1852 enforcing legislation for the 13th Article defined those citizens proclaimed as "negroes and mulattoes." The policy-makers may have thought that being more explicit was redundant since the public understood exactly the meaning of these racial terms. After all, Euramericans created, administered and enforced the laws in this country based entirely upon the doctrine of racial supremacy: they and those who shared their culture and skin coloring were the chosen people. Pursuant to this precept, persons of African black ancestry were perceived as being less than human and denigrated as "blacks," "Negroes," or "niggers." In the South during slavery and later with Jim Crow segregation these concepts became translated into the "one-drop rule," meaning that a Negro was any person with a single drop of "African blood."[19]

With persons of mixed blood, however, the commonly held beliefs varied a bit. Originally, the term "mulatto" was used to designate the offspring of a "pure African negro" and a "pure white." In time, the term came to include the children of unions between whites and so-called "mixed Negroes." For example, both Booker T. Washington and Frederick Douglass having African and white parents were called mulattoes.

For a time the term "colored" was used to refer only to mulattoes, especially those of lighter complexions. Later it became a more socially acceptable term for darker Negroes, including unmixed Blacks. With widespread racial mixture, "Negro" came to mean any slave or descendant of a slave, no matter how much mixed. Eventually in the United States, the terms mulatto, colored, Negro, Black, and African American all came to mean people with any known black African ancestry.

In March, 1852 the Indiana law regulating marriages was updated to conform with the new constitutional changes. The revised version repeated the provisions from earlier legislation which voided marriages "when one of the parties is a white person, and the other possessed of one-eighth or more of negro blood."[20] Thus, as was done in so many states, Indiana continued to classify legally as a "Negro" any person who had seven white (European) grandparents but <u>one</u> of African heritage. This law remained on the books until 1965!

Introduction

NOTES

1. Charles Kettleborough, *Constitution Making in Indiana*, 1916, (Reprint, Indianapolis: Indiana Historical Bureau, 1975), II, 84-125.

2. John D. Barnhart and Donald F. Carmony, *Indiana: From Frontier to Industrial Commonwealth*, 1954 (Reprint, Indianapolis: Indiana Historical Bureau, 1979), II, 88-90.
   By 1850 there were 11,262 free colored persons living in the state, less than one percent of its total population of 988,416. They resided in all but two of the existing counties, with the largest concentrations in Wane, Vigo, Randolph, Marion, Clark, Floyd, Jefferson, and Knox Counties.

3. *Report of the Debates and Proceedings of the Convention for the Revision of the Constitution of the State of Indiana, 1850*, H. Fowler, Reporter (Indianapolis: A. H. Brown, Printer to the Convention, 1850), 231.

4. Emma L. Thornbrough, *The Negro in Indiana Before 1900*, (Indianapolis: Indiana Historical Bureau, 1957), 64.

5. *Report of the Debates and Proceedings. . .*, 247.

6. Ibid., p. 574.

7. Amendents to repeal Article XIII were proposed in the legislature and defeated in 1855, 1865, 1873-75, and 1877. Finally in 1879, both the House and Senate passed the amendment which was submitted to the voters on April 5, 1880. It failed to have a majority of votes cast. After the State Supreme Court decided the amendment was neither adopted or rejected, it was resubmitted to the voters at special election on March 14, 1881, received the necessary majority, and declared in force by proclamation on March 24, 1881. Charles Kettleborough, *Constitution Making in Indiana*, III:385-386.

8. The colonization aspect of Article XIII was spelled out by the legislature in "An Act providing for the colonization of Negroes and Mulattoes and their descendants. . ." approved April 28, 1852. *Revised Statues of Indiana* (Indianapolis: J. P. Chapman, State Printer, 1852), Vol. I, 222-3.

9. *Revised Statutes of Indiana 1852*, 1:375-76.

AN ACT to enforce the 13th Article of the Constitution.
[*Approved June 18, 1852*]

Section 1. Be it enacted by the General Assembly of the State of "Indiana, That it shall not be lawful for any negro or mulatto to come into, settle in, or become an inhabitant of the State.

Sec. 2. The clerk of the several circuit courts in this State shall (give) notice, by publication in the newspaper in their respective counties having the greatest circulation, and if no newspaper be published therein, then by printed hand-bills posted up in three of the most public places in each township of each county, requiring all negroes and mulattoes who were inhabitants of the State prior to the first day of November, A. D. 1851; and entitled to reside therein, to appear before him for registry.

Sec. 3. It shall be the duty of each clerk of the said circuit courts to provide a suitable book, to be called the register of negroes and mulattoes, on which he shall record the name, age, description, place of birth and residence of each and every negro mulatto who may present himself or herself before him for the purpose of being registered, and also, the names of the witnesses by whom the right to such negro or mulatto to reside in the State of Indiana shall have been proven.

Sec. 4. The clerk of the said circuit court, when any negro or mulatto shall come before him for the purpose of being registered, shall have the power to cause to come before him such witnesses as may be necessary to prove the right of inhabitation of such negro or mulatto, by process of subpeona, and shall proceed to hear and determine the right of such negro or mulatto.

Sec. 5. When the right of any such negro or mulatto shall have been proven to the satisfaction of such clerk, he shall register the said negro or mulatto in his register of negroes and mulattoes, and shall also issue to such negro or mulatto a certificate, under the seal of the said court, and attested by such clerk, setting forth the facts contained in the register; which certificate shall be conclusive evidence of the facts therein stated in all prosecution against the employers of negroes and mulattoes, unless it is shown that said employer had notice that the same was obtained by fraud or other undue means, or was not genuine, and the same shall be *prima facie* evidence only in all other cases, and shall be issued to such negro or mulatto without charge.

Sec. 6. All contracts made with negroes or mulattoes who shall have come into the State of Indiana subsequent to the first day of November, A. D. 1851, are hereby null and void.

Sec. 7. Any person who shall employ a negro or mulatto who shall have come into the State of Indiana subsequent to the thirty-first day of October, in the year one thousand eight hundred and fifty-one, or shall hereafter come into the said State, or who encourage such negro or mulatto to remain in the State shall be fined in any sum not less than ten dollars nor more than five hundred dollars.

Sec. 8. This act shall apply only to contracts made with negroes and mulattoes subsequent to the passage of this act.

Sec. 9. Any negro or mulatto who shall come into or settle in this State contrary to, and in violation of the provisions of the constitution, and of the first section of this act, shall be fined in any sum not less than ten, nor more than five hundred dollars.

10. *Indiana Acts, 1867*, chap. 128, sec. 1; p. 360.

Introduction

11. Francis S. Philbrick (ed.), *The Laws of Indiana Territory, 1801-1809* (Illinois Historical Collections, Vol., 21, Springfield, 1930. Reprinted by Indiana Historical Bureau, 1931), 136-39.

12. Jacob P. Dunn, *Indiana: A Redemption from Slavery* (American Commonwealth Series, revised ed., Boston, 1905), 441.

13. These registers have been microfilmed and are located in the Indiana State Library. They are summarized in Emma Lou Thornbrough, *The Negro in Indiana*, 10-13. The one for Knox County was published in *The Hoosier Genealogist*, Vol. 17, #3, September, 1977, and by June Barekman, *Registers of Negro Slaves & Masters for 1805-1807 Knox County: Indiana Territory* (Chicago: Barackman Family Association, 1970).

14. *Inventory of the County Archives of Indiana*, published 1939-1942 for selected counties by The Historical Records Survey, Indianapolis. Not every county's inventory was published, and the collection which I checked in the Monroe County Public Library, Bloomington, Indiana contained sixteen volumes.

Comments to this effect, "formerly the clerk kept a negro register" were found in following publications: No. 2 Allen County (Fort Wayne), p. 144; No. 11 Clay County (Brazil), p. 131; No. 18 Delaware County (Muncie), 145; No. 25 Fulton County (Rochester), p. 165; No. 38 Jay County (Portland); No. 50 Marshall County (Plymouth), p. 162; No. 53 Monroe County (Bloomington), p. 155; No. 55 Morgan County (Martinsville), p. 151; No. 65 Posey County (Mount Vernon), p. 148; No. 73 Shelby County (Shelbyville), p. 145; No. 79 Tippecanoe County (Lafayette), p. 167; No. 87 Warrick County (Boonville), p. 146; and No. 90 Wells County (Bluffton), p. 160.

No listing of a Negro Register was found in No. 28 Greene County (Bloomfield), No. 80 Tipton County (Tipton) and No. 82 Vanderburgh County (Evansville).

15. Efforts to locate these registers over the past ten years have included: checking in person with the county clerk, recorder, or commissioners at the courthouse; collections in local libraries, historical and/or genealogical society; Indiana State Archives; Indiana State Library; Allen County Public Library; Indiana Historical Society Library and files in the Black History Project.

16. Ebenezer Tucker, *History of Randolph County, Indiana* (Chicago: A. L. Kingman, 1882), 198.

17. The 1850 U. S. Population data for African Americans enumerated in the Indiana counties under consideration were: (1) Bartholomew 82, (2) Floyd 574, (3) Franklin 209, (4) Gibson 217, (5) Harrison 91, (6) Hendricks 36, (7) Jackson 214, (8) Jefferson 568, (9) Jennings 323, (10) Knox 530, (11) Martin 96, (12) Ohio 37, (13) Orange 251, (14) Switzerland 66, (15) Washington 252, Total: 3,546.

18. Fred Landon, "Negro Migration to Canada after 1850," in *Journal of Negro History*, 5 (1920), 22-36. Also, Charles H. Money, "The Fugitive Slave Law of 1850 in Indiana," in *Indiana Magazine of History*, 17 (1921), 159-98 and 257-297.

19. A recent excellent discussion of racial terms by F. James Davis, *Who is Black? One Nation's Definition* (University Park, PA.: The Pennsylvania State University Press, 1991). The clasic study on this subject is Edward B. Reuter, *Race Mixture: Studies in Intermarriage and Miscengenation*, (New York: Whittlesey House, 1931; reprint Negro Universities Press, 1969), especially the essay, "Racial Amalgamation in the United States," 27-57.

20. *Revised Statutes of Indiana* (1852), Chap. 67, sec. 2 (2), 361.

LOCATION OF NEGRO REGISTERS 1852-1865

(X) LOCATED

(O) MISSING

REGISTER OF NEGROES AND MULATTOES IN BARTHOLOMEW COUNTY, INDIANA

Names	Age	Description	Place of Birth	Residence	Names of Witnesses	Date Registered
Oxendine, Daniel	37	Mulatto man, five feet nine and a half inches high, rather rawboned, medium size; rather light complexion; good teeth, two out; has a small moleon the right side of upper lip.	Robeson Co, NC	Bartholomew Co	John A. Abbott Randolph Griffith	19 Aug 1853
Jones, William Riley	40	Mulatto man (dark) five feet three inches and a half high; has a scar about 3/4 inch long on the right hand; is rather dark mulatto; rather square built and has round features.	Robeson Co, NC	Bartholomew Co	George B. Gaines a respectable citizen of said County.	22 Aug 1853
Jones, Lucy Ann	40	Mulatto woman, five feet two inches high; her right arm is very much crooked having been broken; rather a dark mulatto; is married & has eight children.	Halifax Co, VA	Bartholomew Co	George B. Gaines a white citizen of said County.	22 Aug 1853
Jones, Irvin	14	Black boy, four feet 11 1/2 inches high and growing; rather a light negro; no scars or marks perceiveable, is son of William Riley Jones Esquire.	Robeson Co, NC	Bartholomew Co	George A. Gaines a respectable citizen of said County.	22 Aug 1853
Jones, Enoch	13	Black boy, four feet 9 1/2 inches high; rather a light negro; has a small scar 1/2 inch long on the back of his left hand near the wrist; is a son of Wm Riley Jones Esquire.	Robeson Co, NC	Bartholomew Co	George A. Gaines a respectable citizen of said County.	22 Aug 1853

Bartholomew County, Indiana

Jones, Thomas	9	Black boy three feet eleven inches high, is rather light negro and seems to be growing; is the son of William Riley Jones Esquire.	Richmond Co, NC	Bartholomew Co	George B. Gaines, a citizen of said County.	22 Aug 1853
Jones, Oliver	7	Black boy, 3 feet and a half inches high but will get higher fast; is rather light negro; nothing remarkable about him in the way of scars. He is son of Wm R Jones.	Richmond Co, NC	Bartholomew Co	George B. Gaines, a citizen of said County.	22 Aug 1853
Jones, Lucinda	5	Black girl, lively and of a light complexion; has a scar on the right side of her neck occasioned by a burn; is daughter of William Riley Jones Esq.	Scott Co, VA	Bartholomew Co	George B. Gaines, a citizen of said County.	22 Aug 1853
Jones, Mary H.	3	Black girl, a plump little darkie, light complexion, without spot or blemish in the way of a scars, etc.; daughter of William Riley Jones Esquire.	Bartholomew Co, IN	Bartholomew Co	George B. Gaines, a citizen of said County.	22 Aug 1853
Jones, Wm. R. Jr.	1	Black boy, plump little nigger baby and too[?] fair to "go through if the breechin'[?] don't break"--no marks or brands perceivable; is a son of Wm R. Jones Sen.	Bartholomew Co, IN	Bartholomew Co	George B. Gaines, a citizen of said County.	22 Aug 1853
Jones, Willis	12	Light negro boy, now four feet and a half high and growing; no particular marks or scars; son of William Riley Jones.	Robeson Co, NC	Bartholomew Co	Geo. B. Gaines, a citizen of said County.	23 Aug 1853

Bartholomew County, Indiana

Name		Description	Origin	County	Witness	Date
Galbraith, Edmund	70	Negro man, 5 feet 8 inches high; has a scar about 2 inches long, caused by a burn on his left breast; is a very peaceable, inoffensive and respectable man.	South Carolina	Bartholomew Co	James Hobbs, and I knew it to be a fact bu myself.	1 Sep 1853
Galbreath, Dianah	50	Black negro woman, 5 feet high; has a small white scar on her left foot; is a very peaceable, inoffensive and respectable woman; is the wife of Edmund Galbraith.	Perquimans Co NC	Bartholomew Co	James Hobbs, and I knew it to be a fact myself.	1 Sep 1853
Turman, Clarissa	53	Negro woman, five feet four inches high, is the wife of Henry Turman.	Clark Co, IN	Bartholomew Co	A. T. Greeno, who says he knew said Clarissa for 35 yrs age up to this time.	12 Sep 1853
Hill, Abraham	53-54	Negro man, 5 ft 7 ins high; has no marks or brands perceivable etc except a very large mouth, laughs remarkably loud when he's tickled; is free soilish in his politics.	Washington Co, VA	Bartholomew Co	James Hobbs, a citizen of said County.	16 Sep 1853
Turman, Harry	53	Mulatto man, 5 feet 7 ins high; has a scar on the left side of his upper lip about an inch long, also a scar on the left part of his forehead of a half circular form.	Rockingham Co, VA	Bartholomew Co	James Hobbs, a citizen of said County.	17 Sep 1853
Blanks, John	54	Mulatto man, 6 feet high; has no hair on the top of his head where hair ought to grow; left wrist is crooked; his right bit toe has been wounded with an ax.	Robeson Co, NC	Bartholomew Co	Edward A. Herod, a citizen of said County.	21 Sep 1853

Bartholomew County, Indiana

Blanks, Christy Ann	18	Mulatto woman, 5 feet 9 inches high; has no marks or brands perceivable; is unmarried.	Robeson Co, NC	Bartholomew Co	Edward A. Herod, a citizen of said County.	21 Sep 1853
Blanks, Willis	21	Mulatto man, 6 ft 2 inches high; has a scar about one inch long on the left side of the left wrist; no other marks perceivable.	Robeson Co, NC	Bartholomew Co	Edward A. Herod, a citizen of said County.	21 Sep 1853
Blanks, Elizabeth	15	Mulatto girl, 5 feet 5 inches high and growing; has a blemish in the ball of the right eye, and a small scar on the right arm; no other marks perceivable.	Robeson Co, NC	Bartholomew Co	Edward A. Herod, a citizen of said County.	21 Sep 1853
Blanks, Eli	13	Mulatto boy, young, likely and growing finely; his hair is nearly straight; no marks or brands perceivable; son of John Blanks.	Robeson Co, NC	Bartholomew Co	Edward A. Herod, a citizen of said County.	21 Sep 1853
Leevy, Alexander	6	Mulatto boy, a bright, active and intelligent boy; no marks perceivable; his father's name in Louis Leevy.	Roberson Co, NC	Bartholomew Co	Edward A. Herod, a citizen of said County.	21 Sep 1853
Wheeler, Ephraim	18	Black boy (or negro), 5 feet 4 inches high; has a scar on his left cheek caused by the kick of a horse; also has a scar about an inch long immediately over left eye; both of his lips have scars on them; teeth good and white.	Johnson Co, IN	Bartholomew Co	James Hobbs, a respectable citizen of said County.	27 Sep 1853
Turman, James	21	Mulatto man, 5 feet and 8 inches high; has a scar about an inch long on his left wrist; also has a scar about 2 inches long near the right temple.	Jennings Co, IN	Bartholomew Co	Nathan Graves, Esq. citizen of said County of Bartholomew.	29 Sep 1853

Bartholomew County, Indiana

Name	Age	Description	Place	County	Witness	Date
Turman, Henry	20	Mulatto, 5 feet 7 1/2 inches high; has a scar made by an axe on the right big toe, no other remarkable marks.	Jennings Co, IN	Bartholomew Co	Nathan Graves, Esq, a citizen of said County.	29 Sep 1853
Turman, Samuel	12	Mulatto boy, a bright intelligent looking boy; appears to be growing finely; has no remarkable marks on his person; is the son of Harry Turman.	Jennings Co, IN	Bartholomew Co	Nathan Graves, Esq, a respectable citizen of said County.	29 Sep 1853
Bolden, Daniel	28	Mulatto, 5 feet 8 inches high; has a scar on the inside of the left arm, below the elbow about one inch long; knuckle of the forefinger of the left hand is knocked out of place.	Ohio	Bartholomew Co	Henry Bryant, a respectable citizen of said County.	30 Sep 1853
Curzy, Edward	43	A light mulatto man; hair black and nearly straight; five feet six and a half inches high; his left leg is crooked having once been broken in the joint of the knee.	Bladen Co, NC	Bartholomew Co	William Atkinson, a citizen of said County.	5 Nov 1853
Curzy, Dolly	26	Mulatto woman, 5 feet 8 inches high; light complexion; tolerably straight dingy black hair; slightly freckled; has a small black mole on the right part of her upper lip; is wife of Edward Curzy & has three children.	Robeson Co, NC	Bartholomew Co	William Atkinson, a citizen of said County.	5 Nov 1853
Curzy, John	4 1/2 yrs.	Light mulatto boy, a very bright, intelligent looking boy; no marks perceivable.	Jennings Co, IN	Bartholomew Co	Wm Atkinson, a citizen of said County.	5 Nov 1853
Curzy, Eliza	3	Mulatto girl; very light complexion, and is quite bright and intelligent looking in her appearance.	Bartholomew Co, IN	Bartholomew Co	Wm Atkinson, citizen of said County.	5 Nov 1853

Bartholomew County, Indiana

Mitchell, Priscilla	45	Negro woman, 5 feet [?] inches high; hair slightly gray, has been married once, but now a widow; never had any children - no particular mark or scars perceivable.	Halifax Co, NC	Bartholomew Co	William H. H. Terrell, a citizen of said County.	10 Nov 1853
Newby, John	21	Negro, about 5 feet 5 inches high; has a small scar on the right side of his forehead and small one on the knucklr of the little finger of the right hand.	Jackson Co, IN	Bartholomew Co	William Ruckle, a citizen of said County.	28 Dec 1853
Newby, Penina	50-60	Negro woman, 5 feet three inches high; no particular marks.	Perquinman Co, NC	Bartholomew Co	Joshua V. Horn	20 Mar 1854
Newby, Jemima	15	Negro girl, five feet five inches high; no particular marks.	Jackson Co, IN	Bartholomew Co	Joshua V. Horn	20 Mar 1854
Hill, Mary Eveline	18	Mulatto girl, 5 feet six and 3/4 inches high; has no particular marks.	Jackson Co, IN	Johnson Co IN	Wm H. H. Terrell	20 Mar 1854
Hill, Catharine	32	Mulatto woman, five feet three inches high - has a small scar over each eye - no other marks perceivable.	Perquinman Co, NC	Johnson Co IN	Joshua V. Horn	20 Mar 1854
Hill, Abraham Augustus	2	Negro boy, a plump little darkie, and, if nothing happens to prevent will make a big one some day - no marks.	Bartholomew Co, IN	Johnson Co IN	Joshua V. Horn	20 Mar 1854
Hill, Susan Henrietta	4	Negro girl, a rightly sprightly little girl; no particular marks at present.	Bartholomew Co, IN	Johnson Co IN	Joshua V. Horn	20 Mar 1854
Hill, Andrew Jackson	8	Negro boy, appears sprightly boy-has a small scar over his left eye and also a small scar on the left cheek.	Bartholomew Co, IN	Johnson Co IN	Joshua V. Horn	20 Mar 1854

Bartholomew County, Indiana

Name	Age	Description	Place	County	Recorder	Date
Osborn, Thomas	15 mos.	Negro boy, a plump little chap and bids fair do well if he lives long enough.	Bartholomew Co IN	Bartholomew Co	Joshua V. Horn	20 Mar 1854
Simmons, Caroline	27	Mulatto woman, 5 feet 8 and a half inches high - the fourth finger next to the little one is off at the 2nd joint of left hand; wife of Lawson Simmons.	Warren Co MS	Bartholomew Co	James Hobbs	10 Apr 1854
Simmons, Susan	36	Mulatto woman, 5 feet 7 inches & 3/4 high; has straight black hair; has a large scar on the right cheek; is the wife of Meredith Simmons.	Henry Co VA	Bartholomew Co	James Hobbs	10 Apr 1854
Simmons, Margaret	22	Mulatto woman, 5 feet 3 inches high; tolerably fair complexion, straight hair - is unmarried.	Brown Co IN	Bartholomew Co	James Hobbs	10 Apr 1854
Simmons, Sarah Jane	14	Mulatto girl, a light mulatto, has straight hair, has a scar on the top of her head caused by a burn, and has a mole on the right side of her upper lip.	Greene CO IL	Bartholomew Co	James Hobbs	10 Apr 1854
Simmons, Betsy Ann	13	Mulatto girl, a very fair, pretty girl, has fine brown hair and rosy cheeks, is the daughter of Lawson Simmons.	Bartholomew Co IN	Bartholomew Co	James Hobbs	10 Apr 1854
Simmons, Mary Ann	9	Mulatto girl, a light mulatto, no particular marks, is the daughter of Lawson Simmons.	Bartholomew Co IN	Bartholomew Co	James Hobbs	10 Apr 1854
Simmons, James	4	Mulatto boy, a bright little boy; no particular marks, son of Lawson Simmons.	Bartholomew Co IN	Bartholomew Co	James Hobbs	10 Apr 1854

Bartholomew County, Indiana

Simmons, Wm. Lawson	4 mos	Mulatto boy-baby, is the son of Lawson Simmons.	Bartholomew Co IN	Bartholomew Co	Isaac S. Boardman, Co Clerk	10 Apr 1854
Oxendine, Priscilla Jane	10	Mulatto girl, is the daughter of Daniel Oxendine.	Robeson Co, NC	Bartholomew Co	James Hobbs	10 Apr 1854
Simmons, Lawson	47	Mulatto man, 5 feet 6 3/4 inches high; bald on the top of his head; is a light mulatto.	Caroline Co, VA	Bartholomew Co	James Hobbs	10 Apr 1854
Simmons, Meredith	37	Mulatto man, six feet one inch and a quarter high; no marks perceivable.	Fayette Co, KY	Bartholomew Co	James Jobbs	10 Apr 1854
Hatcher, John	40	Mulatto man, 5 feet 6 1/4 inches high, dark mulatto Color.	Dowlington District, SC	Bartholomew Co	James Hobbs	4 Oct 1855
Hatcher, Sophia	38	Mulatto woman, 5 feet 3 inches high, dark mulatto, no particular marks.	Nashville, TN	Bartholomew Co	James Hobbs	4 Oct 1855
Hatcher, George W. Griffith	3	Mulatto babe, a smart good looking chubby little fellow, dark mulatto, no particular marks.	Columbus, IN	Columbus IN	James Hobbs	4 Oct 1855
Oxendine, Sarah L. Almyena	9	Bright mulatto girl, daughter of Daniel Oxendine - no marks perceivable.	Robeson Co, NC	Bartholomew Co	Thomas Hays	5 Oct 1855
Oxendine, Senith	7	Dark mulatto, the daughter of Daniel Oxendine and no marks perceivable.	Bartholomew Co, IN	Bartholomew Co	Thomas Hays	5 Oct 1855

REGISTER OF NEGROES AND MULATTOES IN FLOYD COUNTY, INDIANA

Names	Age	Description	Place of Birth	Residence	Names of Witnesses	Date Registered
Richard Johnson	72	Light complexion, height 5 ft 8 ins	Baltimore, Md	New Albany	Robt M Weis	NA
Redford E Turner	36	Light complexion, height 5 ft 8 ins	Floyd Co, Ind	Floyd Co, Ind	Amy Bradley	NA
Drury Mayhoe	40	Light complexion, scar on forehead.	Virginia	Floyd Co, Ind	NA	NA
George Winters	52	Very Black, six feet high	Virginia	Floyd Co, Ind	W A Scribner	NA
Maria Winters	43	Mulatto	Philadelphia	New Albany	NA	NA
Thomas Locklayer	60	Light brown	North Carolina	New Albany	Doc Ev	NA
Lukey Locklayer	55	Light brown	East Tenn.	New Albany	John B Winstandly	NA
Sarah A Whiteman	27	Light brown	Alabama	New Albany	Frank Gwin	NA
Amanda Locklayer	19	Light brown	Alabama	New Albany	Doc Ev	NA
James Locklayer	15	Very black, scar in forehead between the eyes	Alabama	New Albany	Doc Ev	NA
Victoria Locklayer	9	Very black	Alabama	New Albany	Doc Ev	NA
Thomas H Whiteman	8	Very black	Alabama	New Albany	John B Winstandly	NA
Susan Whiteman	4	Very black	Alabama	New Albany	John B Winstandly	NA
Peter Winson	38	Black & Pox marks, 2 scars on top of head	Virginia	New Albany	M. Akins	NA
Elizabeth Winson	22	Light complexion strait hair	South Carolina	New Albany	NA	NA
Mary Jane Winson	6	Light complexion strait hair	South Carolina	New Albany	NA	NA

Floyd County, Indiana

Name	Age	Description	Birthplace	Residence	Owner	
Washington R Runnells	7	Light (quite) complexion	South Carolina	New Albany	NA	NA
Richard Runnells	14	Spanish complexion, strait hair	South Carolina	New Albany	Peter Wigscent (?)	NA
James Russell	35	Bright complexion, scar on right side of neck. Scars on left hand	North Carolina	New Albany	NA	NA
Louisa A Russell	--	--	--	--	--	--
Jane E Mitchem	22	Black, scars on right arm.	Ind.	New Albany	NA	NA
Solomon Duncan	21	Light complexion, scar on left eyebrow	Kentucky	New Albany	I. N. Akin	N
Catherine Mitchem	32	Dark, a scar on the right hand	Ind.	New Albany	--	NA
Frances Menows(?)	18	Black, scar on left shoulder	Ind.	New Albany	--	NA
Henry Thergood	52	Black ---	Born in Virginia	Floyd Co, Ind	--	NA
Barbra Thergood	12	Yellow	Floyd Co, Ind	Floyd Co, Ind	--	NA
Zachariah Thergood	9	Yellow	Floyd Co, Ind	Floyd Co, Ind	--	NA
Mary Catharine Thergood	5	Yellow	Floyd Co, Ind	Floyd Co, Ind	--	NA
Rebecca Jane Thergood	4	Yellow	Floyd Co, Ind	Floyd Co, Ind	--	NA
Henry Thergood [Jr]	3 mos	Yellow	Floyd Co, Ind	Floyd Co, Ind	--	NA
Adam Bunch	53	Black, near six feet high	Virginia	Floyd Co, Ind	--	NA
Nancy Bunch	--	--	--	--	--	--
Gabriel Baldwin	75	Black, 5 feet eleven inches high	Kentucky	New Albany	Robt M Wier	NA
Anna Baldwin	76	Dark mulatto	Maryland	New Albany	Robt M Wier	NA
John Anderson	30	Black, scar on the top of the head; not very tall	Baltimore, Maryland	New Albany	Richard Johnson	NA

Floyd County, Indiana

Name	Age	Description	Origin	Residence	Witness	
Frank Thompson	25	Black, 5 feet 11 1/2 inches high	Corydon, Indiana	New Albany	Thomas Leslie	NA
John Keller	18	Mulatto, low in stature	South Carolina	New Albany	Steve Winson(?)	NA
Beverly Harris	20	Black, front tooth out & scar on forehead & on right ankle	New Albany	New Albany	I N Akin	NA
Thomas Cook	23	Black, scar on right side of the face, & scars on right arm.	New Albany	New Albany	I N Akin	NA
Daniel Madden	21	Scar on left ---	Bloomington, Ind	New Albany	I N Akin	NA
William Carpenter	30	Yellow	North Carolina	New Albany	I N Akin	NA
Danderfield Brust	35	Black, scar on left side of hand & right cheek	Louisiana	New Albany	I N Akin	NA
Samuel Cooper	25	Yellow, scar on right wrist & one under nose	Tennessee	New Albany	I N Akin	NA
Washington Mitchum	23	Black, scars on the forefinger of the right hand	Corydon, Ind	New Albany	I N Akin	NA
Charles Spencer	22	Black, scar in the forehead	Jeffersonville, Ind	New Albany	I N Akin	NA
Robert Hood	25	Light Black, Scar on forehead	Jennings Co, Ind	New Albany	I N Akin	NA
Richard Harris	58	Black, scar on forehead & left hand	Virginia	New Albany	I N Akin	NA
Mahala Harris	44	Black	Kentucky	New Albany	I N Akin	NA
Thomas Harris	14	Dark Brown	New Albany	New Albany	I N Akin	NA
Virginia Harris	12	Dark Brown	New Albany	New Albany	I N Akin	NA
Paulina Harris	8	Dark Brown	New Albany	New Albany	I N Akin	NA
Clarerietta Harris	5	Dark Brown	New Albany	New Albany	I N Akin	NA
Enoch Harris	3	Dark Brown	New Albany	New Albany	I N Akin	NA

Floyd County, Indiana

Name	Age	Description	Origin	Residence	Reference	
Johnson Mitchum	26	Black, Scar on left hand, about six feet high	Harrison Co, Ind	New Albany	I N Akin	NA
John Finley	27	Yellow, Scar on calf of right leg	Virginia	New Albany	I N Akin	NA
William R Boyd	36	Scar on lower lip & left forefinger	North Carolina	New Albany	I N Akin	NA
James Roach	60	Dark Brown, Scar on lower lip & on breast & straight finger on left hand	North Carolina	New Albany	I N Akin	NA
Peterson Boyd	34	Black, Scar on breast	Indiana	Floyd Co, Ind	I N Akin	NA
Absolom Truitt	16	Black, scar in forehead & left cheek	New Albany	New Albany	I N Akin	NA
Lewis Mitchum	16	Black, scar on each cheek bone	New Albany	New Albany	I N Akin	NA
George Finley	21	Yellow, hands darker than face	Harrison Co Ind	New Albany	I N Akin	NA
William J Greenlee	48	Dark Brown, height 5 feet 6 inches	Pennsylvania	New Albany	I N Akin	NA
Mary Greenlee	49	Dark Brown strat hair	Pennsylvania	New Albany	I N Akin	NA
Mary E Greenlee	24	Dark Brown and left eye gray, straight hair	Pennsylvania	New Albany	I N Akin	NA
Sarah J Greenlee	23	Dark Brown, Scar on forehead over right eye, strait hair	Pennsylvania	New Albany	I N Akin	NA
Ann Wasuba Pell	21	Light mulatto strait hair	Pennsylvania	New Albany	I N Akin	NA
William P Q Greenlee	19	Light mulatto strait hair	Pennsylvania	New Albany	I N Akin	NA
Harriet M Greenlee	16	Light mulatto strait hair	Pennsylvania	New Albany	I N Akin	NA
George G Greenlee	14	Light mulatto strait hair	Pennsylvania	New Albany	I N Akin	NA
Susan E Greenlee	7	Light mulatto strait hair	Floyd Co, Ind	New Albany	I N Akin	NA
Anna Belle Hurst	3	Light mulatto strait hair	Floyd Co, Ind	New Albany	I N Akin	NA
Mary Frances Pell	1	Light mulatto strait hair	Floyd Co, Ind	New Albany	I N Akin	NA

Floyd County, Indiana

Name	Age	Description	Birthplace	Residence		
William Terrell	22	Six feet high, his features --- African	Floyd Co, Ind	New Albany	I N Akin	NA
Crankey Freeman	58	Tall & light copper color	Georgia	New Albany	I N Akin	NA
Harrison Mitchum	35	5 feet 6 1/2 inches high, scar on the right side of his upper lip	Indiana	New Albany	I N Akin	NA
Benjamin Harper	37	5 feet 6 1/2 inches high, brown Black complexion	Georgia	New Albany	Doe'y Erickman	NA
Elizabeth Mitchum	27	Brown black complexion	Indiana	New Albany	Robt M Wier	NA
Sarah H Vanderburg	7	Very black	Indiana	New Albany	Robt M Wier	NA
Mary S Vanderburg	6	Brown black	Illinois	New Albany	Robt M Wier	NA
Eliza Webb	44	Brown black	Kentucky	New Albany	Robt M Wier	NA
Irenia (?) Robertson	22	Light mulatto	Indiana	New Albany	Robt M Wier	NA
Hannah Mitchum	41	Very Black	Virginia	New Albany	Robt M Wier	NA
James Munick	36	Black and badly pox marked	Virginia	New Albany	Benj Huddleston	NA
Matilda Mitchum	30	Light copper color & quite fleshly	Virginia	New Albany	Benj Huddleston	NA
Robert Webb	68	Very black	Virginia	New Albany	Robt M Wier	NA
Anthony Munick	32	Scar on left foot	Virginia	New Albany	Robt M Wier	NA
James E Links	21	Scar in forehead and left hand	Indiana	Floyd Co, Ind	Sam'l M Bolin	NA
Kenoway Griffin	55	Scar---	Maryland	New Albany	Robt M Wier	NA
Everett Massie	52	Black, warts off the fore finger of right hand, scar on left wrist	Ohio	New Albany	I N Akin	NA
Maria Massie	44	Black, two scars on left arm and at the elbow	Maryland	New Albany	I N Akin	NA
Mary L Massie	23	Black	New Albany	New Albany	I N Akin	NA

Floyd County, Indiana

Hiram D Massie	2	Light Black		New Albany	I N Akin	NA
George Massie	1	Light Black		New Albany	I N Akin	NA
Lewis Terrill	34	Black, scar across the right foot, between -- & instep	Louisville, Ky	New Albany	I N Akin	NA
Patsy Terrill	44	Black, mark on the back	North Carolina	New Albany	I N Akin	NA
James E Carter	21	Yellow, scar on left cheek, sometimes a barber.	New Albany	New Albany	I N Akin	NA
Josephine C Terrill	14	Black & heavy set	New Albany	New Albany	I N Akin	NA
Paul H Terrill	12	Black & heavy set	New Albany	New Albany	I N Akin	NA
Elijah Terrill	10	Black & heavy set	New Albany	New Albany	I N Akin	NA
Nancy Ann Terrill	8	Black & heavy set	New Albany	New Albany	I N Akin	NA
Benjamin L Terrill	6	Black & heavy set	New Albany	New Albany	I N Akin	NA
James Carter	24	Yellow, mark on left arm near elbow, looks something like a fish.	Indiana	New Albany	I N Akin	NA
Elizabeth Harper	27	Black, scar on forehead at edge of hair.	Georgia	New Albany	G T Werner	NA
James Harper	7	Yellow, scar on left hip.	Indiana	New Albany	G T Werner	NA
John Harper	38	Black, 5 feet 3 1/2 inches high.	Georgia	New Albany	Doc. Evidence	NA
Michael White	31	Black, scar under right eye & in the groin.	Kentucky	New Albany	"	NA
Jane White	24	Black, mark on the face.	Indiana	New Albany	"	NA
Alexander White	9	Yellow	Indiana	New Albany	"	NA
John W. White	1	"	Indiana	New Albany	"	NA
Sarah Bailey	16	Black, broad front teeth.	Jeffersonville, Indiana	New Albany	"	NA

Floyd County, Indiana

Henry Mitchum	27	Black, scar on upper lip & scar on foot.	New Albany	New Albany	I N Akin	NA
Benjamin Franklin	39	Light yellow small mark on the nose & scar on the left knee, mark on left arm.	New Albany	New Albany	I N Akin	NA
Eliza Rickman	30	Very light yellow	New Albany	New Albany	I N Akin	July 18, 1853
Hezikiah Rickman	8	"	"	"	I N Akin	"
Shadrach Rickman	6	"	"	"	I N Akin	"
Anna Belle Rickman	4	"	"	"	I N Akin	"
William E. Rickman	3	"	"	"	I N Akin	"
Catherine Finley	19	Light yellow, scar by right eye & under right arm.	Alabama	New Albany	I N Akin	"
Lucinda J. Hood	27	Light copper color	Georgia	New Albany	George Foreman	"
Chas. Fielding Simonton	33	Light mulatto 5 feet 6 inches high, scar on forehead at edge of hair.	North Carolina	New Albany	W W Tuttle	July 19, 1853
Catherine Simonton	26	Light mulatto	Tennessee	New Albany	W W Tuttle	"
Elizabeth Simonton	6	Rather dark	Ohio	New Albany	W W Tuttle	"
Anna Eliza Bolin	19	Jet black mark under the left eye scar on right wrist.	Cincinnati, Ohio	New Albany	W W Tuttle	"
John Finley	53	6 feet 1 inch high 2 scars on right cheek.	Virginia	New Albany	Robt M. Weir	"
Susan Massey	18	Yellow, strait hair, scar on right side of the head.	North Carolina	New Albany	Cornelius Watson	July 20, 1853
Cornelius Watson	26	Black, a scar on the right arm, scar on lower lip.	Virginia	New Albany	Daniel Massey	"

Floyd County, Indiana

Name	Age	Description	Origin	Residence	Witness	Date
Nancy L. Watson	21	Black, scar on left wrist.	New Albany	New Albany	"	"
Joseph S. Watson	5 mos.	Yellow, only one hand with fingers.	New Albany	New Albany	"	"
Henry Freeman	25	Light Black, scar on right cheek & on middle finger of right hand & over right eye.	Jeffersonville, Indiana	New Albany	"	"
Jane Freeman	23	Light Black, scar on the forehead.	New Albany	New Albany	Henry Freeman	"
John S. Freeman	7	Light Black	New Albany	New Albany	"	"
Mary L. Freeman	5	"	New Albany	New Albany	"	"
James H. Freeman	2	"	New Albany	New Albany	"	"
Sarah Jane Freeman	5 mos.	"	New Albany	New Albany	"	"
Anderson Goings	36	Light mulatto, scar on the little finger of left hand through the nail.	Indiana	New Albany	I N Akin	"
Emma Medad	23	Yellow, scar under chin.	Virginia	New Albany	Alexander Pell	July 21, 1853
William Rollins	7	Yellow	Ohio	New Albany	"	"
Alexander Pell	28	Dark yellow	Indiana	New Albany	I N Akin	"
Levina Stewart	44	Very large and light complexion, scar over right eye.	East Tennessee	New Albany	I N Akin	"
Elizabeth Stewart	24	Nearly white, low in stature, small scar over right eye.	Indiana	New Albany	I N Akin	"
Turther Stewart	28	Light brown	Indiana	New Albany	I N Akin	"
Thomas Stewart	25	"	"	New Albany	"	"
Uriah Stewart	23	Scar on the left cheek & right temple.	"	New Albany	"	"

Floyd County, Indiana

Name	Age	Description		Place		Date
Mary Ellen Stewaet	11	Light brown	"	New Albany	"	"
Catherine Stewart	4	Yellow, scar on the right forehead.	"	New Albany	"	"
Celetina Stewart	2	Light yellow	"	New Albany	"	"
Martin Finley	23	Dark brown, scar on the left thigh and right knuckle.	"	New Albany	"	"
Leroy Nelson	14	Light mulatto scar on the forefinger of the right hand.	Indiana	Floyd County	I N Akin	"
Hardin Finley	26	Mulatto, scar on left foot light scar on nose.	Indiana	New Albany	"	July 22, 1853
William Edwards	20	Black, scar by right corner of right eye and of sleepy appearance.	Kentucky	New Albany	W. W. Goodwin	"
Martha A. Milton	23	Light mulatto, scar over the right eye and left hand.	Indiana	Floyd County	Silas E. Ivy	"
Frances Runnolds	37	Indian complexion. Freckled face.	South Carolina	Clark Co., Ind.	Peter Winson	July 25, 1853
Caroline Runnolds	11	Bright complexion delicate features, small blue mark in center of forehead.	"	"	"	"
Cecelia Runnolds	11	Very bright color, strait hair.	"	"	"	"
Evaline Runnolds	7	"	"	"	Peter Winson	July 25, 1853
Zachariah J. Runnolds	4	"	"	"	"	"
George Scott	14	Chestnut color	"	"	"	"
Darling Scott	12	"	"	"	"	"
John H. Freeman	18	Black, knot besides right ear.	New Albany	New Albany	I N Akin	"
Isaac Mukes	27	5 feet 6 inches high, dark brown.	Kentucky	Floyd County	R. W. Weir	July 27, 1853

Floyd County, Indiana

Name	Age	Description	Born	Residence	Witness	Date
Lucy Brown	28	Light mulatto, mark on left side of the nose.	Louisiana	New Albany	A. F. Israel	"
Martha Jane Stewart	20	Light mulatto	Virginia Born free	New Albany	I N Akin	"
Maezina Stewart	7 mos	"	New Albany	New Albany	"	"
Moses B. Hursh	22	Yellow, warts on right eye.	Kentucky	New Albany	"	"
Walter P. Miller	37	Black, six feet 1 1/2 inches in height, 3 front teeth out. Scar on right hand.	Connecticut	New Albany	Washington Mitchum	"
Abraham Mitchum	37	Black, two scars on left leg, hands scarified, scar on forehead & right leg.	Indiana	New Albany	"	"
Daniel Sims	23	Yellow, small on left cheek & ___ on right knee.	Indiana	Floyd County	"	July 28, 1993
Joseph Hawkins	21	Black (rather light)	Louisiana	Floyd County	"	"
Samuel Flinn	52	Light mulatto, scar on left hand by the thumb.	South Carolina	Harrison County, Indiana	"	"
Harriet Mitchum	40	Black, scar on left arm.	Louisville, Kentucky	New Albany	Robert Webb	July 29, 1853
Louisa Flinn	32	Very light complexion.	South Carolina	Harrison County, Indiana	Edward Bailey	"
James Flinn	9	"	"	"	"	"
Anna Flinn	9	"	"	"	"	"
Zion Flinn	5	Dark compllexion	"	"	"	"
Mary Ellen Flinn	3	"	"	"	"	"
Samuel S. Flinn	2	Light mulatto	Indiana	"	"	"
Hugh Eustis	53	Brown color, small scar above the nose & on left thumb.	North Carolina	Floyd County	I N Akin	July 30, 1853

Floyd County, Indiana

Name	Age	Description	Birthplace	Residence	Witness	Date
James Richards	68	Dark brown, scar over right eye, club footed & over six feet high.	Virginia	New Albany	"	"
John Fulton	66	Dark brown, six feet high, scar on right cheek.	Pennsylvania	Floyd County	"	August 1, 1853
Patty Fulton	56	Black	North Carolina	Floyd County	"	"
Parthenia Deal	16	Bright mulatto	Indiana	Floyd County	"	"
John Foster	25	Yellow, J.F., heart & arrow & M.G. on right arm.	Tennessee	New Albany	John Ross	"
John Ross	30	Black, scar on right leg, two on breast, no nail on big toe of left foot, scar on right hand.	Floyd County	Floyd County	I N Akin	"
Edward Medad	27	Dark brown, & scars over right eye & one on the right thigh & mark on right hand, scar on side of nose.	Philadelphia, Penn.	Floyd County	Henry Turner	"
William Rollins	8	Scarified marks on the cheeks & jaws.	Cincinnati, Ohio	Floyd County	"	"
Edward Bailey	42	Dark brown, 5 feet six inches high, scar on left arm.	Tennessee	Floyd County	P. G. Stewart	"
Silena Bailey	21	Light mulatto, mole under right eye.	Alabama	Floyd County	"	"
Ann Jenkins & now Ann Porter	25	Dark mulatto, scar on right cheek.	New Albany	New Albany	James Burks	August 4, 1853
Thomas Wilson	73	Black, 5 feet 3 inches high and very heavy set.	Virginia	New Albany	Robt. M. Weir	"
Maria Wilson	45	Heavy set & right eye out.	Louisville, Ky.	New Albany	"	"
Samuel Stubblefield	66	Black, scar on left wrist.	VCirginia	New Albany	"	"
Mary A. E. Bunch	4	Dark brown	Indiana	New Albany	I N Akin	August 6, 1853

19

Floyd County, Indiana

Name	Age	Description	Birthplace	Residence	Evidence	Date
Charlotte Bunch	1	" "	Indiana	New Albany	"	"
Pleasant Lucas	34	5 feet 11 inches high, Bright mulatto, 2 moles on left side of the face.	Georgia	Floyd County	Doc[ument] Ev[idence]	"
William Harper	22	Black, pox marked bad, scar on the right side of the chin.	"	"	"	"
Middleton Harper	24	Light mulatto, lightly pox marked, scar over and under right eye.	"	"	"	"
Sally Harper	26	Dark brown	"	"	"	"
Rebecca Harper	7	Bright mulatto	"	"	"	"
Barbara A. Harper	28	"	"	"	"	"
Alexander Harper	7	"	"	"	"	"
Martha A. Harper	11	"	"	"	"	"
Henry Harper	13	"	"	"	"	"
James Lucas	39	Bright mulatto. Scar on right temple.	Virginia	New Albany	I N Akin	August 8, 1853
Ellen Lucas	39	Bright mulatto	South Carolina	New Albany	"	"
Rebecca Lucas	12	" Strait hair.	New Albany	New Albany	"	"
Harriet Lucas	10	Bright mulatto	New Albany	New Albany	"	"
Parmelia Lucas	7	Brown	New Albany	New Albany	"	"
Elmina Lucas	5	Bright mulatto	New Albany	New Albany	"	"
Angeline Lucas	3	Bright mulatto	New Albany	New Albany	I N Akin	"
Milton Lucas	7 mos	" "	New Albany	New Albany	"	"
Cecilia Cook	63	" Scar on right temple.	Georgia	New Albany	"	"

Floyd County, Indiana

Name	Age	Description	Birthplace	Residence		Date
Cassandra Wetherington	45	Dark mulatto	Maryland	New Albany	"	
Cecilia Johnson	44	Black	Pennsylvania	New Albany	Cassandra Washington	"
Mary Ann Wetherington now Mary A. Jamison(?)	18	Light brown, small scar on left side of face.	New Albany	New Albany	"	
Joshua Wetherington	17	Dark, scar on right side of forehead.	New Albany	New Albany	"	
Elizabeth Washington	29	Bright mulatto, thick lips.	Ohio	New Albany	"	
Emma U. Washington	9	Bright mulatto	New Albany	New Albany	"	
Cecilia A. Washington	6	Dark complexion	New Albany	New Albany	"	
Elizabeth McIntosh	39	Dark brown, mole on the back of the right hand.	Kentucky	New Albany	"	August 11, 1853
Husson McIntosh	35	Dark brown	Maryland	New Albany	"	"
Anna McIntosh	12	Dark brown	North Carolina	New Albany	I N Akin	
Mary F. McIntosh	7	"	Indiana	New Albany	"	
Janie McIntosh	2	"	"	New Albany	"	
William McIntosh	3 mos	"	"	New Albany	"	
Nathaniel Carter	22	Light mulatto, quite a small scar on lower lip.	Indiana	Floyd County	S. M. Bolin	August 13, 1853
Susan Carter	18	Brown mulatto straight black hair.	Tennessee	Floyd County	"	
Melissa F. Carter	8 mos	Light mulatto	Floyd County	Floyd County	"	

Floyd County, Indiana

Name	Age	Description	Birthplace	Residence	Owner	Date
Henry Goins	35	Light brown, scar on forehead & on lower lip, little finger on right hand crooked, scar left wrist.	Virginia	Floyd County	John Foster	August 15, 1853
Si Mitchum	23	Dark brown, scar on right side of mouth & right leg.	Indiana	New Albany	Cornelius Watson	Aug 16, 1853
George Willis	55	Dark brown, scar on right eye.	Kentucky	New Albany	"	"
Evaline Willis	28	Dark	Virginia	New Albany	"	"
Thomas W. Willis	10	Light complexion, scar on right foot.	Harrison Co., Ind.	New Albany	"	"
Mary A. Willis	4	Dark complexion.	Clark Co., Ind.	New Albany	"	"
Burkett Manly	47	Quite light, scar on forehead, scars on right hand, on right foot & left lleg.	North Carolina	New Albany	"	Aug 18, 1853
Elizabeth Manly	15	Brown complexion, scar on forehead.	Virginia	New Albany	"	"
James Manly	16	Brown, scar on left leg.	Tennessee	New Albany	"	"
William Manly	11	Brown	"	New Albany	"	"
John Manly	13	"	"	New Albany	"	"
Thomas Manly	9	"	"	New Albany	"	"
Medora Manly	6	"	New Albany	New Albany	"	"
Sarah Manly	3	"	"	New Albany	"	"
Charles Manly	2	"	"	New Albany	"	"
Sylvia Manly	42	", scar on forehead.	Virginia	New Albany	"	"
Sarah Ann Lucas	22	Dark broiwn	Ohio	New Albany	"	Aug 19, 1853
Peter Ross	23	Black. Both little fingers crooked.	Floyd County	Floyd County	John Ross	Aug 20, 1853
Matilda Mitchum	30	Yellow	Virginia	Floyd County	"	Aug 22, 1853

Floyd County, Indiana

Name	Age	Description	Origin	Residence	Witness	Date
William A. Mitchum	10	Brown, scar on the left side of his breast.	Floyd County	New Albany	Matilda Mitchum	"
Joseph H. H. Mitchum	8	Brown	"	New Albany	"	"
Aquila R. Mitchum	7	", scar in front of head.	"	New Albany	"	"
John S. Mitchum	4	Rather dark.	"	New Albany	"	"
George T. Mitchum	1	Brown	"	New Albany	"	"
Richard R. Finley	23	Brown on right eye & top of forehead, scars	Alabama	New Albany	I N Akin	Aug 23, 1853
Charles A. Willis	28	Light complexion, scar near right eye & scar on left wrist two marks on breast.	Kentucky	New Albany	Preston Finley	Aug 24, 1853
Eliza Willis	22	Brown, delicate figure.	Philadelphia	New Albany	"	"
George W. Johnson	33	Brown. Small pox marks in face.	Ohio	New Albany	"	"
Mary Johnson	19	Brown, scar on left cheek.	New Albany	New Albany	"	"
Peter Ross	64	Very Black rather tall.	North Carolina	Floyd County	I N Akin	Aug 26, 1853
Solomon Ross	18	Black, scar on left wrist & on nose.	Floyd County	Floyd County	"	"
Eli Ross	16	Dark brown scar on left leg.	"	"	"	"
Jerome Ross	18	" "	"	"	"	"
Charlotte Johnson	22	Brown, two teeth out --- of the mouth.	Pennsylvania	New Albany	Wm Carpenter	Aug 29, 1853
Elija Sanders	18	Light complexion, scar on left cheek.	Kentucky	New Albany	"	"
Otha James Clair	32	Brown, scar on left cheek and over right eye.	Ohio	New Albany	"	"
Susannah Finley	29	Brown color	"	New Albany	Preston Findley	"

Floyd County, Indiana

Name	Age	Description	Place			Date
Hellena Findley	12	Light brown	New Albany	New Albany	"	"
Preston Findley	30	Brown, scar between eyes & on right arm.	Indiana	"	I N Akin	"
James W. Findley	10	Brown	"	"	"	"
Charles H. W. Findley	8	Brown	Cincinnati, Ohio	"	"	"
Alexander D. Findley	6	"	"	"	"	"
Randolph T. Findley	4	"	New Albany	"	"	"
Mary Finley	36	Yellow small scar on left arm.	Virginia	New Albany	"	Aug 30, 1853
William H. Finley	10	Black	New Albany	New Albany	"	"
Othello Finley	7	"	"	"	"	"
Thomas J. Finley	6	"	"	"	"	"
Lucinda J. Finley	5	Brown (dark)	"	"	"	"
Mary J. Finley	21	Black	"	"	"	"
Patsy Ann Duncan	27	Light brown, rotten teeth in front of mouth.	Harrison Co., Indiana	"	I N Akin	Aug 31, 1853
Martha Finley	22	Black	New Albany	"	Elija Sanders	Sept 2, 1853
Claridge U. A. Finley	5	Rather light and scar on left cheek.	"	"	"	"
Victoria N. Sanders	4	Very bright	New Orleans, La.	"	"	"
Belle W. Sanders	3	" "	Louisville, Ky.	"	"	"
Jonathan Taylor	27	Brown, scar on right wrist & on right hand little finger.	Kentucky	"	"	"
Joseph Thomas	55	Black 5 ft 11 inches high in stockings.	North Carolina	New Albany	James Russell	Sept 3, 1853

Floyd County, Indiana

Name	Age	Description			Date
Elizabeth Thomas	45	Brown complexion	Virginia	New Albany	"
Joseph Thomas [Jr.]	25	Black	Ohio	"	"
Harriet Thomas	23	Brown complexion	New Albany	New Albany	"
Isabella Thomas	16	"			"
		Foregoing allowed by County Board Sept 6, 1853			
Leonard Carter	21	Black, scar on left foot	Floyd County	Floyd County	Jesse Mukes	Sept 8, 1853
Hardin Finley	25	Dark brown, scar on right cheek & nose & on right foot.	New Albany	New Albany	"	Sept 10, 1853
Edward Rickman	30	Quite light, scar on forehead & right cheek.	Virginia	New Albany	I N Akin	Sept 13, 1853
William H. Handy	23	Light brown, right leg amputated above the knee & cork leg.	Kentucky	New Albany	"	"
George Washington	36	Scar on the left side of cheek, nose anf forehead. Very Black.	Baltimore, MarylanD	New Albany	"	Sept 17, 1853
Reuben Mukes	60	Light mulatto, scar on right hand & on forehead.	Kentucky	Floyd County	"	Sept 28, 1853
Fanny Mukes	48	Brown complexion scar on lleft side of head.	Virginia	"	"	"
John Mukes	13	Brown complexion, scar on left side of forehead.	Floyd County	"	"	"
Lucinda Townsell	4	Yellow complexion	Kentucky	"	"	"
William Hood	21	Dark compllexion, scar under left jaw, heavy set.	Indiana	New Albany	Allison Mitchum	Oct 1, 1853
Marianna Campbell	11	Quite light, scar on right thigh.	Indiana	New Albany	John Findley	Oct 8, 1853

Floyd County, Indiana

Name	Age	Description	Origin		Signer	Date
Catherine Findley	48	Brown, pretty large.	Virginia	"	"	Oct 19, 1853
George W. Hayden	24	Dark brown, scar on back of right hand & small one on left hand.	Indiana	"	Thomas Cook	Oct 19, 1853
Isaac Findley	35	Dark brown, scar on left shoulder & scar over left eye.	Kentucky	"	I N Akin	Nov 1, 1853
Julia Ann Findley	8	Black	Illinois	New Albany	Isaac Findley	Nov 1, 1853
Mary C. Findley	9	"	"	"	"	Nov 1, 1853
Silas Weaver	25	Black, scar on left cheek.	Maryland	New Albany	Robt. M. Weir	Nov 2, 1853
Emanuel G. Greenlee	22	Scar on little finger of right hand, mulatto.	New Albany	New Albany	Richard Harris	"
Allison Mitchum	28	Dark brown	Harrison Co., Indiana	New Albany	I N Akin	Nov 15, 1853
Osborne Hillgem	22	" " & quite small.	Kentucky	New Albany	I C Morden	"
John Scott {John Fuller is the proper name}	18	Light mulatto, scar on left wrist & on the left side of forehead.	South Carolina	New Albany	Peter Miston	Nov 21, 1853
John Lochler	39	Dark Brown, scar on right side of chin, over left eye, & right thigh.	North Carolina	"	I N Akin	Nov 25 1853
Shadrick Henderson	26	Light brown	Tennessee	"		Nov 30, 1853
Missy Jackson	22	" "	Ohio	"		Dec 2, 1853
Sampson Lowery	26	Very Black, scar on right cheek, on the throat and on left corner of left eye.	Indiana	"	Absolum F Long	Dec 16, 1853
Alice Lockler	30	Very Black, scar on the inside of right arm.	Virginia	"	John Lockler	Feb 13, 1854
Hester A. Mitchum	23	Dark Brown	New Albany	New Albany	Salem P. Town	Mar 27, 1854

Floyd County, Indiana

Name	Age	Description			Date
Amelia R. Mitchum	40	Dark brown, scar on left hand & left side of the face.	Crawford Co., Ind.	S P Town	April 22, 1854
Amelia Ann Mitchum	20	Dark brown, hight about 5 ft 8 in.	---	"	"
Ellen Jenks	17	Very black	New Albany	"	"
Aaron Mitchem	15	Dark brown, three scars on forehead, one on upper lip.	"	Milly Mitchem	April 26, 1854
Rebecca Bentley	24	Light, scar on left wrist, nearly white.	Louisiana	A W Bentley	May 6, 1854
Rosanna Hood	45	Dark brown	Clark Co., Indiana	Elizabeth Harper	May 29, 1854
Mary Jane Porter	22	Dark brown, scar on back of both hands hardly perceptible.	New Albany	Roseanna Hood	May 31, 1854
Nancy Hawkins	18	Very Black, small.	Louisiana	Wm. A. Fuller	June 12, 1854
Edward Mitchum	13	Light brown, scar on right wrist.	New Albany	S. P. Town	June 13, 1854
Shadrick Hays	41	Light brown, left wrist was broken.	Warren Co., Ky.	Smith Ronsor	July 5, 1854
Elva C. Hays	18	Very light, scar on left upper lip and strait hair.	Floyd County	"	"
Sarah Frances Hays	9 mos	Light brown & strait hair.	Floyd County	"	"
Mary Ross	24	Very Black, with sharp nose, not very large.	Floyd County	Rachel Lacy	July 18, 1854
Thomas Ross	22	Very Black, medium size	Floyd County	"	"
Mary F. Simeril	16	Very Black, hump on the shoulders.	Madison, Ind.	Robert Bonner	Aug 4, 1854
John Adams	34	Light brown, 5 feet 2 inches high. Scar in corner of right eye & one on right knee.	Baltimore	S. P. Town	Aug 7, 1854

Floyd County, Indiana

Name	Age	Description			Date
John Baxter	21	Black, scar on both middle fingers & scars on right forefinger & left thumb & scar on the underside of left wrist.	Kentucky	New Albany	H. W. Smith	Aug 26, 1854
Amy Williams	28	Dark brown.	Jefferson Co., Ky.	New Albany	Elias Thompson	Oct 23, 1854
Eliza J. Foree	26	Dark brown with scar on right cheek.	Floyd County	New Albany	Preston Finley	Nov 25, 1854
Cora E. Campbell	13	Light brown, scar on her forehead & right arm.	Floyd County	New Albany	Cornelia A. Finley	Jan 18, 1855
Cornelia A. Finley	17	Light brown, large.	Floyd County	New Albany	S. P. Town	"
Harriet Robertson	40	Very large, dark brown. Scar under the chin and on instep of right foot.	Virginia	New Albany	"	Jan 25, 1855
George Tolliver	30	Very Black, three fingers on left hand been broken, scar on the right side of face.	Knox Co., Indiana	Clark County	John H. Tolan	March 2, 1855
Albert Butler	19	Yellow, Scar in forehead between the eyes.	Floyd County	New Albany	S. P. Town	Mar 29, 1855
Elias T. Findley	22	Quite Brown, scar on the forehead and left leg.	New Albany	New Albany	Milly Mitchem	April 11, 1855
Jacob Mitchem	42	Very Black, left thumb crooked, 2 fingers on right hand crooked & one on the left hand.	Kentucky	New Albany	S. P. Town	"
Julia Ann Brent	26	Dark Brown, scar over left eye.	New Albany	New Albany	S. P. Town & Eliza Webb	April 17, 1855
Robert Armstrong Brent	9	Light Brown	New Albany	New Albany	Eliza Webb	"
William D. Brent	3	Very Black, left eye imperfect.	New Albany	New Albany	"	"
Carrie A. B. Brent	8 mos	Light brown	"	"	"	"

28

Floyd County, Indiana

Name	Age	Description	Place	Place 2	Witness	Date
Charity E. Mitchem	6	Light brown, scar on left side of face.	"	"	"	"
Zachariah Mitchem	20	Light brown about 5 feet 7 or 8 inches, some pock marks on face, rather slim built.	Corydon, Ind.	New Albany	Saml. Watson	April 19, 1855
Philip Hawkins	18	Very Black, mark of a cut on the belly.	Louisiana	Floyd County	S. P. Town	May 15, 1855
James Ford	35	Dark brown, scar on right wrist, scar in corner of left eye.	Pennsylvania	Floyd County	Jacob Mitchem	May 21, 1855
James W. Parsons	23	Dark brown, scar on forehead & under the chin, flesh mold on left shoulder.	Pennsylvania	Floyd County	"	"
Paris T. Robinson	17	Dark brown about 5 feet high, rather slender with some dark spots on the face & something resembling a scar near left ear, scar on left wrist.	Kentucky	Floyd County	S. P. Town	May 21, 1855
David Simrall	57	Black, about 5 ft 8 ins, stout, well built, has a scar on his head.	Virginia	Floyd County	Doc[umentary] evidence	July 17, 1855
Sally Simrall	57	Black, good size with a scar over the right eye.	"	"	"	"
Jonathan Heard	22	Dark brown, about 5 feet 3 inches high, thin, scars on the right leg.	Indiana	Floyd County	Andrew Jackson	Sept 24, 1855
Nancy Campbell	24	Mulatto, large in size, little toe of the left foot off, mark in corner of left eye.	Evansville, Indiana	New Albany	Peter Vincent	Oct 10, 1855
Morgan Campbell	37	Copper color, small size, front teeth lower jaw right side out, scar on top of head. Two toes grown together on each foot.	Indiana	New Albany	"	"
Susan Gibson	6	Dark cop[per] color.	Kentucky	New Albany	Geo. Winters	Nov 3, 1855

Floyd County, Indiana

Name	Age	Description	Origin	Residence	Contact	Date
Benjamin Thomas	31	Very Black, scar on left hand and on forehead over right eye.	Indiana	New Albany	John Findly	Dec 18, 1855
Phoebe Harris	14	Light brown	Indiana	New Albany	Wm. Hood	"
John Bonds	19	Light brown, and slim built	Vigo County, Ind.	New Albany	John H. Freeman	Dec 19, 1855
William Henry Harris	17	Dark brown, scar over left eye.	New Albany	New Albany	Mary J. Hood	Jan 4, 1856
James N. Mitchem	19 mos	Light brown	New Albany	New Albany	John Findly	Jan 16, 1856
Alice J. Robison	6	Light mulatto	Clark County	New Albany	Eliza Webb	Feb 6, 1856
Franklin A. Blockwell	21	Light mulatto, about 5 ft 8 inches.	Cincinnati	New Albany	Amelia Mitchem	March 3, 1856
Cynthia Ann Milton	7	Mulatto, quite delicate.	New Albany	New Albany	S. P. Ford	March 11, 1856
Daniel Mitchem	21	Dark brown scar on right leg.	New Albany	New Albany	Washington Mitchem	March 20, 1856
Frederick L. Wilson	18	Very Black, crippled in left arm, 2 scars on same arm.	New Albany	New Albany	R. M. Wier	March 22, 1856
Moses Mitchem	17	Light mulatto, blind in left eye, scar on right arm.	New Albany	New Albany	Ephriam Kearns	"
Sarah Carpenter	24	Very black, small frame, scar on left hand.	New Albany	New Albany	S. P. Ford	April 26, 1856
John M. Wilson	21	Very Black, scar over each eye and one on forehead.	New Albany	New Albany	Robert M. Wier	June 2, 1856
Thomas Frederick Howard	17	Very Black	New Albany	New Albany	Peter Vincent	Aug 23, 1856
Mary Ellen Wilson	19	Dark Brown, scar on left side of neck.	Evansville, Ind.	New Albany	Nancy Campbell	Sept 5, 1856

Floyd County, Indiana

Name	Age	Description	Birthplace	Residence	Sponsor	Date
Alexander Milton	29	Light Brown, scar on big toe of right foot, 1 scar near instep of left foot.	North Carolina	New Albany	Lewis Terrell	Dec 31, 1856
Daniel H. Coffin	23	Light brown, both little fingers crooked.	Jennings County, Ind.	New Albany	Jonathan Hood	Feby 3, 1857
Eliza J. Tolbert	17	Black, scar on forehead over left eye & scar on upper lip.	Kentucky	New Albany	Nancy Campbell	Mar 25, 1857
Elias Tolbert	35	Dark brown, scar on top right side of head & scar on lleft side of under jaw.	Virginia	New Albany	"	"
Richard Weaver	19	Very Black, scar on back of lleft hand.	Kentucky	New Albany	Abraham Miller	"
Wilson Mitchem	33	Dark brown, strait hair, small scar on back of right hand.	Indiana	New Albany	Oliver W. Littell	Mar 27, 1857
Oliver Payne	10	Light brown, scar on inside of left leg below knee.	Indiana	New Albany	Panancy Griffin	May 15, 1857
William Henry Payne	38	Brown, cross eyed, pretty large.	Virginia	New Albany	"	"
James Parham	29	Black, rather large scar on left hand near the thumb, small mole on nose between eyes.	"	New Albany	"	May 21, 1857
Algeria Parham	24	Yellow rather slim.	"	New Albany	"	"
George H. Parham	7 mos	Bright yellow, mark on right eye.	Indiana	New Albany	"	"
Hannibal Carter	22	Bright yellow about 5 feet five inches, slim built.	New Albany	New Albany	Geo. W. Castor	June 11, 1857
John Fuller	23	Light mulatto, scar on left wrist and on left side of f0orehead.	South Carolina	New Albany	Si Mitchem	June 16, 1857
Enos Munsey	18	Yellow, scar on left side of neck.	Missouri	New Albany	Elias Findley	July 2, 1857

Floyd County, Indiana

Name	Age	Description	Birthplace	Residence	Owner/Other	Date
Peter Findley	30	Black, heavy set, scar on corner of left eye.	Virginia	New Albany	Wm. Carpenter	Aug 6, 1857
William D. Morris	30	Yellow, 6 feet 1 inch high, scar on corner of right eye.	Indiana	New Albany	Saml. Flin	Aug 7, 1857
William W. Morris	8	Light mulatto	Indiana	New Albany	"	"
Louisa V. Morris	4	Light mulatto	Indiana	New Albany	"	"
James F. Morris	1 1/2	Light mulatto	Indiana	New Albany	"	"
Francis Reed	18	Light mulatto, small size, left forefinger crooked.	Kentucky	New Albany		Aug 11, 1857
Thompson Mitchem	29	Dark brown, scar on left cheek and on back of right hand.	Harrison Co., Ind.	New Albany	Johnson Mitchem	Aug 28, 1857
George Reese	32	Dark brown, rather heavy set, small scar or mark on forehead between the eyes.	Bowling Green & Warren Co, Kentucky	New Albany	Preston Findley	Aug 31, 1857
Thomas Cordron	21	Bright yellow, scar over left eye and has some pock marks.	Indiana	New Albany Floyd County	John Findley	Sept 15, 1857
Thomas I. Brown	37	Dark brown 2 scars on left arm above elbow, scars on right arm and on body.	Kentucky	"	Wilson Mitchem	Sept 21, 1857
Peter Bird	37	Light brown, scar on corner of each eye & scar on left shoulder.	South Carolina	New Albany	Tho. J. Brown	Sept 23, 1857
Sarah Jane Shaw	37	Very light, tall and slim, mole on right cheek and corner of left eye.	Henry Co., Ky.	New Albany	Marion Winters	Sept 30, 1857
Henry Harper	16	Bright mulatto, mole on right side of nose and left side of neck.	Georgia	New Albany	Peter Bond	Oct 13, 1857
Anthony Ergum	18	Black, scar on back of left hand and one near the thumb on same hand.	Indiana	New Albany	Thompson Mitchem	Oct 17, 1857

Floyd County, Indiana

Name	Age	Description	Birthplace	Residence	Owner	Date
Thomas H. Cay	21	Light brown, 2 scars on breast and one scar on back.	Indiana	New Albany	Henry Clay	Oct 22, 1857
Ann E. Brown	28	Dark brown both little fingers crooked.	Kentucky	New Albany	Tho. J. Brown	"
Lewis J. Brown	11	Dark brown color	Indiana	New Albany	"	"
John E. P. Brown	6	Dark brown color	Indiana	New Albany	"	"
Frances A. Brown	4	Dark brown color	Indiana	New Albany	"	"
Martha A. Brown	2	Dark brown color	Indiana	New Albany	"	"
Elias Findley	42	Dark brown color, scar on back of right hand near forefinger.	Virginia	New Albany	John Findley	Nov 24, 1857
James W. Findley	15	Dark brown color, scar on back of left hand.	Tennessee	New Albany	John Findley	"
Andrew Jackson	30	Light mulatto scar on left arm and scar on right leg.	Virginia	New Albany	Jacob Anthony	Nov 25, 1857
Amelia Jackson	51	Brown color, scar on back of right hand.	Indiana	New Albany	"	"
Andrew Leroy Jackson	15	Light brown color, small mark on his breast.	Indiana	New Albany	"	"
Sarah M. Jackson	12	Light brown, scar on right side of nose and on back of left hand.	Indiana	New Albany	"	"
Amelia M. Mitchem	15	Light brown color, scar on right side of neck, scar on back of left hand right arm crooked.	Indiana	New Albany	Catharine Findley	Dec 26, 1857
Malinda Mitchem	38	Light brown color, heavy set. Four small scars on back of right hand.	Indiana	New Albany	"	"

Floyd County, Indiana

Martin Davis	48	Light Mulato	Mississippi, Jefferson Co.	Floyd County	Tho. H. Collins	Jan 19, 1858
Jesse Davis	20	Very light mulato, 2 scars on upper lip.	Same	Same	Same	Same
William Davis	18	Very light mulato, scar on right hand near the thumb.	"	"	"	"
Mary Davis	17	Very light mulato	Mississippi, Jefferson Co.	Floyd County	"	"
Adaline Davis	14	Very light mulato	"	"	"	"
Eliza Jane Davis	11	Very light mulato	"	"	"	"
John Davis	8	Very light mulato	"	"	"	"
Mary Jane Findley	19	Light mulatto	Indiana	New Albany	Amelia R. Mitchhem	Jan 30, 1858
Winney Mitchem	21	Dark brown scar in corner of the right eye.	Indiana	New Albany	Jeanna Robison	Feb 20, 1858
Richard H. L. Mitchem	5	Light brown	New Albany	New Albany	"	"
Beverly L. Mitchem	3	Dark brown, scar over one of her eyes.	New Albany	New Albany	"	"
John C. N. Fowles	26	Light mulatto, has a scar on back of right leg above the ankle.	Philadelphia, Pa.	New Albany	S. P. Town	Mar 16, 1858
Mary Ann Hord	19	Dark brown, quite small in size. Scar on under jaw of right side & scar over left eye on forehand.	Indiana	New Albany	Ann Eliza Bowlin	Mar 26, 1858
James Baker	40	Light mulatto, scar on left wrist. Crippled in left leg.	Maryland	Floyd County	Jacob Anthony	Apr 7, 1858
Nancy Finley	41	Dark brown color, rather small, no marks or scars.	South Carolina	Floyd County	I. F. W. Finley	May 8, 1858

Floyd County, Indiana

Name		Description				Date
Ephraim Keller	48	Black, one upper fronth tooth out, scar on left leg.	Oldem Co, Kentucky	Floyd County	Eli Ross	Aug 25, 1858
William R. Keller	23	Black, rather small, scar on left wrist.	Oldem Co, Kentucky	Floyd County	"	"
Mary Ann Sims	26	Dark brown complexion & small scar in forehead.	Indiana	Floyd County	Peter Wincent	Aug 26, 1858
Daniel Sims	2	Dark brown, a scar on each littlle finger.	Indiana	Floyd County	Mary Ann Sims	"
Eliza George	46	Dark brown color, very heavy set.	Scott Co, Kentucky	Floyd County	Mary Finley	Dec 2, 1858
Mary A. Finley	27	Dark brown complexion, heavy set.	Kentucky	Floyd County	Eliza George	"
Frances George A/C Rendand(?)	17	Dark brown heavy set.	Kentucky	Floyd County	"	"
Henry Justice	13	Light mulatto	Indiana	Floyd County	Bledsoe Hardin	Dec 15, 1858
Henry Clay	52	Light brown, heavy set, scar over left eye.	Kentucky	Floyd County	Geo. C. Shively Jr.	Jan 3, 1859
Eliza B. Clay	12	Light brown, rather heavy set.	Missouri	New Albany	"	"
Harriet A. Clay	6	Light brown slender built.	New Albany	Floyd County	"	"
Florence B. Clay	4	Light brown heavy set.	New Albany	Floyd County	"	"
Henrietta Clay	2	Light brown	New Albany	Floyd County	"	"
Mary Ann Clay	39	Light brown quite small.	Ohio	Floyd County	"	"
James Clark	43	Dark brown complexion, quite small, scar under left eye, scar on left side of forehead.	New Albany	Floyd County	John H. Freeman	April 21, 1859
Rachael Hagen	43	Dark brown complexion, medium size, no marks or scars perceivable.	Georgia	Floyd County	A. C. Pullon	June 1, 1859

Floyd County, Indiana

Name	Age	Description	Origin	Residence	Witness	Date
Alice Fisher	26	Dark Brown, has a scar on left arm.	Alabama	Floyd County	"	"
Mary J. Blackburn	22	Dark brown complexion, no marks or scars perceivable.	Alabama	Floyd County	"	"
Malileta C. Winson	6	Light mulatto, short hair.	Jeffersonville, Indiana	Floyd County	Peter Winson	Blank
Wm. Henry Winson	1	Light mulatto short hair.	New Albany	Floyd County	"	"
Ann M. Clouston	29	Dark Brown complexion scar on left arm at elbow & has a mole on center lip.	Kentucky	Floyd County	J. L. Davis	"
Joseph W. Clouston	10	Dark Brown, has a scar on left side of his face, produced by a burn.	Floyd County	Floyd County	Ann M. Clouston	Sept 9, 1859
Wm. H. Woodall	32	Very light complexion, strat hair, five feet 11 inches high.	Indiana	Floyd County	John H. Freeman	Oct 3, 1859
Henry H. White	22	Light complexion, slender built & a preacher of the Gospel of the Baptist.	Clark Co, Indiana	Floyd County	Edward Rickman	Nov 4, 1859
Wesley Finley	19	Dark brown complexion, scar on right side of chin, scar on left thum.	Indiana, Harrison Co.	Floyd County	Martin Finley	Jan 12, 1860
Laura Bell Caster	18	Dark brown, scar on left wrist.	Clark Co, Indiana	Floyd County	Henry Carter	April 2, 1860
Sarah C. Jacobs	19	Dark brown complexion & tall.	Mississippi	Floyd County	"	"
James Jacobs	22	Light brown complexion, small scar on right wrist.	"	"	"	"
Emily Findley	11	Light mulatto strait black hair delicate features.	New Albany	New Albany	Ann Porter witness on oath	Aug 9, 1860
Laderia Ann Porter	21 mos	Light mulatto strait hair.	New Albany	New Albany	"	"

Floyd County, Indiana

Name	Age	Description	Birthplace	Residence	Witness	Date
John Hancock	22	Light Brown, scars on left thum, right thum short & thicker than left thum.	New Albany	New Albany	Edward L. Cooper witness on oath.	"
James Barkley	29	Dark brown, scar on back of left hand, scar on back joint of middle finger of right hand, scar on left leg.	Pennsylvania	New Albany	Danl Coffin witness on oath	"
John Taylor	33	Black, heavy set forefinger cut off at middle joint on lefft hand, scar on left cheek burn.	Pennsylvania	New Albany	Daniel Coffin oath.	Aug 10, 1860
Isabella Coffin	28	Light mulatto, short black hair.	Indiana	New Albany	"	"
Leonidus M. Henderson	9	Light mulatto, short black hair.	New Albany	New Albany	"	"
Samuel Henderson	5	Light mulatto Curly hair.	New Albany	New Albany	"	"
Rebecca A. Coffin	11	Light mulatto Curly hair.	Madison, Indiana	New Albany	"	"
Rebecca J. Taylor	22	Very light complexion, red hair.	Floyd County	New Albany	John Findley on oath	"
Frances Mitchem	21	Dark Brown bushy hair.	New Albany	New Albany		"
Caroline Findley	6	Dark brown	Born in Arkansas on the 4th of Oct 1854 while her mother was chambermaid on a boat running on Arkansas River.	New Albany	"	
John Demines	21	Very light curly hair, scar on left thum, quite small.	Mississippi	New Albany	Afft of John Ward	"
John Ward	29	Very black, scar on top of head.	Kentucky	New Albany	Afft of John Demines	"
Joseph Hollon	40	Very Black, scar on left hand also over right eye & on lefft side of forehead.	Madison, Indiana	New Albany	Afft of Daniel Coffin	"

Floyd County, Indiana

Mary Jane Ward	Abt 4 years	Dark brown	New Albany	New Albany	John Ward father of Mary J. Ward
Harry Merrill	40	Light brown complexion, mark of "H. M. & E. M." in indelible ink on right arm.	Corydon, Harrison Co, Ind.	New Albany	Afft of Oliver W. Littrel	"
Sarah Merrill	27	Very light complexion strait black hair.	Indiana	Floyd County	Afft of Harry Merrill	"
Mary Susan Mitchem	75	Mulatto, light brown complexion, has a white spot or catarack on right eye.	Indiana	Floyd County	Afft of Amelia R. Mitchem	"
Thomas A. Mitchem	13	Dark brown small scar near lid left eye.	New Albany	New Albany		"
Florence F. Mitchem	3	Light complexion	New Albany	New Albany	"	"
Juliet A. Blackwell	26	"	New Albany	New Albany	"	"
James Price	44	Dark brown, scar on nose and throat rather small.	Clark Co., Indiana	New Albany	Afft of Daniel Coffin	"
Washington Braxson	23	Light complexion, scar on right side of neck.	Madison, Indiana	New Albany	"
William Lewis	44	Dark, scar on his hand, small mole on chin, first joint of little finger on right hand crook.	Louisiana	New Albany	Afft of Geo. Wintors	"
Harriet Goens	19	Light brown scar under right eye.	Indiana	New Albany	Afft of Lavina Stewart	"
Jane Franklin	30	Dark brown complexion.	Indiana	New Albany	Richard Johnson' Afft.	"
John D. Mitchem	20	Dark brown complexion, scar on right cheek bone.	Corydon, Indiana	New Albany	Afft of Oliver W. Littell	"
Benjamin F. Barker	22	Dark brown scar on left arm between shoulder & elbow.	Vanderburg Co, Indiana	New Albany	Afft of Uriah Stewart	"

Floyd County, Indiana

Emeline Weaver	27	Dark brown complexion, rather heavy set, scar on right forefinger, scar on right shin, scar near right eye.	New Albany	New Albany	Afft of Abraham Miller	Aug 11, 1860
Mary Ann Mitchem	18	Dark brown, rather heavy set, small mole on lid of left eye & small mole under chin.	New Albany	New Albany	Afft of Malinda Mitchem	"
Lucinda Jane Mitchem	17	Dark brown heavy set, small scar on right arm.	New Albany	New Albany	Same as above	"
Amanda J. Locklayer	20	Light brown complexion.	Indiana	New Albany	Afft of Peter Bird	"
Sarah E. Bird	24	Light brown, rather heavy set.	Georgia	New Albany	Same as above	"
Lucinda E. R. Bird	13	Light Brown, some small pock marks on her nose.	"	New Albany	"	"
Edward L. Bird	5	Light Brown scar preceivably a burn on top of hand.	New Albany	New Albany	"	"
Patsey Harper	61	Light brown, scar on right side of nose.	Henry Co, Virginia	New Albany	Afft of Edwin Bird	"
Elizabeth Goen	65	Dark brown, heavy set, scar on left foot.	"	New Albany	"	"
John Goen	27	Light mulatto, very large. 3 scars on forehead & scar on right wrist.	Indiana	New Albany	Afft of Elizabeth Goen	"
Jesse Goen	24	Light mulatto, thum of left hand off at first joint.	Indiana	New Albany	Same as above	"
Adam A. Goen	12	Very light mulatto, light hair, left hand crippled by a shot.	Indiana	New Albany	"	"
Lucinda Harper	42	Light brown scar on right cheek.	Indiana	New Albany	"	"

Floyd County, Indiana

Name	Age	Description	Birthplace	Residence	Affidavit/Witness
Sarah A. Harper	14	Light mulatto, sccar of burn on left cheek.	Indiana	New Albany	Afft of Lucinda Harper
Sylvania Harper	9	Light mulatto small scar under left jaw.	Indiana	New Albany	"
John W. Harper	11	Bright mulatto, scar on right shoulder.	Indiana	New Albany	Afft of Patsey Harper
Susan Richards	47	Light brown, scar on forehead right side, scar on right shoulder.	Kentucky	New Albany	Afft of Ann Baty
Jonnetta Richards	11	Light brown, pock mark on left arm between elbow and shoulder.	New Albany	New Albany	Afft of Susan Richards
Hannah Richards	9	Light brown, black mark on left hip.	Indiana	New Albany	"
Martha J. Jones formerly Martha J. Watson	27	Very Black, small scar on bust, & scar on skin of right leg.	Virginia	New Albany	Witness Mary J. Dove
Mary J. Dove	33	Light mulatto, scar on forehead above left eye.	Crawford Co, Indiana	New Albany	Afft of Martha J. Jones
William A. Dove	34	Very black, quite small, scar on right hand, is a Methodist Preacher.	Pennsylvania	New Albany	Mary J. Dove
Martha Flinn	5	Bright mulatto, strait hair.	New Albany	New Albany	Afft of Saml Flinn
Edmonia D. Flinn	22 mos	Bright mulatto, strait hair.	New Albany	New Albany	"
Job Townsend	35	Dark brown scar on left cheek occasioned by a burn.	Delaware	New Albany	Afft of Mary A. Townsend
Indiana Worthington	20	Light brown	New Albany	New Albany	"
Edward Carter	18	Dark brown, scar in corner of left eye, scar on left forefinger.	New Albany	New Albany	Witness Mary Blackburn

Floyd County, Indiana

Name	Age	Description			
William Wadkins	43	Dark brown, scar on left arm between elbow & arm, left thum been displaced, scar on forehead over left eye.	Virginia	New Albany	Harriet Burns, affidavit
Wm. W. Edwards	5	Black (child)	New Albany	New Albany	Child of Wm Wadkins & Jane E. Wadkins formerlly Jane E. Mitchem
John W. Wadkins	6 mos	Black (child)	New Albany	New Albany	Same
William Harding	60	Dark brown, has large scar under chin.	Pennsylvania	New Albany	Afft. of Geo. Bishop
Eliza Harding	45	Dark brown, quite small	Louisiana	New Albany	Wm. Harding the husband of Eliza
Delphine Wright	32	Light mulatto	Pennsylvania	New Albany	Wm. Harding the father of Delphine
Mary A. Johnson	22	Bright mulatto large black mark between shoulders.	New Albany	New Albany	Same proof
Edward Harding	21	Dark brown rather small size.	New Albany	New Albany	Proof of Wm. Harding father of Edward
Joseph Harding	16	Dark brown	New Albany	New Albany	same proof
Virginia I. H. Harding	12	Dark brown	New Albany	New Albany	"
Sarah Harding	7	Dark brown	New Albany	New Albany	"
Sullivan G. Harding	2	Dark brown	New Albany	New Albany	"
Delphy Mitchem	49	Very light mulatto, scar across right hand.	Virginia	New Albany	Aff of Oliver W. Littells
Sarah Jane Mitchem	18	Light brown scar under left ear.	Harrison Co, Ind.	New Albany	Same proof

Floyd County, Indiana

Name	Age	Description		Residence		
Dedda A. Mitchem	16	Dark brown, rather large.	"	New Albany	"	
Clara C. Mitchem	12	Very light mulatto.	New Albany	New Albany	"	
Barbar Rielor	58	Very black, very thick upper lip produced by cancer.	Kentucky	New Albany	Daniel McIntire & wife	
Ellen Mitchem	17	Bright mulatto, scar on right middle finger.	New Albany	New Albany	Johnson Worthington afft	"
Nancy Ann Harper	20	Bright mulatto medium size.	Indiana	New Albany	same proof	"
Nancy Mayhoe	35	Bright mulatto, small size, strait black hair.	Tennessee	Floyd County	Samuel W. Wood Afft	Aug 13, 1860
William Mayhoe	16	Light brown scar on back joint of left fore finger & mole in corner of right eye.	Indiana	Floyd County	same proof	"
Drury Mayhoe	12	Very light mulatto, scar on two fingers of left hand, near the end.	Indiana	Floyd County	"	"
Minerva Mayhoe	11	Very light mulatto scar over left eye.	Indiana	Floyd County	"	"
Temperance Weaver	60	Very Black, face very much marked with small pox.	Maryland	Floyd County	Eliza J. Talbot afft.	Aug 13, 1860
Daniel W. Weaver	18	Very Black, 2 marks of a cut on left side.	Indiana	New Albany	same proof	"
Arthur Weaver	15	Very Black, scar under right jaw & on neck under chin.	Indiana	Floyd County	same proof	"
Eliza Gray	25	Light mulatto, short heavy set, scar over left eye.	Indiana	Floyd County	"	
Mary J. Cousins	21	Light mulatto quite tall.	Indiana	Floyd County	Afft of Wm. A. Love	Aug 15, 1860

Floyd County, Indiana

Isabella Goens	21	Dark brownn, strait hair, scar under chin.	Kentucky	New Albany	Afft of Cecilia Cook	Aug 20, 1860
Pleasant Devol	29	Very Black scar in left corner of left eye, right hand neen broken near back joint of forefinger.	Corydon, Indiana	New Albany	John L. Mitchem	Sept 19, 1860
Martha J. Devol	24	Dark Brown, rather heavy set, small scar over left eye.	New Albany	New Albany	"	"
Anna Bell Devol	4	Dark Brown	New Albany	New Albany	"	"
John Clifton	36	Dark brown, forefinger of right hand off, scar on nose, left hand crippled.	Tennessee	New Albany	William DeMarr	Nov 6, 1860
Andrew J. Findley	16	Dark brown, scar on right hand, back of forefinger.	Tennessee	New Albany	Elias Findley	Dec 28, 1860
James S. Findley	23	Dark brown rather large, scars on left thum, scar near left eye.	Floyd County	Floyd County	Josiah Findlley	Jan 19, 1861
James Lindsey	24	Light brown complexion about six feet high has a small mole in corner of left eye.	Louisville, Ky.	Floyd County	Afft of Hamilton R. Multhins	Jan 21, 1861
Margaret Jane Lee	25	Dark brown complexion, no marks or scars.	Virginia	Floyd County	Jane Porter	Feb 8, 1861
James K. Hilyard	31	Light brown about five feet 3 inches	Pennsylvania	Floyd County	George Winks	May 4, 1861
Washington King	40	Dark brown rather heavy set, scar of burn on left arm & small scar or mole on left eye.	Tennessee	Floyd County	Levi Mann	May 21, 1860
Mary Ann Finley	38	Dark brown rather heavy set, scar on left jaw, fore finger on right hand cut off at first joint.	Georgia	Floyd County	John L. Finley	June 3, 1861

Floyd County, Indiana

Name	Age	Description	Birthplace	Residence	Owner/Other	Date
Virginia Finley	20	Light brown, rather slim heavy head of hair.	Arkansas	Floyd County	Same	"
Preston Carter	21	Light mulatto, scar on top of head, face poc marked.	Floyd County	Floyd County	James Ross Aft	Nov 23, 1861
Ann M. Carter	49	Light mulatto strait hair, rather fleshy.	Chilacothe, Ohio	New Albany	Wm. W. Taley	Aug 30, 1862
John Wilson	19	Light brown	Lafayette, Indiana	New Albany	Charles I. Withs	Oct 20, 1862
Claiborne Goins	26	Light mulatto, hair mainly strait, 6 feet high, thum on left hand is off.	Lawrence Co, Ind.	Floyd County	W. W. Taley	Dec 22, 1862
Jasper Finley	15	Light brown, no scars	Tennessee	Floyd County	Elias Finley	Dec 31, 1862
Sina DeMars	35	Long hair, dark mulatto and measures about 5 feet 2 1/2 unches in height.	Kentucky Oct. 2, 1829	New Albany	W. W. Taley	Mar 5, 1863
Margaret B. DeMars	5	Light mulatto	Floyd County 3rd day Aug 1857	Floyd County	Sina Dewars	"
Jack Hollon	28	Black, plaited hair, scars above left thumb, also on nose.	Jefferson Co, Ind.	New Albany	Claiborne Goins	Mar 11, 1863
Andrew Wood	21	Black, scar from a burn on left cheek.	Jennings Co, Ind.	New Albany	John Wood	March 23, 1863
Frederick D. Wood	3	Dark brown, hair about half curly.	Floyd County	New Albany	"	"
Julia Finley	16	Light brown, small scar above left eye, hair mainly strait.	Illinois	New Albany	May C. Finley	April 6, 1863
May C. Finley	18	Nutmeg brown, scars on face from smallpox.	Illinois	New Albany	Julia Finley	"
Mary Jane Wood	29	Very black, 5 feet 5 inches high, hair curly.	Clark Co, Ind.	New Albany	Jonathan Wood	May 9, 1863

Floyd County, Indiana

Name	Age	Description				Date
Victoria E. Parham, dau of James & Alzera	5	Curly hair very black.	Floyd County	New Albany	Alzera Parham	June 12, 1863
Joseph A. Parham cild of same	3	Curly hair rather light.	Floyd County	New Albany	"	"
James F. Parham child of same	1	Light brown	Floyd County	New Albany	"	"
Nelson Fisher	48	Black, scar on left hand & on the nose, thick lips, cook & steward.	Nashville, Tenn.	New Albany	Edward Baily	June 16, 1863
Margaret Fisher child of Nelson Fisher	4	Light, hair half strait.	New Albany	New Albany	"	"
William Fisher child of Nelson Fisher	3	Blaack	New Albany	New Albany	"	"
May Fisher Child of Nelson Fisher	5 mos	Bright mulatto	"	"	"	"
Newton Finley	16	Black, black curly hair, 5 ft 10 or so in. high, no perceptible scars.	Tennessee	Harrison Co, Ind.	John Finley	Sept 11, 1863
Isaac H. Briggs	24	Light mulatto. Scar on right eye, 5 ft 7 1/2 inches high.	Harrison Co, Ind.	Floyd County	Tho. J. Brown	Dec 16, 1863
Edward Mitchem	18	Light brown. Scar on hand, about 5 ft 4 in in height.	Bennettsville, Ind.	Floyd County	Joel Worthington	Jan 21, 1864
Martha A. Smith	36	Dark brown, about 5 feet 2 in. in height. No scars.	Floyd County	Floyd County	Josephine Mitchem	March 22, 1864
Josephine Mitchem	19	Light brown, scar on right cheek, about 5 ft 3 in in height.	Clark Co, Ind.	Floyd County	Martha A. Smith	"
Charles Mitchem	21	Light brown 5 ft 9 in high.	Bennettsville, Ind.	Floyd County	Ed Midham	April 23, 1864

Floyd County, Indiana

Joseph A. Cousins	29	Dark, with a litttle indication of mulatto blood, about 5 ft 10 in, scar on chin.	Cumberland Co, Ky.	Blank	Blank
Paul Finley	45	Dark brown, about 6 feet high, scar over right eye.	Indiana	Floyd County	P. M. Kopley	Nov 15, 1864
William Graham	25	5-7 in high-light brown, scar over right eye & under chin.	Indiana	Floyd County	M. M. Newton	Dec 3, 1864
Levi T. Russell	21	About 5 ft 10 high, lleft forefinger off, very light brown, brown hair.	New Albany	Floyd County	Jas. Russell	Feb 20, 1865

REGISTER OF NEGROES AND MULATTOES IN FRANKLIN COUNTY, INDIANA

Names	Age	Description	Place of Birth	Residence	Names of Witnesses	Date Registered
Fant, Willis	41	Negro of a yellow complexion about five feet ten inches high.	KY	Franklin Co, IN	John C. Burton Andrew Grob	None given
Scott, Philip	73	Negro colour black about five feet ten inches high.	VA	Franklin Co, IN	Andrew McClary Thomas Gard	None given
Banks, Britton	72 about	Negro dark complexion tinged with yellow. Hair gray five feet eight inches high.	NC	Franklin Co, IN	Benjamin D. Goodwin Henry George	None given
Morgan, Matthew	52	Negro dark complexion tinged with yellow, hair sprinkled with grey five feet eight inches high.	NC	Franklin Co, IN	Robert Pugh William Maxwell	None given
Freeman, Archibald	42	Negro colour black about five feet eight inches high.	NC	Franklin Co, IN	Robert Pugh William Maxwell	None given
Bass, Alexander	32	Mulatto rising six feet high.	NC	Franklin Co, IN	Robert Pugh William Maxwell	None given
Williams, Jesse	24	Mulatto five feet ten inches high.	NC	Franklin Co, IN	William Maxwell Israel Goble	None given
Hays, James	39	Negro colour black about five feet nine inches high.	NC	Franklin Co, IN	William Maxwell Israel Goble	None given
Brayboy, Stephen	34	Mulatto, about five feet six inches high, hair rather strait.	NC	Franklin Co, IN	William Maxwell Israel Goble	None given
Donaldson, Dary	53	Negro colour black about five feet two inches high, has crooked thumbs.	SC	Franklin Co, IN	Israel Goble Andrew J. Ross	None given

Franklin County, Indiana

Name	Age	Description	Origin	Location	Witnesses	Date
Sibley, Henry	53	Negro colour black about five feet six inches high, a crooked finger on the hand hand [sic], left forefinger stiff, a small scar on the right eyebrow.	VA	Franklin Co, IN	William Robinson James Fordice	None given
Edington, Gustavus I.	41	Mulatto, about five feet eight inches high, rather heavy set.	VA	Franklin Co, IN	George M. Byram Nathaniel McCrookshank Samuel Murphy	None given
Hood, Josiah	30	Negro man, black colour, strait hair, about five feet four inches high.	PA [crossed out] On the Ocean	Franklin Co, IN	Jacob Guard Hiram Prison	July 5, 1853
Short, Henry	49	Negro black color about five feet ten inches high.	MD	Franklin Co, IN	Richard Tyner William T. Tyner	July 7, 1853
Holley, Rode	60	Negro light complexion, gray hair about five feet eight inches high.	VA	Franklin Co, IN	Michael Batzner Isaac Jones	July 7, 1853
Smith, Benjamin	46	Negro black color a small scar on upper lip about five feet seven inches high.	NJ	Franklin Co, IN	Branson Samson Oliver M. Bartton	July 27, 1853
York, Joshua	34	Negro light complexion a large scar on the left side of his neck, about 5 feet six inches high.	Franklin Co, IN	Franklin Co, IN	William Robeson Richard S. Sims	September 16, 1853
Morgan, Nancy	42	Mullatto woman light complexion about five feet nine inches high.	NC	Franklin Co, IN	Robert Pugh John S. Simpson	None given
Morgan, Sophonia Ann	12	Mulatto girl light complexion.	NC	Franklin Co, IN	Robert Pugh John S. Simpson	None given
Morgan, James Wesley	14	Mulatto boy.	NC	Franklin Co, IN	Robert Pugh John S. Simpson	None given
Morgan, Joseph	11	Mulatto boy.	NC	Franklin Co, IN	Robert Pugh John S. Simpson	None given

Franklin County, Indiana

Name	Age	Description	From	To	Signed by	Date
White, James B.	26	Negro about five feet nine inches high, good looking.	NC	Franklin Co, IN	Robert Pugh John S. Simpson	None given
Holley, Sarah	60	Mullatto woman rather dark tinged with yellow, about five feet five inches. All upper teeth out except one.	VA	Franklin Co, IN	Aaron Ailes	April 8, 1856
Holley, Nancy	17	Dark mulatto girl, about five feet six inches high, rather slender & good looking.	Franklin Co, IN	Franklin Co, IN	Aaron Ailes	April 8, 1856
Holley, Sanford	20	Dark mulatto boy about six feet high, rather slender made, black curly hair, rather good looking.	Franklin Co, IN	Franklin Co, IN	Aaron Ailes	April 8, 1856
Short, Jane	18	Mulatto, black hair, welll made about five five [sic] in high and good looking.	Dearborn Co, IN	Franklin Co, IN	Aaron Ailes	April 8, 1856
Short, Henry	12	Dark mulatto about four feet nine inches high, slim built, good looking.	Dearborn Co, IN	Franklin Co, IN	James Evans James Johnson	Oct 31/56

REGISTER OF NEGROES AND MULATTOES IN GIBSON COUNTY, INDIANA
(Legend: NR = not recorded. NA = not available, page missing.)

Names	Age	Description	Place of Birth	Residence	Names of Witnesses	Date Registered
Greer, Ann	32	Negro woman, stout built, light complexion, born in Richmond City, Virginia.	Richmond City, VA	Gibson Co, IN	Levi Greer	None given
Greer, Henry	16	Negro boy, 5 1/2 ft high, stout built, light complexion.	Marengo Co, AL	Gibson Co, IN	Levi Greer	None given
Greer, Allen	13	Mulatto, light built, very light complexion	Marengo Co, AL	Gibson Co, IN	Levi Greer	None given
Greer, Willis	11	Mulatto boy, light built, light complexion, 4 1/2 ft high.	Marengo Co AL	Gibson Co, IN	Levi Greer	None given
Greer, Harriet Caroline	4	Very light mulatto, 3 ft high, light built & very light complexion.	Marengo Co, AL	Gibson Co, IN	Levi Greer	None given
Greer, Martha	27	Negro, stout built 5 1/2 ft high, dark complexion.	NC	Gibson Co, IN	Levi Greer	None given
Greer, Zilpy	8	Negro girl, 4 ft 4 in high, light built, dark complexion.	Marengo Co, AL	Gibson Co, IN	Levi Greer	None given
Greer, Mary Lizer	4	Negro girl, 3 ft high, light built, dark complexion.	Marengo Co, AL	Gibson Co, IN	Levi Greer	None given
Morris, Elizabeth	40	Mulatto, spare built, light complexion 5 ft 2 in high.	Wake Co, NC	Gibson Co, IN	John McCoy	None given
Morris, Mary Elizabeth	5	Mulatto girl, light built, dark complexion 3 1/2 ft high.	Gibson Co, IN	Gibson Co, IN	Elizabeth Morris	None given
Hunt, Sarah	33	Mulatto, spare built, light complexion, 5 ft 5 in high.	Wake Co, NC	Gibson Co, IN	Elizabeth Morris	None given

Gibson County, Indiana

Name	Age	Description	Origin	Residence	Bondsmen	Notes
Like, Jacob	30	Negro, stout built, dark complexion, 5 ft 10 in high.	Jackson Co, Missouri(?)	Gibson Co, IN	Joel Lyles & Soloman Russell	None given
Stewart, Joel	38	Mulatto, stout built, dark complexion, 5 feet 8 in high.	Mecklenburg Co, VA	Gibson Co, IN	Willis Hargrove	None given
King, Alexander	47	Mulatto, spare built, dark complexion, 4 ft 10 inches.	VA	Gibson Co, IN	Joel Stewart	None given
Stewart, Lucy	25	Mulatto, slim built, dark complexion, 5 ft 5 inches high.	Franklin Co, IL	Gibson Co, IN	Joel Stewart Alex King	None given
Stewart, Elijah	12	Mulatto, slim built, dark complexion, 4 ft 10 inches.	Gibson Co, IN	Gibson Co, IN	Joel Stewart Alexander King	None given
Wilson, Elijah	18	Dark mulatto, spare built, dark complexion, 5 ft 6 ins high.	TN	Gibson Co, IN	Joel Stewart Alexander King	None given
Stewart, William Henry	9	Dark mulatto boy, slim built, dark complexion, 4 ft 2 ins high.	Gibson Co, IN	Gibson Co, IN	Joel Stewart Alex King	None given
Stewart, Mary Louisa	7	Dark mulatto girl, spare built, dark complexion, 3 ft 10 in high.	Gibson Co, IN	Gibson Co, IN	Joel Stewart Alex King	None given
Stewart, Solomon	1 yr 7 mos	Dark mulatto child, spare built, dark complexion.	Gibson Co, IN	Gibson Co, IN	Joel Stewart Alex King	None given
Harris, Henry	36	Mulatto stout built, dark complexion, 5 ft 9 inches high.	Buford Co, NC	Gibson Co, IN	Hugh H Patten	None given
Cole, Henry	45	Mulatto, spare built, dark complexion, 6 ft high.	Pittsylvania Co, VA	Gibson Co, IN	Joel Stewart	None given
McCan, Peter	45	Negro stout built, light complexion 5 ft 6 1/2 in high.	Che[s]ter District, SC	Gibson Co, IN	John McCoy	None given
Russel, Emeline	21	Mulatto, short built light complexion 5 ft 1 in high.	Franklin Co, IL	Gibson Co, IN	Joel Stewart	None given

Gibson County, Indiana

Russel, James M.	4 mos	Mulatto babe, light complexion.	Gibson Co, IN	Gibson Co, IN	Joel Stewart	None given
Waldon, Henry	53	Mulatto, light built, light complexion, 5 ft 7 in high.	Chatham Co, NC	Gibson Co, IN	Joel Stewart	None given
Russel, Wooddy	25	Negro, light built, light complexion, 6 ft 1 in high.	Franklin Co, IL	Gibson Co, IN	Joel Stewart	None given
Russel, Solomon	21	Negro, light built, light complexion, 6 ft 1 in high.	Franklin Co, IL	Gibson Co, IN	Joel Stewart	None given
Patten, Sally	30	Negro, bony corpulent, light complexion, 5 ft 3 in high.	Richmond, VA	Gibson Co, IN	Dr. H. H. Patten	None given
Patten, Mary Jane	15	Mulatto, light built, light complexion, 5 ft 1 1/2 in high.	Russellville, KY	Gibson Co, IN	Dr. H. H. Patten	None given
Cheevis, John	76	Mulatto, light built, light complexion, 5 ft 6 1/2 in high.	Mecklenburg Co, VA	Gibson Co, IN	John Embree	None given
Cheevis, James	26	Mulatto, light built, light complexion, 5 ft 7 1/2 in high.	Carroll Co, TN	Gibson Co, IN	John Embree	None given
Wimbley, Anderson	33	Negro, light built, Black complexion, 5 ft 7 in high.	TN	Gibson Co, IN	John Embree	None given
Wimbley, Firite	23	Negro, light buillt, Black complexion, 5 ft 7 in.	TN	Gibson Co, IN	John Embree	None given
Henderson, Taburn	23	Mulatto, spare built, light complexion, 5 ft 4 in high.	Saline Co, IL	Gibson Co, IN	James Cheevis	None given
Cheevis, Sarah J.	18	Mulatto, Spare built, very light complexion, 5 ft 3 in high.	Grayson Co, VA	Gibson Co, IN	James Cheevis	None given
Williams, Tabitha	70	Mulatto, stout built, light complexion, 5 ft 3 in high.	Halifax Co, VA	Gibson Co, IN	James Cheevis	None given

Gibson County, Indiana

Rusk, Robert	35	Negro, stout built, Black complexion, 5 ft 7 1/2 in high.	Knox Co, IN	Gibson Co, IN	Morris Rhea	None given
Rusk, Haarriet	39	Mulatto, light built, light complexion, 5 ft 2 in high.	Baltimore City, MD	Gibson Co, IN	Morris Rhea	None given
Soven, James Henry	12	Mulatto, light built, light complexion.		Gibson Co, IN	Morris Rhea	None given
Rusk, Morris	3	Negro, dark compllexion, light built.		Gibson Co, IN	Morris Rhea	None given
Rusk, Sarah E.	2	Negro, dark complexion.		Gibson Co, IN	Morris Rhea	None given
Miles, Virginia	16	Mulatto, dark complexion, light built, 5 feet high.	New Orleans, LA	Gibson Co, IN	Morris Rhea	None given
Rhea, Morris	55	Mulatto, light complexion, light built, 5 ft 7 in high.	Sullivan Co, TN	Gibson Co, IN	Robert Rusk	None given
Lyles, Mary Ellen	25	Mulatto, dark complexion, light built, 5 ft 4 inches high.	Gibson Co, IN	Gibson Co, IN	Tabitha Ferguson	None given
Ferguson, Taqbitha	40	Negro, llight complexion, light built, 5 ft 3 1/2 in high.	TN	Gibson Co, IN	Mary E. Lyles	None given
Lyles, Joshua	52	Negro, llight complexion, light built, 6 ft 1 1/2 in high.	Henry Co, VA	Gibson Co, IN	Joseph Lyles Joel Lyles	None given
Lyles, Joseph	24	Negro, light complexion, light built, 5 ft 9 in high.	Robertson Co, TN	Gibson Co, IN	Joshua Lyles Joel Lyles	None given
Lyles, Joel	22	Negro, light complexion, stout built, 5 ft 7 in high.	Robertson Co, TN	Gibson Co, IN	Joshua Lyles & Joseph Lyles	None given
Lyles, Clapanty [Cleopatra]	50	Mulatto, light complexion, light built, 5 ft 1 in high.	Albemarle Co, VA	Gibson Co, IN	Joshua Lyles, Joseph Lyles & Joel Lyles	None given
Lyles, Mildred	16	Mulatto, dark complexion, light built, 5 ft 1 1/2 in high.	Robertson Co, TN	Gibson Co, IN	Joshua Lyles, Joseph Lyles & Joel Lyles	None given

Gibson County, Indiana

Lyles, Mahala	11	Mulatto, dark complexion, light built, 4 ft 6 in high.	Gibson Co, IN	Gibson Co, IN	Joshua Lyles, Joseph Lyles & Joel Lyles	None given
Lyles, Angeline	20	Mulatto, dark complexion, stout built, 5 ft 1 1/2 in high.	Robertson Co, TN	Gibson Co, IN	Joshua Lyles, Joseph Lyles & Joel Lyles	None given
Lyles, Drucilla	18	Mulatto, dark complexion, stout built, 5 ft 4 in high.	Robertson Co, TN	Gibson Co, IN	Joshua Lyles, Joseph Lyles & Joel Lyles	None given
Lyles, Isaac	13	Mulatto, dark complexion, light built, 4 ft 6 in high.	Gibson Co, IN	Gibson Co, IN	Joshua Lyles, Joseph Lyles & Joel Lyles	None given
Lyles, Jacob	10	Mulatto, dark complexion, light built, 4 ft 3 in high.	Gibson Co, IN	Gibson Co, IN	Joshua Lyles, Joseph Lyles & Joel Lyles	None given
Lyles, Jonathan	8	Mulatto, dark complexion, light built, 4 ft 1 1/2 in high.	Gibson Co, IN	Gibson Co, IN	Joshua Lyles, Joseph Lyles & Joel Lyles	None given
Lyles, Joshua Junior	3	Mulatto, dark complexion, light built.	Gibson Co, IN	Gibson Co, IN	Joshua Lyles, Joseph Lyles & Joel Lyles	None given
Lyles, Peggy Ann	4	Negro, dark complexion, light built.	Gibson Co, IN	Gibson Co, IN	Joshua Lyles, Joseph Lyles & Joel Lyles	None given
Miles, Susan	65	Negro, dark compllexion, stout built, 4 ft 11 1/2 in high.	VA	Gibson Co, IN	Alex Devin	None given
Cole, Thos.	36	Negro, light complexion, stout built 6 feet high.	Pittsylvania Co, VA	Gibson Co, IN	John McCoy	None given
Lyles, Arthelea	13	Negro, dark complexion, light built, 4 ft 6 in high.	Vanderburgh Co, IN	Gibson Co, IN	Thomas Cole	None given
Nash, Alexander	28	Mulatto light complexion, light built, 5 ft 8 1/2 in high.	Mecklenburg Co, VA	Gibson Co, IN	James Cheevis	None given
Nash, Margaret	24	Mulatto, very light complexion, 5 ft 5 1/2 in high.	Carrol Co, TN	Gibson Co, IN	James Cheevis	None given

Gibson County, Indiana

Name	Age	Description	Birthplace	Residence	Witness	Remarks
Nash, John Calvin	7 mos	Mulatto very light complexion.	Gibson Co, IN	Gibson Co, IN	James Cheevis	None given
Russel, Solomon	60	Negro, stout built, dark complexion, 5 ft 8 in high.	Wake Co, NC	Gibson Co, IN	Joel Stewart	None given
Ashby, Richard	65	Negro, light built, dark complexion, 5 ft 8 in high.	NC	Gibson Co, IN	Dr. H. H. Patten	None given
Ashby, Mary Sr.	63	Mulatto, light built, dark complexion, 5 ft 4 in high.	VA	Gibson Co, IN	Dr. H. H. Patten	None given
Ashby, Mary Jr.	13	Mullatto, very dark complexion, 5 ft 4 in high.	Hopkins Co, KY	Gibson Co, IN	Dr. H. H. Patten	None given
Holmes, John	48	Negro, dark complexion, light built, 5 ft 7 in high.	Queens Co, NY	Gibson Co, IN	Joshua Embree	None given
Lyles, Alfred	38	Mulatto, light complexion, light built, 5 ft 10 in high.	KY	Gibson Co, IN	John McCoy	None given
Lyles, Barbara J.	27	Mulatto, very light complexion, light built, 5 ft 1 in high.	Gibson Co, TN	Gibson Co, IN	Alfred Lyles & Henry Waldon	None given
Lyles, Louisa	7	Mulatto, very light complexion, light built.	Gibson Co, IN	Gibson Co, IN	Alfred Lyles & Henry Waldon	None given
Lyles, William Henry	3	Mulatto, very light complexion, light built.	Gibson Co, IN	Gibson Co, IN	Alfred Lyles & Henry Waldon	None given
Lyles, John Thomas	1 yr 6 mos	Mulatto, very light complexion, light built.	Gibson Co, IN	Gibson Co, IN	Alfred Lyles & Henry Waldon	None given
Lyles, Mary Ann	2 mos	Mulatto, very light complexion, light built.	Gibson Co, IN	Gibson Co, IN	Alfred Lyles & Henry Waldon	None given
Lyles, Eleanor	15	Mulatto, dark complexion, light built, 5 ft high.	Vanderburgh Co, IN	Gibson Co, IN	Alfred Lyles & Henry Waldon	None given

Gibson County, Indiana

Name	Age	Description	Origin	Residence	Contact	Other
Walden, Lucy	50	Mulatto, dark complexion, stout built, 5 ft high.	Mecklenburg Co, NC	Gibson Co, IN	Henry Walden	None given
Walden, Lydia Ann	15	Mulatto, light complexion, light built, 3 ft 2 in high.	Gibson Co, TN	Gibson Co, IN	Henry Walden	None given
Lyles, Mary Elizabeth	13	Mulatto, light complexion, light built, 4 ft 10 in high.	Gibson Co, TN	Gibson Co, IN	Henry Walden	None given
Walden, Henry D.	11	Mulatto, light complexion, light built.	Gibson Co, TN	Gibson Co, IN	Henry Walden	None given
Walden, Green Jackson	8	Mulatto, light complexion, light built.	Gibson Co, IN	Gibson Co, IN	Henry Walden	None given
Walden, James Warren	4	Mulatto, light complexion, light built.	Gibson Co, IN	Gibson Co, IN	Henry Walden	None given
Stewart, Mathew Henderson	15	Mulatto, light complexion, light built, 5 ft 2 in high.	IL	Gibson Co, IN	Townsend Glascoe	None given
Artus, Phoebe	20	Mulatto, dark complexion, light built, 5 ft 6 in high.	Robertson Co, TN	Gibson Co, IN	Joel Stewart	None given
Artus, Eliiza Jane	3	Mulatto, dark complexion, light built.	Robertson Co, TN	Gibson Co, IN	Joel Stewart	None given
Hardiman, Martha	15	Mulatto, dark complexion, light built, 5 ft 2 in high.	Robertson Co, TN	Gibson Co, IN	Joel Stewart	None given
Lyles, Anna	11	Mulatto, dark complexion, light built, 5 ft 4 in high.	Robertson Co, TN	Gibson Co, IN	Tabitha Lyles	None given
Wimbly, Sarah	20	Negro, dark complexion, light built, 5 ft 5 1/2 high.	Robertson Co, TN	Gibson Co, IN	Tabitha Lyles	None given
Glascoe, Townsend	53	Negro, dark complexion, light built, 5 ft 6 high.	KY	Gibson Co, IN	John McCoy	None given
Glascoe, Harriet	37	Mulatto, light complexion, stout built, 5 ft 8 in high.	IN	Gibson Co, IN	Enoch Jones & Townsend Glascoe	None given

Gibson County, Indiana

Name	Age	Description	Origin	Associated Names	Notes
Stewart, Nancy Ann	12	Mulatto, light complexion, light built.	Coles Co, IL	Gibson Co, IN	Enoch Jones & Townsend Glascoe	None given
Stewart, Susan	9	Mulatto, light complexion, light built.	Coles Co, IL	Gibson Co, IN	Enoch Jones & Townsend Glascoe	None given
Stewart, Elizabeth Ann	6	Mulatto, light complexion, light built.	Clark Co, IL	Gibson Co, IN	Enoch Jones & Townsend Glascoe	None given
Glascoe, Charles Green	4	Mulatto, dark complexion, light built.	Gibson Co, IN	Gibson Co, IN	Enoch Jones & Townsend Glascoe	None given
Glascoe, Clarissa Emeline	1 1/2	Mulatto, dark complexion, light built.	Gibson Co, IN	Gibson Co, IN	Enoch Jones & Townsend Glascoe	None given
Jones, Enoch	77	Negro, dark complexion, light built, 5 ft 9 1/2 in high.	Fairfield Co, SC	Gibson Co, IN	Townsend Glascoe	None given
Artus, Hardy	30	Negro, dark complexion, light built, 5 ft 10 in high.	Robertson Co, TN	Gibson Co, IN	Anderson Wimbly	None given
Stephenson, Jacob	55	Mulatto, light complexion, stout built, 5 1/2 ft high.	Fairfield Co, SC	Gibson Co, IN	Aaron L. Smith	None given
Stephenson, James Wesley	8	Mulatto, light complexion, light built.	Fairfield Co, SC	Gibson Co, IN	Aaron L. Smith	None given
Stephenson, Harrison	14	Mulatto, light complexion, light built, 4 ft 10 in high.	Fairfield Co, SC	Gibson Co, IN	Aaron L. Smith	None given
Lucas, Julia Ann	11	Mulatto, light complexion, light built.	Gibson Co, IN	Gibson Co, IN	Elizabeth Morris Sarah Hunt	None given
Hunt, Mary Elizabeth	8	Mulatto, light complexion, light built.	Gibson Co, IN	Gibson Co, IN	Elizabeth Morris Sarah Hunt	None given
Hunt, William Calvin	5	Mulatto, light complexion, light built.	Gibson Co, IN	Gibson Co, IN	Elizabeth Morris Sarah Hunt	None given

Gibson County, Indiana

Nolcox, Mary Jane	8	Mulatto, light built and very light complexion.	Gibson Co, IN	Gibson Co, IN	Joel Stewart & Tabitha Ferguson	None given
Nolcox, Nancy Sue	6	Mulatto, light built and very light complexion.	Gibson Co, IN	Gibson Co, IN	Joel Stewart & Tabitha Ferguson	None given
Nolcox, Louisa	3	Mulatto, light built and very light complexion.	Gibson Co, IN	Gibson Co, IN	Joel Stewart & Tabitha Ferguson	None giveN
Nolcox, Weston	41	Mulatto, stout built, light complexion.	Montgomery Co TN	Gibson Co, IN	Joel Stewart & Tabitha Ferguson	None given
Nolcox, Elizabeth G.	31	Mulatto, light built and very light complexion.	SC	Gibson Co, IN	Weston Nolcox, Tabitha Ferguson, Joel Stewart	None given
Nolcox, John Weston	11 mos	Mulatto, light built and very light complexion.	Gibson Co, IN	Gibson Co, IN	Weston Nolcox, Tabitha Ferguson, Joel Stewart	None given
Lyles, Isabella	10	Negro, light built and light complexion.	Vanderburg Co, IN	Gibson Co, IN	Joel Stewart & Tabitha Ferguson	None given
Lyles, Tabitha Elizabeth	4	Mulatto, light built and very light complexion.	Gibson Co, IN	Gibson Co, IN	Joel Stewart & Tabitha Ferguson	None given
King, Araminta	28	Negro, light built and light complexion, 5 ft 1 1/2 in high.	VA	Gibson Co, IN	Alexander King	None given
King, Lucy Ann	10	Negro, light built and very light complexion.	Gibson Co, IN	Gibson Co, IN	Alexander King	None given
King, Eliza Jane	8	Negro, light built and very light complexion.	Gibson Co, IN	Gibson Co, IN	Alexander King	None given
King, Nancy Louisa	6	Negro, light built and very light complexion.	Gibson Co, IN	Gibson Co, IN	Alexander King	None given

Gibson County, Indiana

King, Mary Amanda	4	Negro, light built and light complexion.	Gibson Co, IN	Gibson Co, IN	Alexander King	None given
King, James Henry	About 2	Negro, light built and light complexion.	Gibson Co, IN	Gibson Co, IN	Alexander King	None given
Cheeves, John	28	Negro, light built, dark complexion, 5 ft 5 in high.	Mecklenberg Co, VA	Gibson Co, IN	David Storment	None given
Oliver, Jacob	42	Negro, light built, light complexion, 6 ft.	Buncombe Co, NC	Gibson Co, IN	John McCoy	None given
Oliver, Sarah	26	Negro, light built, dark complexion, 5 ft high.	Lexington, KY	Gibson Co, IN	Jacob Oliver	None given
Oliver, Lewis	15	Mulatto, light built and very light complexion.	Marshall Co, AL	Gibson Co, IN	Jacob Oliver	None given
Oliver, Mary Ann	8	Mulatto, light built, dark complexion.	Hopkins Co, KY	Gibson Co, IN	Jacob Oliver	None given
Oliver, Benjamin	6	Negro, light built and light complexion.	Gibson Co, IN	Gibson Co, IN	Jacob Oliver	None given
Oliver, Nancy Jane	4	Negress, light built and light complexion.	Gibson Co, IN	Gibson Co, IN	Jacob Oliver	None given
Oliver, Lucy	1	Negress, light built and very light complexion.	Gibson Co, IN	Gibson Co, IN	Jacob Oliver	None given
McCallister, Rebecca	21	Negress, stout built, dark complexion, 5 ft 4 in high.	Gallatin Co, IL	Gibson Co, IN	Jacob Oliver, Ferite Wimbly	None given
McCallister, Elizabeth	5	Negress, light built and light complexion.	Gibson Co, IN	Gibson Co, IN	Jacob Oliver, Ferite Wimbly	None given
McCallister, James	2	Negro, light built and light complexion.	Gibson Co, IN	Gibson Co, IN	Jacob Oliver, Ferite Wimbly	None given

Gibson County, Indiana

Name	Age	Description	Birthplace	Residence	Witness	Remarks
McCallister, William Henry	5 mos	Mulatto, light built and light complexion.	Gibson Co, IN	Gibson Co, IN	Jacob Oliver / Ferite Wimbly	None given
Wimbly, Virginia	24	Mulatto, light built and very light complexion, 5 ft 3 in high.	MS	Gibson Co, IN	Ferite Wimbly	None given
Wimbly, Octavia	3	Mulatto, light built and dark complexion.	Gibson Co, IN	Gibson Co, IN	Ferite Wimbly	None given
Wimbly, Jasper Newton	1	Mulatto, light built and light complexion.	Gibson Co, IN	Gibson Co, IN	Ferite Wimbly	None given
Hueston, Joseph	42	Mulatto, stout built, and yellow complexion, 5 ft 6 in high.	Knox Co, IN	Gibson Co, IN	Joseph Lyles	None given
Green, Charles Lewis	20	Negro, stout built, and dark complexion, 6 ft high.	Gibson Co, IN	Gibson Co, IN	John McCoy	None given
Jones, Elizabeth	60	Negress, stout built, light complexion, 5 ft 2 1/2 in high.	VA	Gibson Co, IN	Ellen Lyles	None given
McDaniel, Emily Ann	12	Negress, stout built, light complexion.	Gibson Co, IN	Gibson Co, IN	Ellen Lyles	None given
Holmes, Rachel	29	Negress, stout built, dark complexion, 5 ft 4 in.	Robertson Co, TN	Gibson Co, IN	John Holmes	None given
Walden, Berry Lawrence	21	Mulatto, light built and light complexion, 5 ft 7 in high.	Gibson Co, TN	Gibson Co, IN	John W. Walden	None given
Walden, John W.	18	Mulatto, light built and light complexion, 5 ft 5 in high.	Gibson Co, TN	Gibson Co, IN	Berry L. Walden	None given
Wimbly, Frances	23	Negress, light built, dark complexion, 5 ft 1 in.	Robertson Co, TN	Gibson Co, IN	Tabitha Ferguson	None given
Lyles, Jefferson	28	Negro, light built, dark complexion, 5 ft 6 in high.	Robertson Co, TN	Gibson Co, IN	Frances Wimbly	None given

Gibson County, Indiana

Name	Age	Description	Origin	Location	Reference	Notes
Lyles, Malinda	30	Mulatto, light built and light complexion, 5 ft 3 in high.	Lawrence Co, IL	Gibson Co, IN	Frances Wimbly Jefferson Lyles	None given
Wimbly, Elizabeth Ann	6	Negress, light built, dark complexion.	Gibson Co, IN	Gibson Co, IN	Frances Wimbly Jefferson Lyles	None given
Wimbly, George	7	Negro, light built, dark complexion.	Gibson Co, IN	Gibson Co, IN	Frances Wimbly Jefferson Lyles	None given
Wimbly, Finetta	4	Negress, light built, light complexion.	Gibson Co, IN	Gibson Co, IN	Frances Wimbly Jefferson Lyles	None given
Wimbly, Sarah Elizabeth	17 mos	Negress, light built, light complexion.	Gibson Co, IN	Gibson Co, IN	Frances Wimbly Jefferson Lyles	None given
Wimbly, Nancy Ellen	4	Negress, light built, dark complexion.	Gibson Co, IN	Gibson Co, IN	Frances Wimbly Jefferson Lyles	None given
Harris, Elizabeth	35	Negress, light built, light complexion.	Rockingham Co, VA	Gibson Co, IN	Henry Harris	None given
Harris, Lutitia	8	Negress, light built, very light complexion.	Gallatin Co, IL	Gibson Co, IN	Henry Harris	None given
Harris, Josephine	5	Negress, light built, light complexion.	Posey Co, IL	Gibson Co, IN	Henry Harris	None given
Harris, Nancy A.	2	Negress, light built, light complexion.	Gibson Co, IN	Gibson Co, IN	Henry Harris	None given
Wimbly, Drury	28	Mulatto, dark complexion, light built, 5 ft 6 in high.	Robertson Co, TN	Gibson Co, IN	Henry Walden	None given
Wimbly, Mary Ann	24	Negress, dark complexion, light built, 5 ft.	Robertson Co, TN	Gibson Co, IN	Anderson Wimbly	None given
Wimbly, David	17	Negro, light complexion, light built, 5 ft.	Robertson Co, TN	Gibson Co, IN	Anderson Wimbly	None given
Wimbly, William M.	2	Negro, light complexion, light built.	Gibson Co, IN	Gibson Co, IN	Anderson Wimbly	None given
Wimbly, John Weston	5 wks	Negro, light complexion.	Gibson Co, IN	Gibson Co, IN	Anderson Wimbly	None given

Gibson County, Indiana

Name	Age	Description	Origin	Residence	Contact	Notes
Long,Seption	48	Negro, dark complexion, light built, 5 1/2 ft high.	MD	Gibson Co, IN	Matthew Henderson	None given
McDaniel, Thomas	52	Negro, dark complexion, stout built, 5 ft 9 1/2 in high.	Logan Co, KY	Gibson Co, IN	Daniel I. McFetridge	None given
McDaniel, Duncan	11	Mulatto, light complexion, stout built.	Gibson Co, IN	Gibson Co, IN	Thomas McDaniel	None given
Watkins, William	16	Mulatto, dark complexion, light built.	IL	Gibson Co, IN	Thomas McDaniel	None given
Perry, Nelson	33	Mulatto, dark complexion, stout built, 6 ft 1 in high.	PA	Gibson Co, IN	Gilly Ann Perry	None given
Perry, Gilly Ann	28	Negress, light complexion, light built, 5 ft 4 in high.	NC	Gibson Co, IN	Nelson Perry	None given
Wimbly, Robert	19	Negro, light complexion, light built, 5 ft 5 in high.	Robertson Co, TN	Gibson Co, IN	John Holmes	None given
Evans, William L.	32	Mulatto, light completion, stout built, 6 ft 2 in high.	Lawrence Co, IL	Gibson Co, IN	Willis Howe	None given
Robinson, Calvin	21	Mulatto, dark complexion, light built, 5 ft 4 in high.	Gallatin Co, IL	Gibson Co, IN	Morris Rhea	None given
Lee, John Wesley	15	Mulatto, light completion, light built, 5 ft 10 in high.	Todd Co, KY	Gibson Co, IN	Morris Rhea	None given
Green, Samuel	22	Negro, dark complexion, stout built, 5 ft 10 in high.	Gibson Co, IN	Gibson Co, IN	Morris Rhea	None given
Long, Sarah J.	22	Negress, light complexion, stout built, 5 ft 4 in high.	Clark Co, IL	Gibson Co, IN	Seption Long / Wm. L. Evans	None given
Long, Martha Ann J.	11	Negress, light complexion, light built.	Vigo Co, IN	Gibson Co, IN	Seption Long / Wm. L. Evans	None given
Long, Noah	7	Negro, light complexion, light built.	Vigo Co, IN	Gibson Co, IN	Seption Long / Wm. L. Evans	None given

Gibson County, Indiana

Name	Age	Description	Origin	Residence	Sponsor(s)	Notes
Long, Solomon	3	Negro, light complexion, light built.	Vigo Co, IN	Gibson Co, IN	Seption Long, Wm. L. Evans	None given
Long, John Wesley	11 mos	Negro, light complexion.	Gibson Co, IN	Gibson Co, IN	Seption Long, Wm. L. Evans	None given
Jones, John	53	Mulatto, very light complexion, light built, 5 ft 10 in high.	Bedford Co, TN	Gibson Co, IN	Nelson Perry	None given
Jones, Pamela	50	Mulatto, very light complexion, light built, 5 ft 5 in high.	Logan Co, KY	Gibson Co, IN	Nelson Perry, John Jones	None given
Jones, Ann Eliza Jane	20	Mulatto, light complexion, light built, 5 ft 3 in high.	Vanderburgh Co, IN	Gibson Co, IN	Nelson Perry, John Jones	None given
Jones, Cornelia	13	Mulatto, light complexion, light built.	Vanderburgh Co, IN	Gibson Co, IN	John Jones	None given
Lyles, Jethro	14	Mulatto, dark complexion, light built.	Vanderburgh Co, IN	Gibson Co, IN	Alex King, Daniel Lyles	None given
Graham, Washington	39	Negro, dark complexion, stout built, 5 ft 10 in high.	Claibourne Co, TN	Gibson Co, IN	John McCoy	None given
Graham, Lucy Ann	26	Mulatto, light complexion, light built, 5 ft 2 1/2 in high.	Vanderburgh Co, IN	Gibson Co, IN	Washington Graham	None given
Graham, Morris R. W.	6 wks	Mulatto, light complexion, light built.	Gibson Co, IN	Gibson Co, IN	Washington Graham	None given
Jones, Octavia	11	Mulatto, light complexion, light built.	Gibson Co, IN	Gibson Co, IN	John Jones	None given
Jones, Minerva Ann	9	Mulatto, light complexion, light built.	Gibson Co, IN	Gibson Co, IN	John Jones	None given
McDaniel, Henderson Green	31	Negro, light complexion, light built, 5 ft 7 in high.	Henderson Co, KY	Gibson Co, IN	Thomas McDaniel	None given
McDaniel, Margaret	34	Mulatto, light complexion, stout built, 4 ft 11 1/2 in high.	VA	Gibson Co, IN	Thomas McDaniel, H. G. McDaniel	None given

Gibson County, Indiana

Name		Description			Remarks
McDaniel, Jane C.	1	Mulatto, light complexion, light built.	Gibson Co, IN	Thomas McDaniel H. G. McDaniel	None given
Mooreland, William	9	Mulatto, light complexion, stout built.	Gibson Co, IN	Thomas McDaniel H. G. McDaniel	None given
Mooreland, Peter Wright	7	Mulatto, light complexion, light built.	Gibson Co, IN	Thomas McDaniel H. G. McDaniel	None given
Mooreland, Edward	5	Mulatto, light complexion, light built.	Gibson Co, IN	Thomas McDaniel H. G. McDaniel	None given
Lyles, Malinda	33	Negress, dark complexion, light built, 5 ft 7 in high.	Gibson Co, IN	Thomas McDaniel H. G. McDaniel	None given
Lyles, Casindany	8	Negress, dark complexion, light built.	Gibson Co, IN	Thomas McDaniel H. G. McDaniel	None given
Lyles, William M.	13	Negro, dark complexion, light built.	Gibson Co, IN	Thomas McDaniel H. G. McDaniel	None given
Cheavis, Saylisa	65	Mulatto, light complexion, stout built.	VA	Henderson G. McDaniel	None given
Greer, John	23	Negro, dark complexion, stout built, 5 ft 10 in high.	Gibson Co, IN	Charles Greer	None given
Greer, Charles	69	Negro, dark complexion, stout built, 5 ft 8 1/2 in high.	King & Queen Co, VA	John Greer	None given
Greer, Kasiah	55	Negro, dark complexion, light built.	SC	Charles Greer John Greer	None given
Roberts, Ellias	38	Negro, dark complexion, light built, 5 ft 10 1/2 in high.	Robeson Co, NC	Joseph Devin	None given
Roberts, Susan	NR	NR	NR	Joseph Devin	None given
Roberts, Sarah	NR	NR	NR	NR	None given

Gibson County, Indiana

Name	Age	Description	Birthplace	Residence	Witnesses	Notes
Roberts, Juletta	NR	NR	NR	NR	NR	None given
Roberts, Mary Jane	NR	NR	NR	NR	NR	None given
Roberts, Joseph	NR	NR	NR	NR	NR	None given
Roberts, Elmira	NR	NR	NR	NR	NR	None given
Malary, James W.	37	Mulatto, light complexion, stout built, 5 ft 9 in high.	VA	Gibson Co, IN	John McCoy / Jesse Moore	None given
Malary, Maria	26	Negress, dark complexion, light built, 5 ft 2 in high.	Warren Co, KY	Gibson Co, IN	John McCoy / Jesse Moore	None given
Malary, Elisha B.	17	Mulatto, light complexion, stout built. Born March 24th 1852.	Gibson Co, IN	Gibson Co, IN	John McCoy / James Malary	None given
Goings, Napoleon	17	Mulatto, dark complexion, stout built.	Lawrence Co, AL	Gibson Co, IN	Henry Harris	None given
Harris, William	11	Mulatto, light complexion, light built.	Gallatin Co, IL	Gibson Co, IN	Henry Harris	None given
Greer, William M.	2 mos	Mulatto, light complexion.	Gibson Co, IN	Gibson Co, IN	Ann Greer	None given
Lyles, Wilson	30	Mulatto, light complexion, light built.	Montgomery Co, TN	Gibson Co, IN	Ellen Lyles / John McCoy	None given
Lyles, Arra Jane	9	Mulatto, light complexion, light built.	Gibson Co, IN	Gibson Co, IN	Ellen Lyles / Wilson Lyles	None given
Graham, Martha A.	14	Mulatto, light complexion, light built.	Gibson Co, IN	Gibson Co, IN	Ellen Lyles / Wilson Lyles	None given
Glascoe, Mary	12	Negress, dark complexion, light built.	Gibson Co, IN	Gibson Co, IN	Ellen Lyles / Wilson Lyles	None given
Lyles, Orvilla	7	Mulatto, dark complexion, light built.	Gibson Co, IN	Gibson Co, IN	Ellen Lyles / Wilson Lyles	None given

Gibson County, Indiana

Name	Age	Description	Birthplace	Residence	Parents	Owner
Lyles, Rachel E.	2	Mulatto, light complexion, light built.	Gibson Co, IN	Gibson Co, IN	Ellen Lyles Wilson Lyles	None given
Lyles, James William	9	Mulatto, light complexion. Born November 30th 1852.	Gibson Co, IN	Gibson Co, IN	Ellen Lyles Wilson Lyles	None given
Wiggins, John	54	Negro, dark complexion, stout built, 5 ft 9 1/2 in high.	Halifax Co, NC	Gibson Co, IN	John McCoy	None given
Wiggins, Sophia	36	Negress, dark complexion, stout built, 4 ft 10 in high.	Gibson Co, IN	Gibson Co, IN	John McCoy John Wiggins	None given
Wiggins, William	19	Negro, dark complexion, stout built.	Gibson Co, IN	Gibson Co, IN	John McCoy John Wiggins	None given
Wiggins, Matilda	14	Negress, light complexion, light built.	Gibson Co, IN	Gibson Co, IN	John McCoy John Wiggins	None given
Wiggins, Harrison	16	Negro, light built, dark complexion.	Gibson Co, IN	Gibson Co, IN	John McCoy John Wiggins	None given
Wiggins, A. Eliza	11	Negress, dark complexion, stout built.	Gibson Co, IN	Gibson Co, IN	John McCoy John Wiggins	None given
Wiggins, John	7	Negro, dark complexion, stout built.	Gibson Co, IN	Gibson Co, IN	John McCoy John Wiggins	None given
Wiggins, Samuel	5	Negro, dark complexion, stout built.	Gibson Co, IN	Gibson Co, IN	John McCoy John Wiggins	None given
Wiggins, Thomas	3	Negro, dark complexion, stout built.	Gibson Co, IN	Gibson Co, IN	John McCoy John Wiggins	None given
Wiggins, Joseph	3 mos	Negro, dark complexion.	Gibson Co, IN	Gibson Co, IN	John McCoy John Wiggins	None given
Clinton, Hueston	17	Mulatto, light complexion, light built, 5 ft 7 in high.	Gibson Co, IN	Gibson Co, IN	John McCoy	None given

Gibson County, Indiana

Lee, James	15	Mulatto, light complexion, light built, 5 ft 8 1/2 in high.	NA	NA	Wilson Lyles	None given
Mallard, Jeremiah	17	Negro, dark complexion, light built, 5 ft 5 in high.	NA	NA	NA	None given
Greer, Elizabeth	28	Negress, dark complexion, stout built, 5 ft 5 1/2 in high.	NA	NA	NA	None given
Greer, Mary Jane	26	Negress, dark complexion, stout built, 5 ft 4 in high.	NA	NA	NA	None given
Stephenson, Ellen	18	Mulatto, light complexion, light built.	NA	NA	NA	None given
Stephenson, Robert	12	Mulatto, light complexion, light built.	NA	NA	NA	None given
Stephenson, Charles	10	Mulatto, light complexion, light built.	NA	NA	NA	None given
Young, Robert	34	Negro, light complexion, light built, 5 ft 11 in high.	NA	NA	NA	None given

(Column headers: Davison Co, TN | Gibson Co, IN | Wilson Lyles | None given)

Note: Page 34 is now missing from this Register. Entries in the index to this document show the following three additional names:

Coates, James

Hamby, Harrison

Tivis, Nelson

REGISTER OF NEGROES AND MULATTOES IN HARRISON COUNTY, INDIANA

Names	Age	Description	Place of Birth	Residence	Names of Witnesses	Date Registered
Mitchum, Thomas	35	Bright mulatto, five feet eleven inches high & well made.	Harrison Co, IN	Harrison Co	Henry W. Heth	None given
Rolls, Rachel	21	A very bright mulatto about 5 feet 7 or 8 inches in height, has large feet, hair with much curly, spare made & large bone.	Meade Co, KY	Harrison Co	Robert Vance Esq.	None given
Mitchum, Emanuel	35	Verry b[l]ack about 5 feet 7 or 8 inches high.	Floyd Co, IN	Harrison Co	Daniel Heddon	None given
Mitchum, Bright	45	Copper collor six feet high well made, stammers when talking.	SC	Harrison Co	James Giles	None given
Mitchum, Loyd	25	Copper color about five feet five inches high, heavy built.	Harrison Co, IN	Harrison Co	William Heth	None given
Finley, Isaac	65	Copper color 5 feet 10 inches high	MD	Harrison Co	Pearson B. Byrne	None given
Mitchum, Joseph	32	Bright copper color 5 feet 10 inches high, well formed.	Harrison Co, IN	Harrison Co	Henry W. Heth	None given
Mitchum, Andrew	43	Black, five feet three inches high; heavy-set and has a small scar on the right arm from a cut.	Hardin Co, Ky	Harrison Co	James Giles	None given
Mitchum, Monian	30	A bright mulatto, and about five feet two inches high; well formed and tolerably quick spoken.	Harrison Co, IN	Harrison Co	James Giles	None given
Mitchum, Jonathan	8	of a brown color and heavy set.	Harrison Co, IN	Harrison Co	James Giles	None given

Harrison County, Indiana

Mitchum, Julie Ann	6	of a brown color	Harrison Co, IN	Harrison Co	James Giles	None given
[Mitchum], Virgin Mary	18	black & five feet 4 inches high	Harrison Co, IN	Harrison Co	James Giles	None given
Oswell, Wright	--	Five feet seven & 3/4 inches high, has a small scar on the left side of his face and also on the right thumb.	MD	Harrison Co	James Giles	None given
Finley, James	60-65	Moderately black, a little stiff in walking and five feet ten inches high.	MD	Harrison Co	James Giles	None given
Finley, Milley	65	Five feet two and a half inches high and tolerably heavy built.	VA	Harrison Co	James Giles	None given
Boon, Sylva	50	A blind woman rather small	Shelby Co, KY	Harrison Co	James Giles	None given
Finley, Solon	23	A dark brown or copper color six feet high, his right eye dont open generally as well as the left eye.	MD	Harrison Co	James Giles	None given
Finley, Oilsey[?]	50	Very large and fleshy, five feet two and a half inches high.	MD	Harrison Co	James Giles	None given
Finley, Caroline	37	Five feet and a half inches in height and a dark brown or copper color.	KY	Harrison Co	James Giles	None given
Mitchum, Martha	52	Five feet two inches high and of a brown or copper color.	IN	Harrison Co	James Giles	None given
Finley, Mary Margaret	53	Copper color and has rather a lanquid look in appearance.	IN	Harrison Co	James Giles	None given
Finley, Harriet Ellen	54	Five feet three inches in height, of brown or copper color & has rather a bashful appearance.	Harrison Co, IN	Harrison Co	James Giles	None given

Harrison County, Indiana

Name	Age	Description	Origin	County	Owner	Notes
Finley, Rebecca	30	Five feet five and one fourth inches in height, of a brown or copper color.	KY	Harrison Co	James Giles	None given
Boone, Lucinda	22	Dark brown color five feet two and a half inches high-has a small mole in the left hand.	KY	Harrison Co	James Giles	None given
Finley, Almyra	22	Dark brown or copper color five feet one & a half inches high, has a lively or pleasant look.	KY	Harrison Co	James Giles	None given
Mitchum, Molly	75	Black and about five feet high.	VA	Harrison Co	James Giles	None given
Mitchum, George	26-27	A tolerably bright mulatto, five feet 4 inches high and has a scar on the side or heel of the left hand near the rist caused by being cut by a sickle.	IN	Harrison Co	James Giles	None given
Finley, Lewis	40	Five feet nine inches high, the left leg about a inch and a quarter the shortest and has a scar on the back or inside of the little finger.	KY	Harrison Co	James Giles	None given
Finley, Dicey	45	Four feet eleven inches high and pleasant countenance.	IN	Harrison Co	James Giles	None given
Finley, Eliza Ann	24	Four feet ten inches and a half high, has a win or not on the back of the left rist and has a pleasant countenance.	Harrison Co, IN	Harrison Co	James Giles	None given
Finley, Nathaniel	19	Heavy set about five feet three high.	Harrison Co, IN	Harrison Co	James Giles	None given

Harrison County, Indiana

Name		Description			Surety	
Finley, Eliza Ann	14	Daughter of Lewis Finley, tolerably black.	Harrison Co, IN	Harrison Co	James Giles	None given
Finley, William Preston	11	A negro boy and son of Lewis Finley.	Harrison Co, IN	Corydon IN	James Giles	None given
Finley, Bell	7	A daughter of Lewis Finley, a negress & good looking child.	Harrison Co, IN	Corydon IN	James Giles	None given
Mitchum, Mitchell	56	Five feet eleven inches high and has a large wen on the side of his neck joining the collar bone.	VA	Harrison Co	James Giles	None given
Mitchum, Dumont	15	Of a bright copper color, the skin on the back of his right hand is curried from a scald, well made & about five feet three inches high.	Harrison Co, IN	Harrison Co	James Giles	None given
Mitchum, Middleton	42	Five feet 9 inches high well formed has a scar on the left eye brow tolerably quick (?) & tolerably black.	Ky	Harrison Co	W. Q. Grisham	None given
Mitchum, Catharine	35	A mulatto about five feet high.	KY	Harrison Co	James Giles	None given
Mitchum, Isaiah	20	Black about five feet 9 inches high well made & quick motioned.	IN	Harrison Co	James Giles	None given
Mitchum, John	6	Of a copper color & son of Littleton Mitchum.	IN	Harrison Co	James Giles	None given
Mitchum, Lucinda	3	Of a copper color & daughter of Littleton Mitchum.	IN	Harrison Co	James Giles	None given
Davidson, John	4	A bright mulatto & son of Elizabeth Davidson.	IN	Harrison Co	James Giles	None given

Harrison County, Indiana

Name	Age	Description	Residence	Location	Witness	Date
Welch, Eli	25	Of a dark brown color about 5 feet 8 or 9 inches high, soare made and little stooped shouldered.	Harrison Co, IN	Harrison Co	Samuel S. Leonard	None given
Mitchum, Catharine	20	A dark copper color about 5 feet 8 or 9 inches high & has a small scar below the right eye, pleasant countenance.	Harrison Co, IN	Harrison Co	James Giles	None given
Mitchum, David	22	About 5 foot 8 or 9 inches high, tolerably black and has a very large scar on his right leg some five inches long.	Harrison Co, IN	New Albany, IN	James Giles	None given
Finley, Nathaniel	20	About 5 feet 5 1/2 inches high, has a small scar on the left eye brow, heavy set & has a pleasant countenance when spoken to.	Harrison Co, IN	Harrison Co	William Heth	None given
Mitchum, John Dumont	18	About 5 feet 8 or 9 inches high, scar on right arm occasioned by a scald.	Harrison Co, IN	Harrison Co	William W. Bean	None given
Welch, Nancy Jane	19-23	5 feet high has a scar upon the upper portion of forehead over the right eye is of a rather dark color, is not very heavy set, has rather a pleasant expression of countenance when spoken to.	Boone Twp, Harrison Co, IN	Harrison Co	G. W. Denbo, Clk.	July 11, 1857
Haden, George W.	27	5 feet 9 or ten inches high, scar upon the back of the right hand; also a scar on the left hand extending or between the thumb & wrist. Dark mulatto, pleasant countenance when spoken to. Well made.	Floyd Co, IN	Corydon, IN	William Applegate	April 30, 1858

Harrison County, Indiana

Name	Age	Description	Origin	Location	Owner	Date
Watson, Willis	18	Bright mulatto of a good countenance and rather intelligent. Quick spoken when spoken to. Five feet eight or ten inches high.	Harrison Co IN	New Albany, Floyd Co, IN	Rebecca Kintner	Jan 11, 1860
Johnson, Louiza	22	Bright mulatto of a good countenance, tolerable intelligent, quick spoken when spoken to, four feet eight to ten inches high; a small scar in the right temple, left eye rather weak.	Louisville, KY	Corydon, IN	Frank S. Adams	None given
Finley, John	42	Five feet eleven inches high. Dark mulatto. Scar rather over his left eye, with a crooked little finger on his right hand.	KY	Floyd Co, IN	William Heth	None given
Mitchum, Cyrus	24	A dark mulatto about five feet 6 or 7 inches high. Hair rather wavy, rather heavy set. Has a scar on the right corner of his upper lip, & also a scar on the inside of his right leg.	Harrison Co IN	Floyd Co, IN	William Heth	None given
Cousins, George	55	A dark mulatto, about five feet 8 or 9 inches high. Hair grey, sprinkled with dark. Has a [k]not on the left side of the neck. Has a scar on the left arm, between the shoulder and elbow.	VA	Harrison Co	Wilford Melton	Oct 12, 1861
Cousins, Cynthiana	39	Mulatto about 5 feet high. Has rather a young look for her age. Hair black, slightly sprinkled with grey. Quick and intelligent. Has a small scar immediately under the angle of the jaw.	Cumberland Co, KY	Harrison Co	Wilford Melton	Oct 14, 1861

Harrison County, Indiana

Name	Age	Description	Origin	Residence	Witness	Date
Mitchum, Rhoda	24	Mulatto, about 4 feet & 10 inches hugh, an intelligent look, has a large scar on the back part of the hand.	Cumberland Co, KY	Harrison Co	Wilford Melton	Oct 14, 1861
Cousins, William	18	Dark mulatto, about 5 feet 8 or 9 inches high, a little deaf.	Cumberland Co, KY	Harrison Co	Wilford Melton	Oct 14, 1861
Cousins, Joseph A.	16	Very dark, with a little indication of mulatto blood. About 5 feet 8 or 9 inches high. A small scar on his chin.	Cumberland Co, KY	Harrison Co	Wilford Melton	Oct 14, 1861
Cousins, Thomas	11	A dark mulatto. Has quite an intelligent look. Seems to be quick.	Cumberland Co, KY	Harrison Co	Wilford Melton	Oct 14, 1861
Mitchum, James H.	23	Dark mulatto, about 5 feet 10 inches. Hair black. A scar on the knuckle of the 3rd finger of the left hand. Quick and intelligent look.	Harrison Co IN	Harrison Co	William Reader	Jan 8, 1863

REGISTER OF NEGROES AND MULATTOES IN HENDRICKS COUNTY, INDIANA
(Based upon data reported in *History of Hendricks County*, 1885)

Names	Age	Description	Place of Birth	Residence	Names of Witnesses	Date Registered
Moss, Lydia or Free	40	Black, common size	Randolph Co, NC	Guilford Twp, Hendricks Co, IN	William E. Carter	Aug 17, 1853
Moss, John Watson	17	Full black, full size for his age, five feet seven or eight inches high and tolerably fleshy.	Randolph Co, NC	Guilford Twp, Hendricks Co, IN	William E. Carter	Aug 17, 1853
Moss, Nathan	15	Full black, large of his age, five feet five inches high and tolerably fleshy.	Randolph Co, NC	Guilford Twp, Hendricks Co, IN	William E. Carter	Aug 17, 1853
Moss, Elizabeth Jane	13	Full black, large of his age, five feet two or three inches high and somewhat fleshy.	Randolph Co, NC	Guilford Twp, Hendricks Co, IN	William E. Carter	Aug 17, 1853
Moss, Thurzey C.	10	Full black and large of her age.	Randolph Co, NC	Guilford Twp, Hendricks Co, IN	William E. Carter	Aug 17, 1853
Moss, Willliam Henry	7	Full black and moderate size for a boy of his age.	Randolph Co, NC	Guilford Twp, Hendricks Co, IN	William E. Carter	Aug 17, 1853
Moss, Lydia Ellen Lavina	8 mos	A mulatto and half white.	Hendricks Co, IN	Guilford Twp, Hendricks Co, IN	William E. Carter	Aug 17, 1853
Pierson, Daniel	50	A dark mulatto, five feet nine inches high, spare in his make, and quick of speech and movement.	Shelby Co, KY	Danville, Hendricks Co, IN	James Christie	Nov 30, 1854

Hendricks County, Indiana

Pierson, Ann	50	A negress, very spare made and tall for a women.	Lincoln Co, KY	Danville, Hendricks Co, IN	James Christie	Nov 30, 1854
Pierson, Charles	28	A very dark mulatto, five feet nine inches high, heavy set, husky voice.	Not given	Danville, Hendricks Co, IN	James Christie	Nov 30, 1854
Pierson, Lewis	21	A dark mulatto, five feet eight inches high, very stout and fat, with a round face.	Not given	Danville, Hendricks Co, IN	James Christie	Nov 30, 1854
Pierson, Jane	--	A very dark mulatto, crippled in her right leg an walks on the toe of that foot.	Not given	Danville, Hendricks Co, IN	James Christie	Nov 30, 1854

REGISTER OF NEGROES AND MULATTOES IN JACKSON COUNTY, INDIANA

Names	Age	Description	Place of Birth	Residence	Names of Witnesses	Date Registered
Mitchell, Alvin	32	Light mulatto, height 5 ft 6 1/2 inches high weight about 185 lbs. Blk eyes	East TN	Brownstown, IN	S. W. Ewing	May 26, 1853
Mitchell, Burgess	26	Light mulatto 5 ft 6 in high weight 130 lbs black eyes strait black hair.	Guilford Co, NC	Brownstown, IN	Fielding S. Johnson	May 27, 1853
Mitchell, John	25	Light mulatto 5 ft 6 in high weight 140 lbs blue eyes curley black hair.	Washington Co, IN	Jackson Co, IN	Fielding S. Johnson	May 27, 1853
Dixon, Samuel	33	Light mulatto 5 ft 7 in high weight 150 pounds curly hair black a scar on the right side of right ancle a scar on the right cheek..	Nachez, MS	Jackson Co, IN near Rockford	Fielding S. Johnson	May 30, 1853
Parker, Moses	64	A black man 5 feet 7 inches weighing 200 pounds a scar on his left upper lip.	Perquimans Co, NC	Jackson Co, IN Jackson Twp	Richard Cox	June 10, 1853
Newby, James	43	A black man 5 feet 6 inches high, weighing 150 pounds, a fellon has been on the 2d finger of the left hand.	Perquimans Co, NC	Jackson Co, IN Jackson Twp	Richard Cox	June 10, 1853
Newby, David	38	A black man 5 feet 7 1/2 inches high	Perquimans Co, NC	Redding Twp, Jackson Co, IN	Richard Cox	June 10 1853
Newby, Martha Ann	32	Dark compllexion & wife of the above named David Newby	Perquimans Co, NC	Redding Twp, Jackson Co, IN	Richard Cox	June 10 1853
Newby, Edmund	14	Born 18th July 1839 dark colour son of David and Martha Ann Newby	Jackson Twp, Jackson Co, IN	Redding Twp, Jackson Co, IN	Richard Cox	June 10, 1853
Newby, Levi	12	Born 28th Dec 1841 very dark colour, son of David and Martha Ann Newby	Jackson Twp, Jackson Co, IN	Redding Twp, Jackson Co, IN	Richard Cox	June 10, 1853

Jackson County, Indiana

Name		Description			Date
Newby, Henry	7	Born 10th June 1853 A dark colour son of David and Martha Ann Newby	Jackson Twp, Jackson Co, IN	Redding Twp, Jackson Co, IN	Richard Cox	June 10, 1853
Parks, Amy	50	A black woman wife of Moses Parks.	Perquimans Co, NC	Jackson Twp, Jackson Co, IN	Richard Cox	June 10, 1853
Newby, Zilpha	42	A light coloured woman aged 42 years & wife of James Newby.	Perquimans Co, NC	Jackson Twp, Jackson Co, IN	Richard Cox	June 10, 1853
Newby, Thompson	21	A black man 5 feet 8 inches high, son of James Newby.	Jackson Co, IN	Jackson Twp, Jackson Co, IN	Richard Cox	June 10, 1853
Newby, Alfred	15	Born 7th April 1838 A dark coloured boy, son of James Newby before described.	Washington Co, IN	Jackson Twp, Jackson Co, IN	Richard Cox	June 10, 1853
Newby, Henry	19	Born in 1835. A light coloured boy & son of James Newby before described.	Jackson Co, Washington Twp, IN	Jackson Twp, Jackson Co, IN	Richard Cox	June 10 1853
Newby, Nancy Jane	13	A black girl 13 years old, daughter of James & Zilpha Newby before described.	Jackson Twp, Jackson Co, IN	Jackson Twp, Jackson Co, IN	Richard Cox	June 10 1853
Bishop, Mitchell	40	A negro man of light complexion 5 feet 10 inches high, 143 pounds weight, a scar on his right cheek.	Lexington, KY	Jackson Twp, Jackson Co, IN	Richard Cox	June 10 1853
Bishop, Mariah	35	Wife of Mitchell Bishop, a dark complexion, scar on the right temple.	Perquimans Co, NC	Jackson Twp, Jackson Co, IN	Richard Cox	June 10 1853
Newby, Isaiah	24	24 years old 19th Apl last 5 feet 7 inches high 147 lbs weight, a small scar on his right cheek bone.	Jackson Twp, Jackson Co, IN	Jackson Twp, Jackson Co, IN	Richard Cox	June 10 1853
Newby, Catherine Elvina	21	A light colour, wife of Isaiash Newby, above described. A scar on her forehead one inch long.	Elbert Co, GA	Jackson Co, IN	Richard Cox	June 10 1853

Jackson County, Indiana

Newby, Willis	32	A negro man 5 feet 8 inches high 160 pounds weight, a scar on hos right fore finger.	Perquimans Co, NC	Jackson Co, IN	Richard Cox	June 10 1853
Newby, Caroline	35	A mulatto woman wife of Willis Newby.	Pittsburgh, PA	Jackson Twp, Jackson Co, IN	Richard Cox	June 10 1853
Newby, Mathew	13	13 years old 8th June 1853. A dark coloured boy son of Willis Newby & Caroline Newby.	Jackson Twp, Jackson Co, IN	Jackson Twp, Jackson Co, IN	Richard Cox	June 10 1853
Newby, Elizabeth Mariah	11	A dark colour daughter of Willis & Caroline Newby.	Jackson Twp, Jackson Co, IN	Jackson Twp, Jackson Co, IN	Richard Cox	June 10 1853
Newby, Sophia	8	A dark negro girl of Willis & Caroline Newby.	Jackson Twp, Jackson Co, IN	Jackson Twp, Jackson Co, IN	Richard A Cox	June 10 1853
Newby, Thomas Edward	5	A negro boy son of Willis & Caroline Newby.	Jackson Twp, Jackson Co, IN	Jackson Twp, Jackson Co, IN	Richard A Cox	June 10 1853
Newby, Bishop Parks	3	A negro boy dark colour son of Willis & Caroline Newby.	Jackson Twp, Jackson Co, IN	Jackson Twp, Jackson Co, IN	Richard A Cox	June 10 1853
Christy, William	27	A negro man of dark colour five feet 8 inches high, 144 lbs weight, a scar on the right eye brow & scar on the left corner of the right eye.	SC	Jackson Twp, Jackson Co, IN	Richard A Cox	June 10 1853
Christy, Mariah Ann	14	A light mulatto, wife of William Christy.	Washington Co, IN	Jackson Twp, Jackson Co, IN	Richard A Cox	June 10 1853
Christy, John Franklin	4	4 years old 11th March 1853. A boy light black colour son of William Christy & Maria Ann Christy.	Washington Co, IN	Jackson Twp, Jackson Co, IN	Richard A Cox	June 10 1853

Jackson County, Indiana

Bishop, Stanford	11	11 years old A boy of dark complexion, son of Mitchell Bishop & Maria Bishop.	Clark Co, IN	Jackson Twp, Jackson Co, IN	Richard A Cox	June 10 1853
Bishop, Sarah Jane	8	A girl 8 years old dark complexion, daughter of Mitchell Bishop & Maria Bishop.	Clark Co, IN	Jackson Twp, Jackson Co, IN	Richard A Cox	June 10 1853
Bishop, Willis Ceraloo	4	A boy light complexion son of Mitchell Bishop & Maria Bishop.	Clark Co, IN	Jackson Twp, Jackson Co, IN	Richard A Cox	June 10 1853
Bishop, Amy Hetty Ann	3	A dark complexion girl, daughter of Mitchell Bishop & Maria Bishop.	Jackson Twp, Jackson Co, IN	Jackson Twp, Jackson Co, IN	Richard A Cox	June 10 1853
Bell, Martin	40	A light mulatto, a scar on the left cheek 5 ft 8 in high 140 lb weight.	Frederick Co, VA	Jackson Co, IN Brownstown Twp	Wm Williams	June 10 1853
Bell, Delania	35	A light mulatto no scars about 5 ft 2 in high weighs 135 lbs.	Guilford Co, NC	Jackson Co, IN Brownstown Twp	Wm Williams	June 10 1853
Bell, Nathaniel	17	A light mulatto, no marks. 5 ft high weighs about 115 lbs.	Jackson Co, IN	Jackson Co, IN Brownstown Twp	Wm Williams	June 10 1853
Bell, Lewis	14	A light mulatto, no marks. 4 ft high weighs about 90 lbs.	Jackson Co, IN	Jackson Co, IN Brownstown Twp	Wm Williams	June 10 1853
Bell, David	13	A light mulatto scar on his right arm.	Jackson Co, IN	Jackson Co, IN Brownstown Twp	Wm Williams	June 10 1853

Jackson County, Indiana

Bell, John	7	A light mulatto, no marks.	Jackson Co, IN	Jackson Co, IN Brownstown Twp	Wm Williams	June 10 1853
Bell, Charlie	3	A light mulatto, no marks.	Jackson Co, IN	Jackson Co, IN Brownstown Twp	Wm Williams	June 10 1853
Anthony, Elijah	51	5 feet 10 inches high, 200 pounds weight, litttle light black complexion & quite gray headed.	Elbert Co, GA	Jackson Co, IN	Samuel P. Mooney	July 25 1853
Anthony, Hannah	43	Yellow complexion under middle size.	Elbert Co, GA	Jackson Co, IN	Samuel P. Mooney	July 25 1853
Anthony, Catherine Elvira	22	Yellow complexion of common size.	Elbert Co, GA	Jackson Co, IN	Samuel P. Mooney	July 25 1853
Anthony, Oliver	8	Yellow complexion	Elbert Co, GA	Jackson Co, IN	Samuel P. Mooney	July 25 1853
Anthony, Maria Jane	20	Yellow complexion	Elbert Co, GA	Jackson Co, IN	Samuel P. Mooney	July 25 1853
Anthony, Sarah Ann	19	Yellow complexion	Elbert Co, GA	Jackson Co, IN	Samuel P. Mooney	July 25 1853
Anthony, Nelly Miss	17	Yellow complexion	Elbert Co, GA	Jackson Co, IN	Samuel P. Mooney	July 25 1853
Anthony, Melisha	16	Yellow complexion	Elbert Co, GA	Jackson Co, IN	Samuel P. Mooney	July 25 1853
Anthony, Elijah [Jr]	13	Yellow complexion	Jennings Co, IN	Jackson Co, IN	Samuel P. Mooney	July 25 1853
Anthony, Noah	11	Yellow complexion	Jennings Co, IN	Jackson Co, IN	Samuel P. Mooney	July 25 1853
Anthony, Nancy	8	Yellow complexion	Jennings Co, IN	Jackson Co, IN	Samuel P. Mooney	July 25 1853
Anthony, Hannah [Jr]	3	Yellow complexion	Jennings Co, IN	Jackson Co, IN	Samuel P. Mooney	July 25 1853
Anthony, Ophelia	1	Yellow complexion	Jennings Co, IN	Jackson Co, IN	Samuel P. Mooney	July 25 1853
Anthony, Jephther	1	Yellow complexion	Jackson Co, IN	Jackson Co, IN	Samuel P. Mooney	July 25 1853

Jackson County, Indiana

Name	Age	Description	Origin	Residence	Registrant	Date
Dudley, Lawney	60	A black man six feet high, scars on his lips & hands, weight 160 pounds.	Culpepper Co, VA	Washington Twp, Jackson Co, IN	Wm Weather	August 6 1853
Dudley, Nicey	42	A dark complexioned negro woman.	Perquimans Co, NC	Jackson Co, IN	William Weather	August 6 1853
Dudley, Sally	15	A dark complexioned negro girl.	Adair Co, KY	Jackson Co, IN	William Weather	August 6 1853
Soyde, Susan Amanda	11	A dark complexioned negro girl.	Washington Co, IN	Jackson Co, IN	William Weather	August 6 1853
Soyde, Jacob Wesley	7	A dark complexioned negro boy.	Washington Co, IN	Jackson Co, IN	William Weather	August 6 1853
Mitchell, Francis	29	A light mulatto man 5 6 1/2 inches high.	Washington Co, IN	Jackson Co, IN	John P. Miller	August 11 1853
Morris, Batch	68	A mulatto man 5 feet 11 inches high 250 pounds.	Newberry District, SC	Jackson Co, IN	Samuel W. Smith	August 29 1853
Cozens, James	39	is a copper bllack 5 feet 4 1/2 inches high 145 pounds.	Franklin Co, VA	Jackson Co, IN	Samuel W. Smith	August 29 1853
Mitchell, Sarah	93	A mulatto woman.	Amelia Co, VA	Jackson Co, IN	George H. Murphy	Sep 3 1853
Waters, Ellen	65	A copper colored woman.	Granville Co, N C	Jackson Co, IN	George H. Murphy	Sep 3 1853
Brannon, Henry	30	A dark mulatto man 5 feet 6 inches high weighs 160 pounds.	Washington Co, IN	Jackson Co, IN	George H. Murphy	Sep 3 1853
Brannon, Delelia	19	A copper colored woman.	Jackson Co, IN	Jackson Co, IN	George H. Murphy	Sep 3 1853
Mitchell, Harrison	37	A light mulatto man, 6 feet high weight 175 pounds. A scar on the side of thhe right eye & temple.	Guilford Co, NC	Jackson Co, IN	George H. Murphy	Sep 3 1853
Mitchell, Laura Ann	20	A light mulatto woman, wife of Harrison Mitchell.	Jackson Co, IN	Jackson Co, IN	George H. Murphy	Sep 3 1853
Waters, William	18	A dark mulatto boy 5 feet 5 inches high weighing 130 pounds.	Jackson Co, IN	Jackson Co, IN	George H. Murphy	Sep 3 1853

Jackson County, Indiana

Name	Age	Description	Origin	Residence	Witness	Date
Mitchell, Mary Maranda	11	A light mulatto girl, daughter of Harrison Mitchell.	Jackson Co, IN	Jackson Co, IN	Medy W. Shields	Sep 3 1853
Mitchell, Hiram	22	A light mulatto man 5 feet 7 in h igh 148 lbs weight.	Jackson Co, IN	Jackson Co, IN	Medy W. Shields	Sep 3 1853
Mitchell, William	26	A mulatto man 5 feet 6 inches high weighing 150 pounds, a scar on the left shoulder.	Guilford Co, NC	Jackson Co, IN	John P. Miller	Sep 20 1853
Morris, Polly	48	A mulatto woman the wife of Batch Morris.	Newberry District, SC	Jackson Co, IN	Clark S. Borden	Sep 21 1853
Penn, Sally	90	A light complexioned colored woman.	SC	Jackson Co, IN	Clark S. Borden	Sep 21 1853
Penn, William	46	A black negro man six feet 4 inches high cross eyes, weighs 180 pounds.	Newberry District, SC	Jackson Co, IN	Clark S. Borden	Sep 21 1853
Penn, Nancy	50	A light complexioned mulatto woman.	Newberry District, SC	Jackson Co, IN	Clark S. Borden	Sep 21 1853
Bird, Eliza Ann	10	A light complexioned mulatto girl, daughter of Peter & Catherine Bird.	Jackson Co, IN	Jackson Co, IN	Clark S. Borden	Sep 21 1853
Bird, George Jefferson	9	A bright complexioned mulatto boy, son of Peter & Catherine Bird.	Jackson Co, IN	Jackson Co, IN	Clark S. Borden	Sep 21 1853
Bird, Mary Ellen	6	A light complexioned mulatto girl, daughter of Peter & Catherine Bird.	Jackson Co, IN	Jackson Co, IN	Clark S. Borden	Sep 21 1853
Patridge, Nancy Ann	11	A light complexioned mulatto girl, daughter of Lucinda Patridge.	Jackson Co, IN	Jackson Co, IN	Clark S. Borden	Sep 21 1853
Cozens, Tabitha	32	A light complexioned negro woman, wife of James Cozens.	Perquimans Co, NC	Jackson Co, IN	Clark S. Borden	Sep 21 1853
Cozens, Mary Ann	15	Daughter of James & Tabitha Cozens, a light complexioned negro girl.	Jackson Co, IN	Jackson Co, IN	Clark S. Borden	Sep 21 1853

Jackson County, Indiana

Cozens, John	13	Son of James & Tabitha Cozens, a light complexioned negro boy.	Jackson Co, IN	Jackson Co, IN	Clark S. Borden	Sep 21 1853
Cozens, Geo. Marshall	12	Son of James & Tabitha Cozens, a light colored negro boy.	Jackson Co, IN	Jackson Co, IN	Clark S. Borden	Sep 21 1853
Cozens, Elizabeth	9	Daughter of James & Tabitha Cozens, a light complexioned negro girl.	Jackson Co, IN	Jackson Co, IN	Clark S. Borden	Sep 21 1853
Cozens, Francis Marion	5	Son of James & Tabitha Cozens, a negro boy.	Jackson Co, IN	Jackson Co, IN	Clark S. Borden	Sep 21 1853
Cozens, Sarah Isabella	3	Daughter of James & Tabitha Cozens, a negro female child.	Jackson Co, IN	Jackson Co, IN	Clark S. Borden	Sep 21 1853
Lamb, Hiram	42	A light mulatto man 5 feet 6 inches high, weight 170 pounds.	Randolph Co, NC	Jackson Co, IN	Samuel P. Mooney	Sep 24 1853
Dudley, Henry	33	A black man negro 5 feet 4 inches high weighing 164 pounds. Scar on the left side of his nose.	Adair Co, KY	Jackson Co, IN	Andrew Cox	Oct 5 1853
Dudley, Sarah	27	A negro woman wife of Henry Dudley.	Cumberland Co, KY	Jackson Co, IN	Andrew Cox	Oct 5 1853
Dudley, William	9	Born 10th June 1843 in Adair County KY & son of Henry Dudley a black boy.	Adair Co, KY	Jackson Co, IN	Andrew Cox	Oct 5 1853
Dudley, Malinda Jane	7	Born 24th March 1846, a black girl daughter of Henry Dudley.	Adair Co, KY	Jackson Co, IN	Andrew Cox	Oct 5 1853
Dudley, Martha Ann	5	Born 1st June 1848 daughter of Henry Dudley a negro girl.	Jackson Co, IN	Jackson Co, IN	Andrew Cox	Oct 5 1853
Dudley, Melissa	3	Born 28th Feby 1852 daughter of Henry Dudley a black negro child.	Jackson Co, IN	Jackson Co, IN	Andrew Cox	Oct 5 1853

Jackson County, Indiana

Name	Age	Description	Origin	Residence	Witness	Date
Dudley, Alice Ann	3 mo	Born 1st Aug 1853 and daughter of Henry Dudley.	Jackson Co, IN	Jackson Co, IN	Andrew Cox	Oct 5 1853
Baker, Milly	57	A black woman 4 feet 1 inch high weight 115 pounds.	Chesterfield Co, VA	Jackson Co, IN	Andrew Cox	Oct 5 1853
Parker, Thompson	23	A black negro man 5 feet 7 inch high, weight 150 pounds. A scar on his forehead.	Washington Co, IN	Jackson Co, IN	Wm. Moore	Oct 5 1853
Patridge, Richard	22	A mulatto man light complexion six feet high 164 pounds.	Floyd Co, IN	Jackson Co, IN	William Goslin	Oct 14 1853
Mitchell, Milton	23	A light mulatto man 5 feet 4 inches high weight 145 pounds.	Washington Co, IN	Jackson Co, IN	Asa Woodmansee	Oct 28 1853
Mitchell, Serena	19	A light mulatto woman, wife of the above named Milton.	Jackson Co, IN	Jackson Co, IN	Asa Woodmansee	Oct 28 1853
Parker, Isaac	68	A negro man 5 feet 4 inches 147 pounds.	Perquimans Co, NC	Jackson Co, IN	Walter Benton	Oct 31 1853
Parker, Flora	58	A negro woman wife of Isaac Parker.	MD	Jackson Co, IN	Walter Benton	Oct 31 1853
Parker, Wright	24	A black man 5 ft 7 inches high 139 lbs. Son of Isaac & Flora Parker.	Washington Co, IN	Jackson Co, IN	Walter Benton	Oct 31 1853
Parker, Mary Ann	18	A black negro girl daughter of Isaac & Flora Parker.	Washington Co, IN	Jackson Co, IN	Walter Benton	Oct 31 1853
Parker, Priscilla	18	A negro girl daughter of Isaac & Flora Parker.	Washington Co, IN	Jackson Co, IN	Walter Benton	Oct 31 1853
Parker, Isaac Jr	17	A black boy 5 ft 8 inches high 130 lbs. Son of Isaac & Flora Parker.	Washington Co, IN	Jackson Co, IN	Walter Benton	Oct 31 1853
Parker, Elizabeth Jane	4	A black girl gran[d]daughter of Isaac & Flora Parker.	Salem, Washington Co, IN	Jackson Co, IN	Walter Benton	Oct 31 1853

Jackson County, Indiana

Goings, George	44	A mulatto man 6 feet high 184 pounds.	Henry Co, VA	Jackson Co, IN	John Ruddick	Nov 5 1853
Goings, John	41	A light mulatto man 6 ft 2 inches high 185 lbs.	Henry Co, VA	Jackson Co, IN	John Ruddick	Nov 5 1853
Goings, Nancy	52	A light mulatto woman & wife of George Goings.	MS	Jackson Co, IN	John Ruddick	Nov 5 1853
Goings, Phebe	30	A light mulatto woman & wife of John Goings.	Washington Co, IN	Jackson Co, IN	John Ruddick	Nov 5 1853
Dockery, Cain	62	A light colored mulatto man weighs 150 lbs 5 feet 8 inches.	Wake Co, NC	Jackson Co, IN	Wm. D. Benton	Nov 9 1853
Dockery, Hannah	64	A light colored woman wife of cain Dockery.	Randolph Co, NC	Jackson Co, IN	Wm. D. Benton	Nov 9 1853
Newby, Louisa Emeline	15	A negro girl daughter of James Newby and Zelpha his wife was born on the 24th day of March 1842.	Jackson Co, IN	Jackson Co, IN	Richard Cox	Feby 21 1854
Newby, Margaret Ellen	11	Daughter of the above named persons born 6th day of June 1844 Negro girl.	Jackson Co, IN	Jackson Co, IN	Richard Cox	Feby 21 1854
Newby, Sarah Isabel	17	Was born 18th day of the March 1847 a negro girl daughter of the above named persons.	Jackson Co, IN	Jackson Co, IN	Richard Cox	Feby 21 1854
Newby, Isaiah Harrison	18	A negro boy son of the above named persons born 16 Jany 1850.	Jackson Co, IN	Jackson Co, IN	Richard Cox	Feby 21 1854
Newby, Mary Ann Elvira	19	A negro girl daughter of the above named James Newby & wife born Dec 28th 1852.	Jackson Co, IN	Jackson Co, IN	Richard Cox	Feby 21 1854

Jackson County, Indiana

Bell, Nathaniel	19 the latter of Nov 1855	5 feet 3 inches high 150 pounds a light coloured mulatto pretty well put up his face rather spotted giving him the appearance of being pock marked.	Brownstown, Jackson Co, IN	Brownstown Twp, Jackson Co, IN ever since his birth.	Frank Emerson Martin Bell	[Not recorded]
Mitchell, Samuel	25	A bright mulatto, five feet five and a half inches high weighs about one hundred and twenty seven pounds.	Near Brownstown, Jackson Co, IN	Madison in Jefferson Co IN	John P. Miller	[Not recorded]

REGISTER OF NEGROES AND MULATTOES IN JEFFERSON COUNTY, INDIANA

Reg No.	Names	Age	Description	Place of Birth	Residence	Names of Witnesses	Date Registered
114	Allen, James H.	29	A Negro about 5 ft 10 ins with scars on back left hand, left sideof forehead, ball of left foot. Spare built.	Shelby Co KY on October 20, 1826.	Madison Twp Jeff Co IN	John Carr, Robert B Craig	13 Jan 1855
86	Allums, Andrew	14 mos	Black. Son of Osberry and Elizabeth Allums who were residents of the State of Indiana prior to the 1st day of November 1851.	Hanover Twp Jefferson Co IN on 16 June 1852.	Near Hanover Jeff Co IN	Osberry Allums, Elizabeth Allums	15 Aug 1853
7	Allums, Asbury	34	A mulatto 5 ft 9 ins high rather stout built large eyes a small scar near mouth, quick spoken and quite a good looking man.	Pekins District SC Born Oct 1st 1819.	Jefferson Co IN	Lydia Ann Beaty	June 27 1853
85	Allums, Elizabeth	[27]	Black. Medium size full round face. Wife of Osberry Allums.	KY 1826.	Near Hanover Jeff Co IN	Washington Stapp David Miller.	15 Aug 1853
14	Allums, Osbery	34	Dark mulatto about 5 ft 8 ins high. Sharp features, pleasant countenance. Twin brother to Asbury Allums.	SC on the 1st Oct 1819.	Jefferson Co IN	Marcus D Lott	June 28 1853
144	Anderson, William I.	49	Negro about 6 ft mulatto with marked Negro features. Scars left cheek, bald headed, stout built. Elijah Anderson's brother.	Fluvanna Co VA 3 June 1811.	Madison Jefferson Co IN	Squire Lockridge	16 Jan 1860
35	Ayers, Thomas	25	Mulatto, 5 ft 8 ins high, broad face, rather heavy build. Long scar on back of left hand, one on right arm, one left shin.	NC on 8th May 1828.	Madison Jefferson Co IN	Benedict B Taylor, Marcus D Lott, Gavitt	July 9 1853

Jefferson County, Indiana

125	Beatty, John H. I.	20	Pale mulatto, wooly sandy colored hair, scar right elbow joint; short neck and inclined to be stooped shoulder; 5 ft 7 ins.	Louisville KY in 1836 or 1837.	South Hanover Jeff Co IN	Asberry Allums	4 Mar 1857
60	Beaty, Henry Clinton	19	Mulatto about 5 ft 6 ins high. Slim build has scar running from center of upper lip to corner of left eye.	Mercer Co KY on 19th September 1834.	10 miles west Madison	John Taylor	Aug 1 1853
5	Beaty, Lydia Ann	45	Mrs Beaty is a mulatto regular features rather above medium height, slender and sprightly, lives 3 miles west of Madison.	King William County VA	Jefferson Co IN	James C Thom & Asbury Allums	June 27 1853
58	Blackburn, Robert	20	Black, about 5 ft 10 ins high, small black scar near left nostrila little stooped shoulder.	Near Lexington KY on 11 April 1833.	Near Hanover Jefferson Co	Nelson Ellington	July 30 1853
87	Blackman, Frances	19	Black low and heavy set round face, being unmarried at this time.	KY on 14 April 1834.	Near Hanover Jeff Co IN	Osberry Allums	18 Aug 1853
131	Borday(?), John Henry	18	Scar on nose, left arm on elbow, dark brown complexion 5 ft 5 1/2 inches high.	Madison Jefferson Co IN	Madison Jefferson Co IN	Wm T Evans	31 Aug 1857
1	Boulain, Woodward	28	Bright Mulatto about 5 ft 10 inch	Jefferson Co IN	Jefferson Co IN	Maston Harris	June 22 1853
52	Boung, Thomas	21	Black, 6 ft high, heavy broad build. Scars on right side of throat, one under left eye.	Fayette Co KY on 22 May 1832.	Near Hanover Jefferson Co	Asbury Allums	July 26 1853
16	Broady, John	34	Black, 5 ft 10 ins high full forehead. No marks discernable except a small scar near the left angle of nose.	Near Lexington KY on 25th December 1817.	Madison Jefferson Co IN	Marcus A Gavit	June 29 1853
6	Brown, Lew	49	Mulatto about five feet three inches in height, spare built. A scar on right shoulder.	King William Co VA	Jefferson Co IN	Lydia Ann Beaty	June 27 1853

89

Jefferson County, Indiana

96	Bull, John	58	Black 6 ft high, has hair. 6 fingers on each hand. The 6th one having been cut off at the second joint of each little finger.	Henry Co VA in 1795.	North Madison Jeff Co IN	George Armstrong	22 Aug 1853
97	Bull, Joseph S.	12	Black, thick lips. Scar on upper lip.	Shelbyville KY in November 1841.	North Madison, Jeff Co IN	John Bull	22 Aug 1853
26	Bunday, Henry	56	Black, 5 ft 11 ins high, high forehead running back from eye. Has scar on hind part of right thigh.	VA in 1797.	Madison Jefferson Co IN	Marcus A Gavit	July 8 1853
98	Burke, Cook	24	Light mulatto, 5 ft 10 ins high. Straight hair round face.	Switzerland Co IN on 14 August 1829.	Madison Twp Jeff Co IN	Charles Conover	24 Aug 1853
53	Carter, Alexander	10	Nearly or quite full blooded Black. Scar on neck and also about mouth from scrofa. Deaf & dumb occasion from sickness.	Madison IN, Jul 19 1843; son of Jacob Carter & Elizabeth Sims.	Madison Jefferson Co IN	Elizabeth Todd & Stepney Stafford	July 26 1853
162	Carter, Morgan	16	Negro black, 5 ft 3 ins, scar on rt wrist, rt leg outside, on outside left leg. Well made, smooth features, round head & face.	Madison Jefferson Co IN	Madison Jefferson Co IN	Robt R Rea, Saml C Humphrey	----
13	Carter, Peter	24	Black, 5 ft 5 ins high. Small scar on joint next the hand on the little right hand finger, heavy built.	Louisville KY on 1st March 1829.	Madison Jefferson Co IN	Andrew Wilson & Copeland P Avion	June 27 1853
116	Causby, Susan	33 1/2	Dark mulatto about 5 feet, pleasant countenance.	VA	Madison Jefferson Co IN	John H Taylor	18 Apr 1855
115	Causby, William	33	Dark mulatto about 6 ft 8 ins. Scar on forefinger rt hand, the nail being split in the center.	Jefferson Co IN on 10 July 1822.	Madison Jefferson Co IN	John H Taylor	18 Apr 1855

Jefferson County, Indiana

	Name	Age	Description	Birthplace	Residence	Witness	Date
109	Chaplain, Gabrella	3	Black, round full face, a child of Charles and Mary Catharine Chaplain.	Near Hanover Jefferson Co IN on 29 May 1851.	South Hanover Jeff Co IN	Gabriel Miller	29 May 1854
110	Chaplain, Eason J.	11 mos	Black	Near Hanover Jefferson Co IN on 19 July 1853.	South Hanover Jeff Co IN	Gabriel Miller	29 May 1854
108	Chaplain, Mary Catherine	22	Black medium size broad forehead. Near sighted.	Woodford Co KY on 13 December 1832	South Hanover Jeff Co IN	Gabriel Miller	29 May 1854
23	Chaplain, Charles	30	Black, 5 ft 7 ins high, piece broken off of upper front tooth, heavy set, laughs easily, high forehead.	MD, 1823.	Jefferson Co IN	William M Dunn, Gabriel Miller.	July 2 1853
25	Clay, Henry Harrison	30	Mulatto six feet one inch high, scar on second joint of thumb on left handm slim built, a little stoop shouldered.	VA on 14 February 1823	Madison Jefferson Co IN	Marcus A Gavit	July 5 1853
10	Clay, William	27	Light mulatto 6 ft high, slender built, thumb on left hand maimed. Full face.	Lunenburgh Co VA January __ 1827.	Madison Jefferson Co IN	Thomas J Martin	June 27 1853
133	Claybrook, John	17	Rather dark complected, 5 ft 6 1/2 ins, scar over lt eye, mole orwart on forefinger rt hand, scar on side of body near breast.	Sparta, White Co TN.	Madison Jefferson Co IN	Thomas J Todd	4 Mar 1858
141	Cosby, John	21	Light complexion. Scar on left wrist above joint. 5 ft 11 ins.	Jefferson Co IN	Madison Jefferson Co IN	E G Leland	4 March 1859
17	Crider, Benjamin	57	Black, heavy build 5 ft 10 ins high. Considerably gray. A mark resembling a black cherry low down on left breast.	NC in 1802.	Madison Jefferson Co IN	Gamaliel Taylor	June 29 1853

Jefferson County, Indiana

19	Crider, John Wesley	4	Black small boy, large head with big forehead, large eyes; very intelligent appearing.	Madison Jefferson Co IN on 26 December 1849	Madison Jefferson Co IN	Benjamin Crider, Lucinda Crider.	June 29 1853
18	Crider, Lucinda	39	Black, slim build, sharp features, high forehead. Upper teeth gone on right side.	Now Tremble Co KY 1814.	Madison Jefferson Co IN	Gamaliel Taylor	June 29 1853
15	Dean, Sandy	50	Black, about 5 ft 7 ins high, heavy built. Raised [by] Genl William O Butler of Carrollton KY.	MD on 28 day of Sept 1803.	Madison Jefferson Co IN	Marcus A Gavit	June 28 1853
106	Dericoat, Absolom	61	Black about 5 ft 5 ins high, gray headed, teeth all sound.	New Castle VA 1792	South Hanover Jeff Co IN	Gamaliel Taylor	19 Oct 1853
134	Ditto, Edward	19	Full blooded Negro; scars on left arm; burn scar near elbow. 5 ft 6 ins, spare built, a pleasant countenace.	Shelbyville KY in 1839.	Madison Jefferson Co IN	Raimus Nettles	13 Mar 1858
21	Ellington, Nelson	30	Mulatto, 5 ft 8 ins high. Scar under left eye, hair nearly straight, lively appearance.	Prince Edward Co VA 1823.	Jefferson Co IN	Gamaliel Taylor	July 2 1853
127	Evans, William T.	30	About 6 ft 1 in, straight built, fair complexion. Scar lt hand back of thumb, oval shape.	Madison Jefferson Co IN	Madison Jefferson Co IN	Robert M Mendall	25 Mar 1857
59	Forson, John R.	27	Black 5 ft 11 ins high, slim build. Scar over left eye in eyebrow and two on calf of left leg.	Bourbon Co KY on 3 November 1826.	Near Hanover Jefferson Co	John Smock	July 30 1853
128	French, Gideon	28	About 5 ft 4 ins, negro, stout built but not fleshy; scar near rt eye, also one near left knee and one near right ankle.	Henry Co KY in 1829	Madison Jefferson Co IN	James N Littlejohn, William E Hillis	28 May 1857

Jefferson County, Indiana

70	French, Strawder	19	Black, 5 ft 3 ins high. Prominent cheek bones. Scar in center forehead, two on right knee, one on left wrist.	Madison Jefferson Co IN on March 1834.	Madison Jefferson Co IN	Stepney Stafford & Isaac Griffin	8 Aug 1853
137	French, William	17	Light complexion, scar forehead above lt eye, about 5 ft 4 ins. Scar on left arm, scar on back of each hand.	Jefferson Co IN	Madison Jefferson Co IN	Thomas Jefferson French	29 March 1858
99	Gardner, Harriet Jane	38	Black, about medium size, hair nearly straight. Wife of Jacob Gardner.	Fayette Co KY on 11 Aug 1815.	Jefferson Co IN	James C Thom	29 Aug 1853
20	Gardner, Isaac	45	Black, slim face and sharp features, 5 ft 10 ins high, prominent mouth.	Caroline Co VA 1808.	Jefferson Co IN	James Y Allison	July 2 1853
112	Gering, William	16	Mulatto boy, spare built tall for his age, of open countenance. Mark on left hand near wrist joint.	Florence AL in October 1838.	Madison Jefferson Co IN	James B Siddall, John Carter	29 Nov 1854
34	Grey, Granderson	22	Black, 5 ft 10 ins high, slim build. Scar on left forearm, wide across cheek bones which are prominent.	KY October 1831.	Jefferson Co IN	Asbury Allums	July 9 1853
68	Griffin, Isaac	50	Black, 5 ft 8 ins high, sharp features, eyes sunken.	MD on 10 March 1803.	Madison Jefferson Co IN	Stepney Stafford	8 Aug 1853
124	Halton, Charles	24	Negro about 5 ft 10 3/4 ins, spare made and well formed, wooly hair, pleasant countenance; scar on fore finger left hand.	South Hanover Jefferson Co IN on 26 February 1833.	Hanover Jeff Co IN	Asberry Allums	16 Feb 1857
147	Hamlet, Anna	20	A scar caused by burn on right hand, rather light complexion. 5 ft two ins, stout built.	TN	Madison Jefferson Co IN	George Hamlet	15 Oct 1860

Jefferson County, Indiana

148	Hamlet, George	30	Negro about 7/8 blood. 5 ft 6 3/4 ins, spare built, tolerably stout guilt. Scar left arm, rt leg near knee cap.	Sparta TN on Oct 12 1830.	Madison Jefferson Co IN	Marcus D Lott	15 Oct 1860
157	Hardgrave, Ann Eldora	13	Negro pure blood, daught of Peter and Rebecca Hardgrave.	Jefferson Co IN on April 12 1847.	Jefferson Co IN	Gamaliel S. Taylor, Chapman Harris	-----
158	Hardgrave, Charles David Vandamore	7	Negro pure blood, son of Peter & Rebecca Hardgrave.	Jefferson Co IN on March 20, 1853.	Jefferson Co IN	Gamaliel S Taylor, Chapman Harris	--
51	Hardgrave, Peter	--	--	--	--	William C Hillis	--
150	Harris, Ann Maria	13	Negro, coarse features, daught of Chapman & Patsey Ann Harris.	Jefferson Co IN on Oct 8, 1847.	Jefferson Co IN	Gamaliel S. Taylor, Chapman Harris	--
103	Harris, Chapman	49	Black, 6 ft high, large eyes, thick lips. Scar on forehead, one on back of right hand.	VA 1804	Near Madison Jeff Co IN	Wm W Woollen	5 Sept 1853
151	Harris, Chapman M.	10	Negro, coarse features. Son of Chapman & Patsy Ann Harris.	Jefferson Co IN on Feb 8 1850.	Jefferson Co IN	Gamaliel S. Taylor, Chapman Harris	--
105	Harris, Charles Walker	10	Black, large eyes with heavy lids.	Jefferson Co IN on 8 December 1842.	Near Madison Jeff Co IN	Wm W Woollen, Chapman Harris	5 Sept 1853
111	Harris, Daniel	44	Dark mulatto about 5 ft high spare built. Pleasant countenance. Scars on rt arm near wrist & elbow; both little fingers deformed.	Harden Co KY on 25 Sept 1810.	Madison Jefferson Co IN	John G Sering, James H Smith, R B Craig	20 July 1854

Jefferson County, Indiana

153	Harris, Elwiza	6	Negro daughter of Chapman & Patsey Ann Harris.	Jefferson Co IN on Aug 6 1854.	Jefferson Co IN	Gamaliel S Taylor, Chapman Harris	--
104	Harris, George Henry	13	Black heavy man, large feet, no marks.	Jefferson Co IN on 8 April 1840.	Near Madison Jeff Co IN	Wm W Woollen, Chapman Harris	5 Sept 1853
155	Harris, Gertrude	2	Negro son [sic] of Chapman & Patsey Ann Harris	Jefferson Co IN on January 28 1858.	Jefferson Co IN	Gamaliel S Taylor, Chapman Harris	--
121	Harris, Henry	25	Negro about 5 ft 9 ins, hair black and curly. Right leg about 3 ins shorter than left. Scar over lt eye, very black complected	Boone Twp Harrison Co IN on 9 Feb 1831.	Madison Jefferson Co IN	John Simons	7 Mar 1856
149	Harris, Mary Elizabeth	15	Negro, coarse features, week eyes from scrofulus. Marks under rt ear. Daughter of Chapman and Patsy Ann Harris.	Madison Jefferson Co IN on December 20, 1845	Jefferson Co IN	Gamaliel S. Taylor, Chapman Harris	--
2	Harris, Maston	36	Bright mulatto 5 ft 10 inch, large.	Harrodsburgh KY	South Hanover, Jeff Co IN	Woodward Boulain	June 22 1853
156	Harris, Patsey Ann	39	Negro (pure blood) 5 ft 2 1/2 ins in height, stout built, mole on left side of chin.	KY betwn Spencer & Shelbyville on 12 April 1821.	Madison Jefferson Co IN	Gamaliel S Taylor	--
154	Harris, Theodore	4	Negro son of Chapman & Patsey Ann Harris	Jefferson Co IN on Sep 9 1856.	Jefferson Co IN	Gamaliel S Taylor, Chapman Harris	--
152	Harris, Virginia A.	8	Negro coarse features, daughter of Chapman & Patsey Ann Harris.	Jefferson Co IN on April 28, 1852.	Jefferson Co IN	Gamaliel S. Taylor, Chapman Harris	--

Jefferson County, Indiana

69	Holton, Joseph	30	Black 5 ft 11 ins high, large thick lips. Scar on right eyebrow One on left shoulder and one on right thigh.	Louisville KY on 4 July 1823.	Madison Jefferson Co IN	Stepney Stafford, Isaac Griffin.	8 Aug 1853
40	Hubbard, Jeremiah	37	Black, 5 ft 9 ins high, heavy stout build, broad face with prominent features.	NC August 1816.	Madison Jefferson Co IN	John H Taylor, Henry Deputy.	July 12 1853
61	Huttals, Elijah F.	28	Black. About 6 ft high stout build, large full features with large eyes.	Henry Co KY on 3 June 1825.	Madison Jefferson Co IN	John G Sering	4 Aug 1853
80	Jackson, Henry	23	Black, 5 ft 7 ins high. Small scar on bridge of nose, one on the right knee, one on rt wrist, one made by bullet near top of head.	Indianapolis IN in August 1830.	Madison Jefferson Co IN	Enoch Burke	12 Aug 1853
143	Jacobs, Charles	72	Negro about 5 ft 6 ins high. Hands mishappen from rheumatism. Spare builkt.	Eastern shore MD in 1757.	Jefferson Co IN	James G. Allison	1 Dec 1859
12	Johnson, David	33	Black, full forehead, quick spoken, five feet nine inches high.	Jefferson Co IN on 23rd day of September 1820.	Madison Jefferson Co IN	John N Taylor	June 27 1853
30	Johnson, James	25	Black or very dark brown color, 5 ft 11 ins high. Slim built. High forehead. Scar inch and half under the leg above knee joint.	Clark Co KY in 1828.	Near Bryantsburg Jeff Co	Jonathan Storms	July 8 1853
76	Johnson, Jane	21	Black large and heavy build, full round face, 5 ft 6-7 ins high. Small scar on cheek under right eye.	Jessamine Co KY on 4 July 1832.	Near Pressburgh, Jeff Co	David Stonestreet	12 Aug 1853
24	Jones, Hester Ann	28	Mulatto, heavy built, a small mole on forehead, large scar on the wrist of right arm.	Bracken Co KY 15th January 1853 [1825].	Madison Jefferson Co IN	Thos Jefferson Martin	July 5 1853

Jefferson County, Indiana

#	Name	Age	Description	Origin	Residence	Witnesses	Date
37	Lott, Cyrus Baptist	24	About 3/4 colored black, 6 ft high, slim, straight and well built, front teeth a little separated.	Near Chillecothe OH on 25 March 1827.	3 miles north Madison	Benedict B Taylor, Marcus A Gavit.	July 9 1853
50	Lott, Henry	30	Black, 7 ft high, slim build. Scar below right eye near nose.	PA on 19 October 1823.	Madison Jefferson Co IN	William Howard	July 25 1853
159	Lott, John [I]	27	Negro black almost 5 ft 9 ins high. Rt arm longer than left. Right leg also larger than left. Scars big toe and on back.	Madison Jefferson Co IN	Jefferson Co IN	John Kirk, John Gerber Jr.	Nov 15, 1861
42a	Lott, John [II]	19	Black about 5 ft 9 ins high, rt arm longer than left. Scar from burn on left leg; cut scar left big toe. [Reg. cancelled in Orig]	Madison Jefferson Co IN	Madison Jefferson Co IN	John H Taylor	July 12 1853
118	Martin, Ann E.	25	A bright handsome mulatto, being a half breed about 5 ft 3 ins, hair dark brownish black wavy; mole near mouth; stout well formed	Lauderdale Co, Florence AL.	Madison Jefferson Co IN	Thomas I Martin	3 July 1855
95	Martin, Sarah Ellen	10	Mulatto, slim built, sharp feature, high forehead, hair straight.	Florence AL on 29 March 1843.	Graysville Jeff Co IN	Thomas J Martin	20 Aug 1853
9	Martin, Thomas Jefferson	30	Mulatto about one half blood, full face, 5 ft 9 ins high. Scar on back right hand near wrist.	Shelbyville TN on the 25th day of June 1823.	Madison Jefferson Co IN	Jas H Smith	June 27 1853
122	Mason, Peter Hampton	17	A boy of color about 5 ft 10 ins, complexion of dark brown color, hair inclined to curl, very slender and well built.	Madison Jefferson Co IN on 9th Jan 1839.	Madison Jefferson Co IN	Robert Rea, Mary Mason	8 July 1856
163	Mayberry John Alexander	38	Negro (not jet black) 5 feet 10 inches high, slender built (about 150 lbs) no particular marks or scars.				--

Jefferson County, Indiana

82	Miller, Ann Mariah	23	Black 5 ft 4 ins high, full round face, short neck.	Franklin Co KY on 25 December 1830.	Near Hanover Jeff Co IN	Washington Stapp, David Miller	18 Aug 1853
22	Miller, Gabriel	53	Black, 5 ft 10 ins high, end of middle finger on right hand cut off.	Woodford Co KY	Jefferson Co IN	Abraham Luck	July 2 1853
107	Miller, Mariah	48	Black, rather large and full face.	Woodford Co KY in 1806.	South Hanover Jeff Co IN	Gabriel Miller	25 Feb 1854
83	Miller, Sarah Ellen	16	Nearly full blood black, hair straighter than usual; high full forehead.	Franklin Co KY on 1 August 1837.	Near Hanover Jeff Co IN	Washington Stapp, David Miller	18 Aug 1853
84	Miller, Susan	14	Black, four feet three inches high, round full face.	Franklin Co KY on 25 November 1839.	Near Hanover Jeff Co IN	Washington Stapp, David Miller	15 Aug 1853
138	Mitchell, Martin	21	About 1/2 Indian and 1/2 Negro (Father & mother being 1/2 Indian and 1/2 Negro). 5 ft 8 3/4 ins high; spare built. Many scars.	New London Jefferson Co IN in 1837.	Madison Jefferson Co IN	Marcus D Lott, Gideon French.	10 April 1858
146	Nettles, Andrew J.	26	5 ft 5 1/2 ins, rather stout built. scars left cheek, on left shoulder blade, rather light complexion.	New Castle KY on January 31 1835.	Madison Jefferson Co IN	James J Sering	24 July 1860
135	Nettles, Raimus	17	Scar on nose between eyes, mark on left arm near elbow; 5 ft 9 1/2 inches high.	Madison Jefferson Co IN	Madison Jefferson Co IN	Edward Ditton	13 March 1858
38	Nolton, Edward	22	Black, 5 ft 9 ins high, round plump features. Two small scars onback of left hand, one on back of right hand.	Louisville KY on 1 Jan 1831.	Madison Jefferson Co IN	Thomas Ayers	July 9 1853

Jefferson County, Indiana

136	Noon[?], Calvin	25	Black, about 5 ft 6 ins high, rather dish faced, some scars on his head.	Madison Jefferson Co IN on 21 July 1828.	Madison Jefferson Co IN	Benedict B Taylor	July 9 1853
32	Overstreet, David	38	Dark brown color, 5 ft 11 ins high, rather lean slim build. Blemish in inside corner of right eye.	Jessamine Co KY on Sept 1815.	Near Bryantsburgh Jeff Co	Jonathan Storms	July 8 1853
71	Overstreet, Edward	61	Dark mulatto about 5 ft 7 ins in height.	Patrick Co VA	Monroe Twp Jefferson CoIN	John Land & Jonathan Storms	10 Aug 1853
93	Overstreet, Gracy Ann	27	Black, above medium size, large face, rather slim build.	Jessamine Co KY on 16 April 1826.	Monroe Twp Jeff Co IN	Jonathan Storms	19 Aug 1853
91	Overstreet, Mary Jane	3	Black. Small delicate features.	Jessamine Co KY on 16 January 1850.	Monroe Twp Jeff Co IN	Jonathan Storms	19 Aug 1853
31	Overstreet, Samuel	40	Black, 5 ft 2 ins high, scar two and a half inches long across forehead.	Jessamine Co KY in 1813.	Near Bryantsburgh Jeff Co	Jonathan Storms	July 8 1853
92	Overstreet, Sarah Elizabeth	23 mos	Black. Large of her age.	Jessamine Co KY on 20 Sept 1851.	Monroe Twp Jeff Co IN	Jonathan Storms	19 Aug 1853
33	Overstreet, William [I]	16	Mulatto, tall and slim build, being about 5 ft 10 ins high. Low forehead.	Jessamine Co KY on April 1837.	Near Bryantsburgh Jeff Co	Jonathan Storms	July 8 1853
29	Overstreet, William [II]	45	Black. 5 ft 2 ins high, very heavy built. Weighs 212-215 lbs.	Jessamine Co KY in 1808.	Jefferson Co IN	Marcus D Lott, Jonathan Storms.	July 8 1853
113	Owen, William	47	Dark mulatto about 5 ft 8 ins. Pleasant countenance.	Gallatin Co KY.	Milton Twp Jeff Co IN	Robert B Craig, John I Craig	4 Jan 1855
41b	Roberts, Abraham [I]	20	Black 5 ft 8 ins high, full face, heavy stout built, scar in center forehead, rt cheek, lt side throat.[Reg cancelled in orig]	Henry Co KY born on 2 day May 1833.	Madison Jefferson Co IN	Wm C Hillis	July 12 1853

Jefferson County, Indiana

142	Roberts, Abraham [II]	26	Negro 5 ft 8 ins, stout built; scars center forehead, rt cheek bone, left side throat, on back of both hands from burns.	Henry Co KY 2 day May 1833.	Madison Jefferson Co IN	Gam S Taylor	15 June 1859
42	Roberts, Elisha	24	Black, 5 ft 8 ins high, well proportioned, round face; small scars upper lip, breast; 3 fingers on right hand crooked.	Henry Co KY on 1 March 1830.	Madison Jefferson Co IN	Wm C Hillis	July 12 1853
117	Roberts, Enoch	25	A Negro 5 ft 7 1/2 ins. Scars right cheek, right arm below elbow on shin left leg, spare, well built, stout.	Henry Co KY about 9 miles from Newcastle on 10 February 1830.	Madison Jefferson Co IN	Robert B Craig, John H Taylor	5 Jun 1855
66	Roberts, Timothy [I]	19	Black, 5 ft 4 ins high, prominent forehead, rather prominent mouth. Scar under left arm, two scars on left hip, 2 over lt eye	Beauford KY in 1834.	Madison Jefferson Co IN	Stepney Stafford	8 Aug 1853
129	Roberts, Timothy [II]	20	About 5 ft 9 ins stout built, two scars over lt eye and one on left side between 3 & 4 ribs.	Bedford KY	Madison Jefferson Co IN		3 June 1857
140	Robinson, James R.	22	Full blooded negro, 5 ft 6 ins high, spare built; scars on rt side chin, back of rt hand, on rt foot betwn 2nd - 3rd toe.	Fluvanna Co VA on 9 February 1837.	Madison Jefferson Co IN	Thomas Clark (Colored man)	8 March 1859
39	Russell, Maria	70	Mulatto, low and heavy set, broad face, low forehead, nose low between the eyes.	Petersburgh VA in 1787.	Madison Jefferson Co IN	Sarah M Daily, Sarah G Steveman.	July 12 1853
45	Shafer, John C.	36	Black 5 ft 8 ins high, slim build. Scar on inside corner of lefteye, ball of left hand much mutilated.	McMinnville TN on 17 Oct 1817.	Madison Jefferson Co IN	James C Thom & John G Sering	July 15 1853

Jefferson County, Indiana

41	Simmoms, John T.	27	Mulatto, 5 ft 10 ins high, slim build with slim sharp features. Scar on left jaw, second finger on lt hand doubled into palm.	Jefferson Co IN on 22 July 1826.	Madison Jefferson Co IN	William C Hillis	July 12 1853
102	Simmons, James B.	9	Mulatto, heavy build, a little cross eyed.	Jefferson Co IN on 26 December 1844.	Jefferson Co IN	Harriet Jane Gardner	29 Aug 1853
100	Simmons, Rebecca Frances	17	Mulatto, rather above medium height, large features.	Fayette Co KY on 6 March 1836.	Jefferson Co IN	James C Thom	29 Aug 1853
101	Simmons, Thomas S.	15	Black. Eyes set back. Prominent forehead.	Jefferson Co IN on 22 January 1838.	Jefferson Co IN	Harriet Jane Gardner	29 Aug 1853
28	Stafford, Polly	57	Black or dark brown color, about 5 ft high, has a scar on the legby knee in front.	VA in 1796.	Madison Jefferson Co IN	John Lund Sr.	July 8 1853
27	Stafford, Stepney	66	Black, heavy set, 5 ft 10 ins high, scar on cheek under lt eye. Scar on back of left hand.	Fayette Co KY in 1787.	Madison Jefferson Co IN	John Lund Sr.	July 8 1853
132	Stapp, Amerlerd (?)	24	Dark mulatto 5 ft 9 ins high, not very fleshy but stout; incline to stoop; small pox scars; scars above wrist.	South Hanover Jefferson Co IN in 1833.	South Hanover Jeff Co IN	Wm A M Henry	16 Nov 1857
65	Stapp, Amstead	22	Nearly Black, 5 ft 10 ins high, stout active build, high forehead Small scar on inside of left wrist.	Near Hanover, Jefferson Co IN on 17 Oct 1831.	Near Hanover, Jeff Co IN	James G Allison	8 Aug 1853
49	Stapp, Horace	32	Full blood Black, about 5 ft 6 ins high, tolerably heavy set. Scar below left temple, and between left eye and left ear.	Scott Co KY in 1821.	Madison Jefferson Co IN	Houston Wood	July 22 1853
81	Stapp, Washington	23	Dark mulatto 6 ft high prominent cheek bones, bow legged.	Hanover Jefferson Co IN in May 1830.	Near Hanover, Jeff Co IN	James C Thom	18 Aug 1853

Jefferson County, Indiana

74	Stonestreet, Benjamin	9	Dark mulatto, spare built mark over his right eye.	Jessamine Co KY in July 1844.	Monroe Twp Jeff Co IN	David Stonestreet & Jonathan Storms	12 Aug 1853
79	Stonestreet, Emily Jane	2 1/2 years	Mulatto full forehead. Nose short and eyes close together and daughter of David and Mary Stonestreet, residents Jeff Co IN.	Jefferson Co IN in January 1851.	Monroe Twp Jefferson Co	David Stonestreet, Jonathan Storms	12 Aug 1853
78	Stonestreet, Mary Ann	12	Mulatto, slim build with slim features, rather a sprightly appearance.	Jessamine Co KY on December 1841.	Monroe Twp Jeff Co IN	David Stonestreet, Jonathan Storms.	12 Aug 1853
73	Stonestreet, Margaret	14	Mulatto spare built large for her age.	Jessamine Co KY in June 1839.	Monroe Twp Jeff Co IN	David Stonestreet & Jonathan Storms	12 Aug 1853
77	Stonestreet, Martha	4	Mulatto, small delicate appearance with finer features than usual.	Jessamine Co KY on 1 April 1849.	Monroe Twp Jeff Co IN	David Stonestreet	12 Aug 1853
72	Stonestreet, Mary	33	Mulatto spare built about 5 ft 3 ins in height.	Jessamine Co KY in 1820.	Monroe Twp Jeff Co IN	David Stonestreet & Jonathan Storms	12 Aug 1853
75	Stonestreet, Nancy	6	Light mulatto, spare built.	Jessamine Co KY in February 1847.	Monroe Twp Jeff Co IN	David Stonestreet & Jonathan Storms	12 Aug 1853
64	Taylor, Ann Eliza	12	Mulatto, slim light figure nose sharper than usual, hair nearly straight. Daughter of John and Elizabeth Taylor.	Mooresville AL on 17 July 1841.	Madison Jefferson Co IN	Jas N Smith	5 Aug 1853
145	Taylor, Charles W.	24		---			16 Feb 1860

Jefferson County, Indiana

160	Taylor, Charles William	27	Negro light complexion about 5 ft 20 ins. American code found on left arm. Name C W Taylor on right arm & also picture of lady.	Fredericksburg VA	Madison Jefferson Co IN	Robt R Rea, Danl McIntire	--
63	Taylor, Elizabeth	38	Mulatto, rather below minimum size, good figure, sharper features than usual, hair nearly strait, scar left jaw.	Franklin Co TN 10 March 1815. Wife of John Taylor.	Madison Jefferson Co IN	Jas N Smith	5 Aug 1853
3	Taylor, John	51	Mulatto Dark	King George Co Va, March 10th 1802.	Madison Jefferson Co IN	John H Taylor	June 25 1853
43	Taylor, Kingsburry	35	Light mulatto half blood, 5 ft 7 1/2 ins, Scar on left hand on joint at finger; burn scar on right thigh.	Nash Co NC	Madison Jefferson Co IN	James G Allison, Festus L Thompson	July 13 1853
57	Taylor, Sarah Ann	6	Mulatto, large eyes, large features, has a black mark near left nostril about the size of a five cent piece.	Jefferson Co IN on 29 August 1847.	Madison Jefferson Co IN	Thomas Jefferson Martin	July 29 1853
123	Taylor, William M.	22	About 5 ft 8 ins, pleasant countenance, light complected; straight hair except ends which is inclined to curl.	Monroeville AL on 9 August 1834.	Madison Jefferson Co IN	John Taylor, Alsterd Stapp	9 Feb 1857
62	Taylor, William M.	19	Dark mulatto, 5 ft 3 ins high, hair nearly strait, slim build.	Mooresville AL on 19 Aug 1834.	Madison Jefferson Co IN	John Taylor	5 Aug 1853
48	Thomason, Charles	28	Black, 5 ft 3 ins high, light build. Scar on rt arm, on top of head, several on breast caused by cupping instrument.	Rowan Co NC on 10 August 1825.	Madison Jefferson Co IN	John G Sering	July 21 1853

Jefferson County, Indiana

139	Thornton, Austin	16	Full bodied Negro, 5 ft 6 1/4 ins; scars middle finger rt hand, forefinger on left hand, on left arm; compactly stout built.	Madison Jefferson Co IN on 7 May 1842.	Madison Jefferson Co IN	Robert R Rea, Henry Thornton	12 April 1858
126	Thornton, Henry	41	Negro 5 ft 5 3/4 ins, spare built; scar under left ear, rt leg above ankle; 2 scars between rt eye and rt ear.	Falmouth VA in 1816.	Madison Jefferson Co IN	James G Allison	17 Mar 1857
44	Todd, Elizabeth	38	Mulatto compactly built, aged about 38 years. Widow of Harrison Todd and of William Sims.	Louisville Jefferson Co KY on 17 October 1817.	Madison Jefferson Co IN	Henry Deputy	July 13 1853
54	Todd, Mary Eliza	2	Nearly full blood with regular features, large black mark under and on right ear, mark under left arm shaped like a strawberry.	Madison Jefferson Co IN on Aug 1, 1851.	Madison Jefferson Co IN	Elizabeth Todd, Stepney Stafford	July 26 1853
136	Todd, Thomas Jefferson	20	Dark complected, 5 ft 6 ins, scar on rt knee joint, on left forefinger, on right ankle.	Florence, Switzerland Co IN.	Madison Jefferson Co IN	William French	29 Mar 1858
55	Todd, William H.	5 mos	Nearly or quite full blooded Black, mark on his right lip of shape of a catfish. Child of Harrison and Elizabeth Todd.	Madison Jefferson Co IN February 13 1853. Now dead.	Madison Jefferson Co IN	Elizabeth Todd, Stepney Stafford	July 26 1853
4	Tyree, Joseph Henry	21	Negro Thumb on left hand mutilated & the following letters and figures inscribed on his right arm: "1832 Jo H T"	Charleston Clark Co IN May 24 1832.	Madison Jefferson Co IN	James C Thom	June 27 1853
47	Tyree, Moses	59	Black, about 5 ft 3 ins high, high forehead, teeth out in front.	Caroline Co VA in October 1793.	Near Hanover Jefferson Co	William M Dunn	July 18 1853
90	Vickery, Emily	45	Black, medium size upper teeth out in front, scar in center of forehead.	SC in 1808.	Madison Jefferson Co IN		18 Aug 1853

Jefferson County, Indiana

89	Vickery, Mary Ann	21	Black, medium size, round full face. Scar on back of left wrist.	SC in 1832.	Madison Jefferson Co IN	18 Aug 1853
8	Wicker, Amos	26	Mulatto 5 ft 5 ins high. Scar left side of throat, high cheek bones, high forehead, resembling features of Western Indians.	Washington Co GA on 3rd day of April 1827.	Jefferson Co IN	June 27 1853
119	Williams, Samuel	31	Mulatto, being a half breed, about 5 ft 6 1/2 ins; scar left corner left eye; left leg shorter than right; spare built.	Donaldsonville LA in 1824.	Madison Jefferson Co IN	25 Oct 1855
120	Williams, William	15	Mulatto one fourth breed, 4 ft 1/2 in high. Scar on neck about two inches long.	TN Dec 1, 1840. Father: Samuel Williams	Madison Jefferson Co IN	7 Nov 1855
11	Wilson, Andrew M.	30	Full blood 5 ft 10 ins high, slim built, high forehead, front teeth stand apart.	Jessamine Co KY on ___ day of ___ 1823.	Madison Jefferson Co IN	June 27 1853
56	Winn, Andrew	50	Mulatto, 5 ft 8 ins high. Scar on muscle of left arm, small moleon left nostril, one of lip 1/2 in from left nostril.	Barren Co KY in 1803.	Madison Jefferson Co IN	July 29 1853
94	Winn, Minerva	32	Mulatto, slim build, sharp features, thin lips, straight hair. Above medium height.	Gainesborough TN in 1821.	Graysville Jeff Co IN	20 Aug 1853
130	Wood, Curtis [I]	18	Rather light complected, scar right arm below elbow on fleshy part; about 5 ft 6 ins.	MS	Madison Jefferson Co IN	3 June 1857
161	Wood, Curtis [II]	21	Negro black 5 ft 6 ins, scar on rt arm, round face, round and well proportioned head, well built.	MS	Madison Jefferson Co IN	--
67	Wood, Vernon	19	Dark mulatto, 5 ft 10 ins high, heavy build. Round face. has a larege scar on left leg.	MS on 16 October 1834.	Madison Jefferson Co IN	8 Aug 1853

		Madison Jefferson Co IN	
	Asmon Allums		
	Archibald Taylor		
	Jno H Taylor		
	John N Taylor		
	William T Evans, David Johnson		
	Thomas J Martin		
	Wm T Evans		
	Robert M Marshall, Rufus Goen Jr		
	Stepney Stafford		

Jefferson County, Indiana

88	Woodfork, Elizabeth	50	Black, small with prominent mouth. Scar under left ear and five on right hip.	Baltimore MD in 1802.	Madison Jefferson Co IN	Gideon Fitch	18 Aug 1853
46	Woodfork, Gabriel	51	Black, 5 ft 5 ins high, rather spare, left hand deformed from being burnt when a child. Scar on breast.	Oldham Co KY in 1802.	Madison Jefferson Co IN	William C Hillis	July 18 1853

REGISTER OF NEGROES AND MULATTOES IN JENNINGS COUNTY, INDIANA

Names	Age	Description	Place of Birth	Residence	Names of Witnesses	Date Registered
Carsey, Dennis	64	A Negro of yellow complexion, black eyes & hair, and of medium height and size.	GA	Jennings Co, IN	Robert D. McCammon James H. Biggs	25 April 1853
Carsey, Ephraim	60	A Negro of yellow complexion, black eyes and hair, and of medium size and height.	GA	Jennings Co, IN	Achilles Vawter David G. Vawter	30 April 1853
Carsey, Alexander	19	A Negro of light yellow complexion, black eyes and hair, and of medium size and height.	Jennings Co, IN	Jennings Co, IN	Achilles Vawter David G. Vawter	30 April 1853
Carsey, Stephen	70	A Negro man of yellow complexion, black eyes and white hair or nearly so. Nearly six feet high, and well proportioned in size. height.	NC	Jennings Co, IN	Robert D. McCammon, Asa Haney	2 May 1853
Carsey, Sally	60	A Negro woman of yellow complexion, with dark eyes and hair, above the medium size.	GA	Jennings Co, IN	Joseph Cowell Thomas J. Story	3 May 1853
Dennis, Peter	41	A mulatto man dark eyes and hair, medium size.	SC	Vernon, Jennings Co, IN	Achilles Vawter Robert D. Mc Cammon	5 May 1853
Dennis, John William	15	A mulatto boy with dark eyes-hair.	SC	Vernon, Jennings Co, IN	Achilles Vawter Robert D. Mc Cammon	5 May 1853
Dennis, Sarah Elizabeth	13	A mulatto girl with dark eyes and hair & light complexion.	SC	Vernon, Jennings Co, IN	Achilles Vawter Robert D. Mc Cammon	5 May 1853

Jennings County, Indiana

Dennis, Mary Eliza	11	A mulatto girl with dark eyes and hair.	SC	Vernon, Jennings Co, IN	Achilles Vawter Robert D. Mc Cammon	5 May 1853
Dennis, James Walter	9	A mulatto boy with dark eyes and hair.	SC	Vernon, Jennings Co, IN	Achilles Vawter Robert D. Mc Cammon	5 May 1853
Dennis, Enoch Wagoner	7	A mulatto boy with dark eyes-hair.	KY	Vernon, Jennings Co, IN	Achilles Vawter Robert D. Mc Cammon	5 May 1853
Dennis, Margaret Ann	4	A mulatto girl with dark eyes and hair.	Jennings Co, IN	Vernon, Jennings Co, IN	Achilles Vawter Robert D. Mc Cammon	5 May 1853
Dennis, Robert Maxwell Johnson	2	A mulatto boy with dark eyes and hair.	Jennings Co, IN	Vernon, Jennings Co, IN	Achilles Vawter Robert D. Mc Cammon	5 May 1853
Dye, Daniel	44	A mulatto man of light yellow complexion, light or blue eyes, medium size.	Warren Co, GA	Jennings Co, IN	Achilles Vawter Robert D. Mc Cammon	11 June 1853
Dye, Nancy Jane	13	A mulatto girl of yellow complexion & pleasant countenance.	Jennings Co, IN	Jennings Co, IN	Achilles Vawter Robert D. Mc Cammon	11 June 1853
Dye, Acquilla Ann	9	A mulatto girl of yellow complexion.	Jennings Co, IN	Jennings Co, IN	Achilles Vawter Robert D. Mc Cammon	11 June 1853
Dye, James William	8	A mulatto boy of yellow complexion and cross eyed.	Jennings Co, IN	Jennings Co, IN	Achilles Vawter Robert D. Mc Cammon	11 June 1853

Jennings County, Indiana

Name	Age	Description			Date
Valentine, Andrew	23	A negro man of medium size, rather good looking and of yellowish complexion.	SC	Jennings Co, IN	Commodore C. Root Wm. B. Hagins	9 July 1853
Harper, Thomas	29	A negro man about five feet and 11 inches high and weighing about 175 and a brown black complexion.	Elbert Co, GA	Jennings Co, IN	Arad Parks John Skinner	9 July 1853
Harper, Riley	28	A negro man of medium size and hight and of light brown complexion.	Elbert Co, GA	Jennings Co, IN	Arad Parks John Skinner	11 July 1853
Norman, Nancy	47	A negro woman of black complexion with some large warts or moles on her face and ears and somewhat corpulent.	Elbert Co, GA	Jennings Co, IN	William B. Hagins David Merrick	11 July 1853
Norman, Augustus	15	A negro boy of black complexion & well grown for his age.	Elbert Co, GA	Jennings Co, IN	William B. Hagins David Merrick	11 July 1853
Norman, Willie	13	A negro boy of black or dark brown complexion.	Elbert Co, GA	Jennings Co, IN	William B. Hagins David Merrick	11 July 1853
Lee, Ellen	--	A mulatto woman of light yellow complexion and medium size.	Jennings Co, IN	Jennings Co, IN	William B. Hagins David Merrick	18 July 1853
McCoppin, Marshall	38	A negro man of black or dark brown complexion & of tall stature.	SC	Jennings Co, IN	William B. Hagins David Merrick	18 July 1853
McCoppin, Sarah	35	A negro woman of black or dark brown complexion & wife of the above named Marshall McCoppin.	Elbert Co, GA	Jennings Co, IN	William B. Hagins David Merrick	22 July 1853
Vickery, James	49	A negro man of black complexion and medium size.	Aberville District, SC	Jennings Co, IN	Thompson Grisson William B. Hagins	22 July 1853
Vickery, Rhoda	49	A negro woman of black complexion and medium size, & wife of the above named James Vickery.	Elbert Co, GA	Jennings Co, IN	Thompson Grisson William B. Hagins	22 July 1853

Jennings County, Indiana

Name	Age	Description	Origin	Signers	County	Date
Anthony, David	53	A negro man of black or very dark brown complexion of medium size and gray hair.	Elbert Co, GA	Thompson Grisson / William B. Hagins	Jennings Co, IN	22 July 1853
Anthony, Charlotte	38	A mulatto woman of medium size & of bright yellow complexion with intelligent countenance and hair nearly straight & smooth.	Elbert Co, GA	Thompson Grisson / William B. Hagins	Jennings Co, IN	22 July 1853
Anthony, William	22	Mulatto man of yellow complexion and of medium size.	Elbert Co, GA	Thompson Grisson / William B. Hagins	Jennings Co, IN	22 July 1853
Hullman, Jasper	10	A mulatto boy of bright yellow complexion & ordinary size.	Elbert Co, GA	Thompson Grisson / William B. Hagins	Jennings Co, IN	22 July 1853
Harper, Grigg	82	A negro man of dark brown complexion and walks lame, and somewhat bald & gray.	Prince Edward Co, VA	Asa Skinner / John Skinner	Jennings Co, IN	22 July 1853
Pettiford, Drury	41	A mulatto man of brown complexion and of medium size.	Stokes Co, N?	Levi W. Todd / David Merrick	Jennings Co, IN	28 July 1853
White, William	50	A negro man of black complexion and of medium size.	VA	Thompson Grisson / William B. Hagins	Jennings Co, IN	30 July 1853
Phillips, Henry	31	A negro man of dark brown complexion, of medium size.	Warren Co, GA	Ebenezer Baldwin / Joseph Fellenger	Jennings Co, IN	1 August 1853
Hill, Ananis	51	A negro man of black complexion of medium size with gray hair.	MD	George M. Payne / Avery W. Bullock	Jennings Co, IN	5 August 1853
Anthony, Nancy	22	A negro woman of brown complexion and medium size.	Jennings Co, IN	Joseph Fellenger / Harvey M. Cowell	Jennings Co, IN	6 August 1853
Phillips, Rosa	23	A negro woman of dark brown complexion of medium size and wife of Henry Phillips.	Jennings Co, IN	Joseph Fellenger / Harvey M. Cowell	Jennings Co, IN	6 August 1853

Jennings County, Indiana

Name	Age	Description	Origin	Residence	Witnesses	Date
Phillips, Elzora	5	A negro girl of dark brown complexion, and small of her age a daughter of Henry Phillips.	Jennings Co, IN	Jennings Co, IN	Joseph Fellenger / Harvey M. Cowell	6 August 1853
Phillips, Cynthia	3	A negro girl of dark brown complexion, and daughter of Henry Phillips.	Jennings Co, IN	Jennings Co, IN	Joseph Fellenger / Harvey M. Cowell	6 August 1853
Phillips, Emily	1	A negro girl of dark brown complexion with cross eyed, and daughter of Henry Phillips.	Jennings Co, IN	Jennings Co, IN	Joseph Fellenger / Harvey M. Cowell	6 August 1853
Hood, John	20	A negro man of dark brown complexion, below medium size.	Jennings Co, IN	Jennings Co, IN	Achilles Vawter / Monroe McMindes	12 August 1853
Harper, Jane	56	A negro woman of dark brown or black complexion, short hair a little gray, medium size.	Elbert Co, GA	Jennings Co, IN	Milton Boner / Harvey Boner	12 August 1853
Hill, Bluford A.	28	A negro man of dark brown complexion, of medium size & intelligent countenance.	Elbert Co, GA	Jennings Co, IN	Ebenezer Baldwin / Smith Vawter	15 August 1853
Newsom, Emily	19	A negro woman of dark brown complexion of medium size.	Jennings Co, IN	Jennings Co, IN	Achilles Vawter / Harvey M. Cowell	15 August 1853
Carsey, Eliza Jane	18	A negro woman of brown complexion, rather tall and good looking.	Jennings Co, IN	Jennings Co, IN	Achilles Vawter / Harvey M. Cowell	15 August 1853
Evans, Zebidee	19	A mulatto man of yellow complexion of medium size, of quick and lively turn.	Halifax Co, NC	Indianapolis, IN	Achilles Vawter / James M. Baldwin	16 August 1853
Carsey, Willis	17	A negro man of dark brown complexion, of medium size and intelligent countenance.	Jennings Co, IN	Jennings Co, IN	Achilles Vawter / James M. Baldwin	16 August 1853

Jennings County, Indiana

Wallace, Elias	19	A negro man of black complexion and a little below of medium height, of intelligent countenance.	Jennings Co, IN	Jennings Co, IN	Joseph Cowell Era Rose	19 August 1853
Henderson, Harrison	42	A negro man of black complexion of medium size and has stoppage in his speech.	Garet Co, KY	Jennings Co, IN	Achilles Vawter Harvey M. Cowell	20 August 1853
Dunlop, Peter	63	A mulatto man of light brown complexion and very tall.	Aberville District, SC	Jennings Co, IN	Harvey Boner Smith Vawter	20 August 1853
Dunlop, Jane	51	A mulatto woman of light brown complexion & tall.	Aberville District, SC	Jennings Co, IN	Harvey Boner Smith Vawter	20 August 1853
Dunlop, Martha	30	A mulatto woman of light yellow complexion & very tall.	Aberville District, SC	Jennings Co, IN	Harvey Boner Smith Vawter	20 August 1853
Dunlop, Nancy	20	A mulatto woman of light yellow complexion & very tall.	Aberville District, SC	Jennings Co, IN	Harvey Boner Smith Vawter	20 August 1853
Dunlop, William	5	A mulatto boy of light brown complexion.	Jennings Co, IN	Jennings Co, IN	Harvey Boner Smith Vawter	20 August 1853
Valentine, Samuel	28	A negro man of dark brown complexion, of medium size.	Aberville District, SC	Jennings Co, IN	Harvey Boner Smith Vawter	20 August 1853
Valentine, Caroline	34	A mulatto woman of yellow brown complexion rather tall.	Aberville District, SC	Jennings Co, IN	Harvey Boner Smith Vawter	20 August 1853
Valentine, Martha	5	A mulatto girl of brown complexion.	Jennings Co, IN	Jennings Co, IN	Harvey Boner Smith Vawter	20 August 1853
Valentine, James	3	A mulatto boy of brown complexion.	Jennings Co, IN	Jennings Co, IN	Harvey Boner Smith Vawter	20 August 1853
Valentine, Jesse	4 mos	A mulatto boy of brown complexion.	Jennings Co, IN	Jennings Co, IN	Harvey Boner Smith Vawter	20 August 1853

Jennings County, Indiana

Carsey, Hulbert	21	A negro man of dark brown complexion and of medium size.	Jennings Co, IN	Harvey Boner Charles Rust	20 August 1853
Carsey, Mariah Jane	19	A mulatto woman of brown complexion, medium size and wife of the above named Helbert Carsey.	Elbert Co, GA	Harvey Boner Charles Rust	20 August 1853
Carsey, George	54	A negro man of dark brown complexion, a little bald on the crown, and of medium size.	Willis Co, GA	Levi W. Todd John S. Barnett	24 August 1853
Brandon, Lemuel	17	A mulatto man of dark brown complexion, of medium size, and intelligent countenance.	Jackson Co, IN	Levi W. Todd Henry House	24 August 1853
Phillips, Wesly	25	A negro man of brown complexion, medium size, and intelligent countenance.	Warren Co, GA	Ebenezer Baldwin Solon Cowell	26 August 1853
Phillips, Joseph	2 1/2	A negro boy of yellowish brown complexion, son of Wesly Phillips.	Jennings Co, IN	Ebenezer Baldwin Solon Cowell	26 August 1853
Phillips, Jesse	21	A negro man of brown complexion, of medium size.	Warren Co, GA	Ebenezer Baldwin Solon Cowell	26 August 1853
Phillips, Silvester	19	A negro man of dark brown complexion, of medium size.	Warren Co, GA	Ebenezer Baldwin Solon Cowell	26 August 1853
Phillips, Stephen	15	A negro boy of dark brown complexion, and of medium size.	Jennings Co, IN	Ebenezer Baldwin Solon Cowell	26 August 1853
Hill, Lewis	69	A negro man of dark brown complexion and of medium size.	Culpepper Co, VA	Achilles Vawter Levi W. Todd	26 August 1853
Hill, Agrippa	15	A negro boy of dark brown complexion, and son of Lewis Hill.	Jennings Co, IN	Achilles Vawter Levi W. Todd	26 August 1853

Jennings County, Indiana

Name	Age	Description	Origin	County	Witnesses	Date
King, Spencer Beverly	19	A negro man of black complexion and medium size.	Jennings Co, IN	Jennings Co, IN	Achilles Vawter / Levi W. Todd	26 August 1853
Henry, Thomas I.	33	A mulatto man of yellowish complexion and gray eyes and of medium size.	Bourbon Co, KY	Jennings Co, IN	Achilles Vawter / George M. Payne	29 August 1853
King, Spencer	68	A negro man of black complexion and medium size, with gray or white hair.	Culpepper Co, VA	Jennings Co, IN	Levi W. Todd / Thomas Walker	30 August 1853
Carsey, Ephram	32	A negro man of dark brown complexion under medium size and walks quite lame.	Jennings Co, IN	Jennings Co, IN	Solon Corwell / Achilles Vawter	30 August 1853
Hill, Jefferson	20	A negro man of dark brown complexion of medium size.	Jennings Co, IN	Jennings Co, IN	James M. Baldwin / Elisha Boner	1 September 1853
King, Emiline	24	A negro woman of black complexion a little above medium size.	Jefferson Co, IN	Jennings Co, IN	Harvey M. Cowell / Achilles Vawter	5 September 1853
Johnson, Thomas L.	29	A negro man of black or dark brown complexion of medium size and stout heavy set, with a scar on his chin.	Jennings Co, IN	Jennings Co, IN	Achilles Vawter / Robert D. McCammon	14 September 1853
Dennis, Margaret	37	A mulatto woman of light yellow complexion, of intelligent countenance & of medium size.	SC	Jennings Co, IN	Achilles Vawter / Joseph Cowell	16 September 1853
Johnson, Judah	72	A negro woman of dark brown or black complexion below the medium height.	TN	Jennings Co, IN	Achilles Vawter / Joseph Cowell	16 September 1853
Johnson, Mary	30	A negro woman of black or dark brown complexion of medium size.	Fauquier Co, VA	Jennings Co, IN	Achilles Vawter / Robert D. McCammon	17 September 1853

Jennings County, Indiana

Johnson, Sarah Esther	4	A negro girl of black or dark brown complexion & daughter of Thomas Johnson and Mary Johnson.	Jennings Co, IN	Jennings Co, IN	Achilles Vawter Robert D. McCammon	17 September 1853
Stafford, Richard	30	A negro man of dark brown complexion of a little below medium size.	Fauquier Co, VA	Jennings Co, IN	Manlove Butler Robert D. McCammon	19 September 1853
Wallace, Isaiah	19	A Negro man of black or dark brown complexion and of medium size.	Jennings Co, IN	Jennings Co, IN	John S. Basnett Lewi W. Todd	19 September 1853
Vickery, Allen	39	A negro man of black complexion about six feet high.	Aberville District, SC	Jennings Co, IN	Achilles Vawter Thomas McGammon	20 September 1853
Vickery, Addis	18	A negro man of black complexion of middle height.	Aberville District, SC	Jennings Co, IN	Achilles Vawter Thomas McGammon	20 September 1853
Vickery, Oliver	17	A negro man of black complexion well grown of his age.	Aberville District, SC	Jennings Co, IN	Achilles Vawter Thomas McGammon	20 September 1853
King, Jane	26	A negro woman of black complexion and of medium size.	Jefferson Co, IN	Jennings Co, IN	Achilles Vawter Thomas McGammon	20 September 1853
Stafford, Martha E.	20	A negro woman of black complexion and of medium size.	Abesville District SC	Jennings Co, IN	Achilles Vawter Thomas McGammon	20 September 1853
Hood, James H.	11	A negro boy of black or dark brown complexion.	Jennings Co, IN	Jennings Co, IN	Achilles Vawter Thomas McGammon	20 September 1853
Hill, Mary Ann	23	A mulatto woman of yellowish brown complexion of middle size.	Elbert Co, GA	Jennings Co, IN	Achilles Vawter Thomas McGammon	20 September 1853
Hood, William	55	A negro man of medium size rather stout of yellowish brown complexion.	Rockingham Co, NC	Jennings Co, IN	Achilles Vawter Elisha Boner	26 Deecember 1853
Hood, Ephraim	59	A negro man of medium size stout built of brown complexion.	Rockingham Co, NC	Jennings Co, IN	Achilles Vawter Elisha Boner	26 Deecember 1853

Jennings County, Indiana

Hood, Mary	16	A negro girl of brown complexion and intelligent countenance and a little below medium size.	Jennings Co, IN	Jennings Co, IN	Achilles Vawter Elisha Boner	27 Deecember 1853
Lee, William	54	A mulatto man of yellowish brown complexion, with light or gray eyes, and of middle size.	Rockingham Co, VA	Jennings Co, IN	Robert D. McGammon Avery W. Bullock	1 February 1854
Newby, James	16	A negro boy of dark brown or black complexion and is tall and well grown for his age.	Jacjson Co, IN	Jennings Co, IN	William B. Hagins Henry L. Arnold	13 February 1854
Edwards, Grace	18	A negro woman of dark brown or black complexion rather below middle size.	Elbert Co, GA	Jennings Co, IN	Joshua Palmer Margaret Palmer	18 August 1854
Hood, Hannibal	41	A mulatto man rather above medium height, full medium & of dark yellow complexion.	Jefferson Co, IN	Jennings Co, IN	Achilles Vawter Robert D. McCammon	19 June 1855
Hood, Fanny	46	A negro woman very tall and of dark brown complexion (large).	VA	Jennings Co, IN	Harvey M. Cowell Elisha Boner	28 January 1856

REGISTER OF NEGROES AND MULATTOES IN KNOX COUNTY, INDIANA

Page No.	Names	Age	Description	Place of Birth	Residence	Names of Witnesses	Date Registered
1	Thomas, Edward	25	Negro man of dark coller round face ca. 5' 5 1/2 in high; barber.	Knox Co, IN	Knox Co, IN	James C. Denny	28 June 1853
1	Newton, Nathaniel	62	Black man of dark color, 5 ft 9 ins high, farmer.	Mecklenburgh Co, VA	Knox Co	Elihu Stout	30 June 1853
2	Springs, Judea	58	Negro woman fleshy heavy-built and dark complexion, 5 ft 5 ins.	KY near Lexington	Knox Co IN	Elihu Stout	1 July 1853
2	Hay, Jesse	29	Mulatto man, 5 ft 5 ins high, high yellow complexion.	Vincennes, Knox Co.	Knox Co.	James C. Denny	1 July 1853
3	Springs, Henry I.	68	Negro man about 5 ft 6-7 ins high, dark complexion, 150 lbs.	Shelby Co, KY	Knox Co, IN	Elihu Stout	1 July 1853
3	Carter, Richard	45	Mulatto, about 5 ft 5 ins, yellow complexion, about 130 lbs.	Knox Co, IN	Knox Co, IN	Thos. J. Beeler	1 July 1853
4	Ember, Tobitha	28	Black man, about 5 ft 9 ins high, dark color, broad flat nose.	Knox Co, IN	Knox Co, IN	John D. Gardner	7 July 1853
4	Rollins, William I.	36	Negro man, fleshy heavy built and dark complexion, 5 ft 10 ins.	Giles Co, TN	Vincennes, Knox Co, IN	N.B. Barron	8 July 1853
5	Whitfield, Harmon	45	Negro man about 5 ft 6 ins, 160 lbs of dark complexion.	Sussex Co, VA	Knox Co, IN	William E. Cooke	22 July 1853
5	Purier, Tousant	56	Mulatto man, about 5 ft 10 1/2 ins, rather light complexion;	Vincennes, Knox Co, IN	Knox Co, IN	N. B. Barron	3 Aug 1853
6	Purier, Sylvia	52	Negro woman; about 5 ft high; dark complexion; 100 lbs. slender.	SC	Knox Co, IN	N. B. Barron	3 Aug 1853
6	Purier, James	20	Negro man, about 5 ft 10 1/2 ins; weighs 170 lbs. rather dark.	Knox Co, IN	Knox Co, IN	N. B. Barron	3 Aug 1853

Knox County, Indiana

	Name	Age	Description	Origin	Residence	Witness	Date
7	Purier, Henry	16	Negro boy, about 5 ft 6 ins, rather dark, weighs about 120 lbs.	Knox Co, IN	Knox Co, IN	N. B. Barron	3 Aug 1853
7	Purier, Charles	13	Negro boy about 5 ft 10 ins, weighs 180 lbs, dark complexion.	Knox Co, IN	Knox Co, IN	N. B. Barron	3 Aug 1853
8	Farmer, Charles	42	Negro man, about 5 ft 3 3/4 ins, dark complexion, about 140 lbs.	SC	Knox Co, IN	Niceton P. Gee	3 Aug 1853
8	Farmer, Edith	32 about	Negro woman, 4 ft 4 ins high, spare built, light complexion.	Shawneetown, IL	Knox Co, IN	Milton P. Gee	3 Aug 1853
9	Farmer, Nancy Jane	10	Negro girl, about 4 ft high, spare built, rather lt complexion.	Shawneetown IL	Knox Co, IN	Milton P. Gee	3 Aug 1853
9	Farmer, Dianna	4	little Negro girl, about 3 ft high, rather dark complexion.	Shawneetown, IL	Knox Co, IN	Milton P. Gee	3 Aug 1853
10	Farmer, London	2	Small Negro boy, about 2 ft 6 ins high of dark complexion.	Shawneetown, IL	Knox Co, IN	Milton P. Gee	3 Aug 1853
10	Cox, Isiah	21	Negro man, 5 ft 1 in high slim built weighs 125 dark complexion.	Knox Co, IN	Knox Co, IN	James C. Denny	3 Aug 1853
11	Brunswick, James	60	Negro man, about 5 ft 6 3/4 ins, about 202 lbs, heavy built, dark.	TN	Knox Co, IN	N. B. Barron	3 Aug 1853
11	Brunswick, Mary	35	Negro woman, about 5 ft 5 ins high, weighs 220, dark complexion.	Vincennes, Knox Co, IN	Vincennes, Knox Co, IN	N. B. Barron	3 Aug 1853
12	Lewis, William	18	Negro boy, 5 ft 3 ins high, 120 lbs; slim built; dark complexion.	Marion Co, IN	Knox Co, IN	Napoleon B. Barron	5 Aug 1853
12	McGilpin, Yorich	43	Mulatto man, 5 ft 7 ins high, 150 lbs, light complexion.	VA	Knox Co, IN	N. B. Barron	5 Aug 1853
13	McGilpin, Lucinda	37	Negro woman, 5 ft 3 ins, 125 lbs, slim built, dark complexion.	VA	Knox Co, IN	N.B. Barron	5 Aug 1853

Knox County, Indiana

13	Day, Wilson	32	Negro man, 6 ft 1 1/2 ins, 190 lbs, well made, light complexion.	Pulaski, TN	Knox Co, IN	N. B. Barron	6 Aug 1853
14	Day, Margaret	27	Negro woman, 5 ft 1-2 ins, 125 lbs, slender, darker than husband.	Vincennes IN	Knox Co IN	B. F. Thom	6 Aug 1853
14	Day, Mary	12	Negro girl, 5 ft high, 110-115 lbs, slim, rather light complexion	Vincennes IN	Knox Co IN	B.F. Thom	6 Aug 1853
15	Day, Elizabeth	5	Negro girl, 3 ft 6 ins, slim built, rather light complexion.	Vincennes IN	Knox Co IN	B F Thom	6 Aug 1853
15	Day, Jesse	3	Negro boy, 3 ft high, rather light complexion.	Vincennes IN	Knox Co IN	B F Thom	6 Aug 1853
16	Purier Jr., Tousant	28	Mulatto man, 5 ft 7 3/4 ins, 173 lbs, stout, heavy built, light.	Vincennes IN	Knox Co IN	M P Gee	6 Aug 1853
16	Purier Jr, Francis	27	Mulatto man, 5 ft 9 3/4 ins, 175 lbs, light complexion.	Vincennes IN	Knox Co IN	M P Gee	6 Aug 1853
17	Purier, Francis	65	Mulatto, 5 ft 8 1/2 ins, 145 lbs, light compl, grey headed, slim.	Vincennes IN	Knox Co IN	Abrm Smith	6 Aug 1853
17	Knight, George	29	Negro man, 5 ft 11 ins, 170 lbs, dark complexion, stout, heavy.	Knox Co IN	Knox Co IN	William Clark	6 Aug 1853
18	Brunswick, Hester Anne	16	Negro woman, 4 ft, 100 lbs, heavy built, dark complexion.	Knox Co IN	Knox Co IN	John M Collins	6 Aug 1853
18	Brunswick, Ophelia	14	About 4 ft high, weighs 80 lbs, slender, light complexion.	Knox Co IN	Knox Co IN	John M Collins	6 Aug 1853
19	Brunswick, Rachael	12	Negro girl, 3 ft 6 ins high, 70 lbs, dark complexion.	Knox Co IN	Knox Co IN	John M Collins	6 Aug 1853
19	Brunswick, Thomas	10	Negro boy, 3 ft 4 ins high, slender 60 lbs, dark complexion.	Knox Co IN	Knox Co IN	John M Collins	6 Aug 1853

Knox County, Indiana

20	Brunswick, Hannah M	8	Negro girl, heavy built rather dark complexion.	Knox Co IN	Knox Co IN	John M Collins	6 Aug 1853
20	Brunswick, Nancy Ann	6	Negro girl, slender built, rather dark complexion.	Knox Co IN	Knox Co IN	John M Collins	6 Aug 1853
21	Brunswick, George Washington	4	Negro boy, bolerably heavy built rather dark complexion	Knox Co IN	Knox Co IN	John M Collins	6 Aug 1853
21	Brunswick, Theodore	2	Negro boy, tolerably heavy built rather dark complexion.	Knox Co IN	Knox Co IN	John M Collins	6 Aug 1853
22	Bellier, Prosper	29	Mulatto man, 5 ft 9 ins, 145 lbs, tall slender built, light comp.	New Orleans, LA	Knox Co IN	N.P.Barron	8 Aug 1853
22	Bellier, Elizabeth	27	Mulatto woman, 5 ft high, 140 lbs, light complexion.	Vincennes IN	Knox Co IN	N.P. Barron	8 Aug 1853
23	Bellier, Josephine	6	Mulatto girl, 4 ft high, slim built, very light complexion.	Vincennes IN	Knox Co IN	N.B. Barron	8 Aug 1853
23	Bellier, John Henry	2	Mulatto boy, light complexion. Trim slender built.	Vincennes IN	Knox Co IN	N B Barron	8 Aug 1853
24	Purier, David	24	Mulatto man 5 ft 8 1/4 ins, 155 lbs, quite light, heavy built.	Knox Co IN	Knox Co IN	James C Denny	8 Aug 1853
24	Purier, George	31	Mulatto man, 5 ft 11 1/2 ins, 170 lbs, light complexion, stout.	Knox Co IN	Knox Co IN	N B Barron	8 Aug 1853
25	Purier Jr., Francis	4	Mulatto boy 3 ft 2 ins, very light, hair light and not much curly	Knox Co IN	Knox Co IN	Francis Purier	8 Aug 1853
25	Clark, Samuel	67	Negro man 5 ft 9 ins heavy built somewhat grey 157 lbs.	KY	Knox Co IN	Elihu Stout	10 Aug 1853
26	Clark, Eliza	29	Negro woman 5 ft 3 ins; 230 lbs; dark complex, scar left arm.	Vincennes IN	Knox Co IN	B F Thom	10 Aug 1853

Knox County, Indiana

	Name	Age	Description	From	To	Filer	Date
26	Brewer, Samuel	13	Negro boy, 100 lbs, heavy fleshy. Stout built, light complexion.	Vincennes IN	Knox Co IN	B F Thom	10 Aug 1853
27	Brewer, George	12	Negro boy, 70 lbs, slender, dark complexion, lame toe rt foot.	Vincennes IN	Knox Co IN	B F Thom	10 Aug 1853
27	Brewer, Edward	11	Negro boy 70 lbs tolerably heavy built, light complexion.	Vincennes IN	Knox Co IN	B F Thom	10 Aug 1853
28	Brewer, Mary Ann	9	Negro girl about 70 lbs, heavy built, dark complexion, scar hip.	Vincennes IN	Knox Co IN	B F Thom	10 Aug 1853
28	Day, Margaret	9	Negro girl, 3 ft 6 ins, slender, dark complexion, scar left leg.	Vincennes IN	Knox Co IN	B F Thom	10 Aug 1853
29	Clark, Wm W.G.W.	27	Negro man 5 ft 6 ins, 150 lbs, stout, heavy, rather dark complex.	Vincennes IN	Knox Co IN	B F Thom	10 Aug 1853
29	Clark, Frances or Mary	23	Negro woman, heavy built, rather fleshy, supposed to weigh 150 lb	Vincennes IN	Knox Co IN	B F Thom	10 Aug 1853
30	Clark, Lovina Mariah	16	Negro woman, 5 ft high, slender, dark complexion, scar left leg.	Vincennes IN	Knox Co IN	B F Thom	10 Aug 1853
30	Clark, Queen Victoria	6	Negro girl, 3 ft high, slender built, dark complexion.	Vincennes IN	Knox Co IN	B F Thom	10 Aug 1853
31	Clark, Milia	54	Negro woman 5ft high weighs 100 lbs, rather light complexion.	SC	Knox Co IN	B F Thom	10 Aug 1853
31	Cottee, Gabriel	15	Mulatto boy, 4 ft 5 ins, light complexion, heavy built.	Knox Co IN	Knox Co IN	Abm Smith	15 Aug 1853
32	Cottee, Antone	20	Colored man 5 ft 5 ins dark brown color, long curled hair.	Knox Co IN	Knox Co IN	Abraham Smith	15 Aug 1853
32	Waller, J W	77	Negro man 5 ft 9 ins 170 lbs Stout Heavy	VA	Knox Co IN	Abraham Smith	16 Aug 1853

Knox County, Indiana

33	Waller, Keziah	60+	Tall, slender built woman, tolerably dark complexion.	VA	Knox Co IN	Elihu Stout	16 Aug 1853
33	Waller, Lydia	21	Stout heavy built rather low, rather dark complexion.	Knox Co IN	Knox Co IN	Elihu Stout	16 Aug 1853
34	Waller, James	19	Negro boy 5 ft 9 ins high, tolerably heavy built.	Knox Co IN	Knox Co IN	Elihu Stout	16 Aug 1853
34	Howard, Rosana	46	Negro woman low heavy built dark complexion.	VA	Knox Co IN	Elihu Stout	17 Aug 1853
35	Howard, Charles	25	Negro man 5 ft 10 ins, 170 lbs; well built, dark complexion.	Knox Co IN	Knox Co IN	Elihu Stout	17 Aug 1853
35	Howard, John	23	Negro man 5 ft 8 ins, 164 lbs, rather dark complexion.	Knox Co IN	Knox Co IN	Elihu Stout	17 Aug 1853
36	Howard, William	20	Negro man 5 ft 5 ins; stout, heavy built, dark complexion.	Knox Co IN	Vigo Co IN	Elihu Stout	17 Aug 1853
36	Howard, Thomas	19	Negro boy 5 ft 5 ins tall, slender built, dark complexion.	Knox Co IN	Knox Co IN	Elihu Stout	17 Aug 1853
37	Howard, Elizabeth M	18	Negro woman rather small height and weight unknow, light complex.	Knox Co IN	Knox Co IN	Elihu Stout	17 Aug 1853
38	Waller, John W	29	Negro man 6 ft 1 in high, 198 lbs, stout. Clear black color.	Knox Co IN	Knox Co IN	Elihu Stout	17 Aug 1853
38	Howard, Mary	13	Negro girl tall and slim built, light complexion.	Knox Co IN	Knox Co IN	Elihu Stout	17 Aug 1853
39	Sims, Cornelius	49	Negro man 5 ft 6 1/2 ins 140 lbs Speaks quick, square built.	VA	Knox Co IN	Thos J Beeler	20 Aug 1853
39	Sims, Elizabeth	33	Negro woman 5 ft 3 ins 120 lbs tolerably dark complexion.	Knox Co IN	Knox Co IN	Thomas J Beeler	20 Aug 1853

Knox County, Indiana

40	Sims, Priscilla Jane	22	Negro woman 5 ft high weighs 120 lbs, dark complexion.	Daviess Co IN	Knox Co IN	Thos J Beeler	20 Aug 1853
40	Sims, Charles	18	Negro boy 5 ft 6 ins, 145 lbs, stout heavy built, dark.	Daviess Co IN	Tippecanoe Co IN	Thos J Beeler	20 Aug 1853
41	Sims, Eleanor	16	Negro girl, low heavy built. Well made. Dark complexion.	Daviess Co IN	Knox Co IN	Thos J Beeler	20 Aug 1853
41	Sims, Sarah	12	Negro girl, slim, slender built, rather lighter complex than fa.	Vincennes IN	Knox Co IN	Thos J Beeler	20 Aug 1853
42	Sims, William	14	Negro boy rather slender built, quick lively turn, dark complex.	Daviess Co IN	Knox Co IN	Thos J Beeler	20 Aug 1853
42	Sims, George W	10	Slim built, quick lively turned, dark complexion.	Vincennes IN	Knox Co IN	Thos J Beeler	20 Aug 1853
43	Sims, Charlotte	6	Negro girl, low heavy built, dark complexion.	Vincennes IN	Knox Co IN	Thos J Beeler	20 Aug 1853
43	Sims, Thomas J	4	Tall, large child for age. One finger crooked, dark complexion.	Vincennes IN	Knox Co IN	Thos J Beeler	20 Aug 1853
44	Solters, Tobias	29	Mulatto man 5 ft 8 1/2 ins 160 lbs light complexion, square blt.	Knox Co IN	Knox Co IN	John W Fitch	20 Aug 1853
44	Solters, Indiana	27	Negro woman 5 ft 4-5 ins, slim built 120 lbs.	Vincennes IN	Knox Co IN	John W Fitch	20 Aug 1853
45	Solters, Eneas Augusta	11 mos	Mulatto boy rather light complexion.	Daviess Co IN	Knox Co IN		20 Aug 1853
45	Newton, Percilia	48	Negro woman dark brown color 5 ft 5 ins, spare built. 130 lbs.	SC	Knox Co IN	James C Denny	22 Aug 1853
46	Walker, Abraham	24	Negro man 5 ft 9 ins, 160 lbs. Dark complexion.	Knox Co IN	Knox Co IN	Samuel Gouchnor	22 Aug 1853

Knox County, Indiana

46	Walker, Christiana	20	Mulatto woman, 5 ft 2 1/2 ins, 120 lbs, light complexion.	NC	Knox Co IN	Samuel Gouchnor	22 Aug 1853
47	Walker, Lyman T	5 mos	Of yellow complexion, stout hearty child of his age.	Vincennes IN	Knox Co IN	Samuel Gouchnor	22 Aug 1853
47	Thomas, Abraham	27	Negro man 5 ft 7 ins, 145 lbs, rather light complexion.	Vincennes IN	Knox Co IN	Samuel Gouchnor	22 Aug 1853
48	Thomas, Eliza	27	Mulatto woman, heavy built, rather light complexion.	Vincennes IN	Knox Co IN	Samuel Gouchnor	22 Aug 1853
48	Knight, Relivis	14	Negro boy rather light complexion, tall & slender built.	Vincennes IN	Knox Co IN	Samuel Gouchenour	22 Aug 1853
49	Knight, Aaron	12	Negro boy heavy built light complexion.	Vincennes IN	Knox Co IN	Samuel Gouchenour	22 Aug 1853
49	Knight, Alevia	9	Negro girl, stout heavy built, light complexion.	Vincennes IN	Knox Co IN	Samuel Gouchenour	22 Aug 1853
37	Howard, Nancy Jane	14	Negro girl, tall slim built rather light complexion.	Knox Co IN	Knox Co IN	Elihu Stout	17 Aug 1853
50	Thomas, William	5	Negro boy, stout square built, dark complexion.	Vincennes IN	Knox Co IN	Samuel Gouchenour	22 Aug 1853
50	Thomas, Sarah Louise	3	Negro girl, stout hearty square built child.	Vincennes IN	Knox Co IN	Samuel Gouchenour	22 Aug 1853
51	Thomas, Laura	4 mos	Negro girl, a stout hearty child light complexion.	Vincennes IN	Knox Co IN	Samuel Gouchenour	22 Aug 1853
51	Embers, Sarah H	28	Mulatto woman, tall and well made, quite light complexion.	OH	Knox Co IN	M P Gee	22 Aug 1853
52	Embers, William P Q	11	About 4 ft 10 ins high, small scar left ear, dark complexion.	Vincennes IN	Knox Co IN	M P Gee	24 Aug 1853

Knox County, Indiana

52	Embers, Charles H	9	Mulatto boy, stout, heavy built, tolerably light complexion.	Vincennes IN	Vincennes IN	M P Gee	24 Aug 1853
53	Embers, Thomas C	6	Mulatto boy, light built; scar back left ear, light complexion.	Vincennes IN	Knox Co IN	M P Gee	24 Aug 1853
54	McGill, Leaver C	20	Mulatto woman 5 ft high, strait and well made, dark complexion.	Washington, Daviess Co IN	Knox Co IN	M P Gee	24 Aug 1853
54	Perkins, Sarah E	18	Mulatto woman, 5 ft high very light complexion, yellow hair.	Vincennes IN	Knox Co IN	M P Gee	24 Aug 1853
55	Perkins, Thomas E	10 mos	Mulatto boy, light complexion, strait hair black color.	Vincennes IN	Knox Co IN	M P Gee	24 Aug 1853
55	White, Carolina	18	Colored woman 5 ft 3 ins high stout heavy dark complexion.	Vincennes IN	Knox Co IN		24 Aug 1853
56	White, Joanna E.	6 mos	Colored child light complexted, black curley hair.	Vincennes IN	Knox Co IN		24 Aug 1853
56	Carter, Melinda	16	Mulatto woman 5 ft high, scars on neck and right hand, dark comp.	Vincennes IN	Knox Co IN	M P Gee	24 Aug 1853
53	Embers, Mariam A	1 1/2	Mulatto, slim built child, light complexion and yellow hair.	Vincennes IN	Knox Co IN	M P Gee	24 Aug 1853
57	Carter, Elizabeth L.	5	Negro girl, stout hearty child crossed eye with left eye.	Vincennes IN	Knox Co IN	M P Gee	24 Aug 1853
57	Knight, Miriam	78	Colored woman, heavy stout built fleshy old woman.	MD	Knox Co IN	M P Gee	24 Aug 1853
58	Knowland, Samuel	78	Negro man, large heavy built, dark complexion, grey headed.	VA	Knox Co IN	Elihu Stout	24 Aug 1853
58	McGill, Arthur	58	Mulatto man 5 ft 8 ins 170 lbs light complexion.	MD	Knox Co IN	John M Clark	24 Aug 1853

Knox County, Indiana

#	Name	Age	Description	Origin	Residence	Witness	Date
59	McGill, Rachel	47	Mulatto woman, stout heavy built, light complexion.	MD	Knox Co IN	John M Clark	24 Aug 1853
59	McGill, Isiah	22	Mulatto man, 5 ft 7 ins high, 160 lbs, light complexion.	Daviess Co IN	Knox Co IN	John M Clark	24 Aug 1853
60	McGill, George A	17	Mulatto boy, 5 ft 3 ins high 120 lbs, light complexion.	Vincennes IN	Knox Co IN	John M Clark	24 Aug 1853
60	McGill, Arabella	11	Mulatto girl, tolerably heavy built light complexion.	Vincennes IN	Knox Co IN	John M Clark	24 Aug 1853
61	McGill, Jernene	7	Mulatto girl, slender built, light complexion.	Vincennes IN	Knox Co IN	John M Clark	24 Aug 1853
61	Perkins, Louisa	15	Mulatto girl, heavy built, light complexion, sandy strait hair.	Daviess Co IN	Knox Co IN	John M Clark	24 Aug 1853
62	McGill, Mary C	4	Mulatto girl, rather heavy well built child light complexion.	Vincennes Knox Co IN	Knox Co IN	John M Clark	24 Aug 1853
62	Stewart, Mathew	16	Negro boy 4 ft 3 ins, slim built, scar near lt eye, dark complex.	Vigo Co IN	Knox Co IN	N B Barron	24 Aug 1853
63	Stewart, Henry H	47	Mulatto man 5 ft 6 ins, 165 lbs, scar rt arm and on left leg.	IN	Knox Co IN	N B Barron	24 Aug 1853
63	Stewart, Rhoda Ann	24	Colored woman 4 ft 6 ins slender, 116 lbs, dark complexion.	Knox Co IN	Knox Co IN	N B Barron	24 Aug 1853
64	Stewart, William H	19	Mulatto boy 4 ft 3 ins, slender built, light complexion.	Vigo Co IN	Knox Co IN	N B Barron	24 Aug 1853
64	Stewart, Yorich G	6 mos	Mulatto child, fleshy, light complexion.	Vincennes Knox Co IN	Knox Co IN		24 Aug 1853
65	Stewart, Keziah	75	Mulatto woman, 5 ft high, slender built, light complexion.	VA	Knox Co IN	N B Barron	24 Aug 1853

Knox County, Indiana

65	Carter, Jane	35	Negro woman 5 ft 6 ins, dark complexion, tolerably heavy built.	Vincennes Knox Co IN	Knox Co IN	N B Barron	24 Aug 1853
66	Carter, Joseph	2	Mulatto boy, heavy stout built child, light complexion.	Vincennes Knox Co IN	Knox Co IN	H H Stewart	24 Aug 1853
66	Gould, Anthony	50	Negro man 5 ft 8 3/4 ins, 170 lbs, dark complexion/	Knox Co IN	Knox Co IN	N B Barron	24 Aug 1853
67	Carter, Augustus	28	Negro man 5 ft 3 1/2 ins, 120 lbs; scars eye and ft hand; dark.	Nelson Co KY	Knox Co IN	John Emison	25 Aug 1853
67	Brooks, Lewis	90	Negro man 6 ft high, very black, has been struck with palsy.	VA	Knox Co IN	N B Barron	25 Aug 1853
68	Brooks, Milley	70	Negro woman, heavy built and fleshy, about 5 ft 3 ins high.	VA	Vincennes Knox Co IN	N B Barron	25 Aug 1853
68	Turner, George Washington	33	Mulatto and part Indian, 5 ft 7 ins, 150 lbs, light complexion.	Vincennes Knox Co IN	Knox Co IN	N B Barron	25 Aug 1853
69	Turner, Synthia P. Ann	22	Mulatto woman, 4 ft 6 ins, 170 lbs, chunkey, light complexion.	Daviess Co IN	Knox Co IN	N B Barron	25 Aug 1853
69	Turner, Theodore	11	Mulatto boy, 3 1/2 ft high, spare slight built, light complexion.	Vincennes Knox Co IN	Knox Co IN	N B Barron	25 Aug 1853
70	Turner, Washington Louis	8	Mulatto boy, 3 ft high, light complexion, 80 lbs.	Vincennes Knox Co IN	Knox Co IN	N B Barron	25 Aug 1853
70	Turner, Sarah Louisa	6	Mulatto child, 3 ft high, light complexion, slender.	Vincennes Knox Co IN	Knox Co IN	N B Barron	25 Aug 1853
71	Turner, Hester	8 mos	Mulatto babe, 2 ft high, light complected and fine child.	Vincennes Knox Co IN	Knox Co IN	N B Barron	25 Aug 1853
71	Turner, Rachel	5	Mulatto girl 3 ft high light complexion slender and well made.	Vincennes Knox Co IN	Knox Co IN	N B Barron	25 Aug 1853

Knox County, Indiana

72	Burgess, Thomas	50	Mulatto man, 5 ft 10 ins, 140 lbs, quite light complexion.	VA	Knox Co IN	Martin Robinson	25 Aug 1853
72	Burgess, Thomas E. W.	18	Mulatto boy, 5 ft 6-8 ins, pleasing dress, good manners, light.	Vincennes Knox Co IN	Knox Co IN	Martin Robinson	25 Aug 1853
73	Burgess, Eliza	53	Mulatto woman, 5 ft 1-2 ins, about 120 lbs, heavy, light complex.	SC	Knox Co IN	Martin Robinson	25 Aug 1853
73	Morris, George P	23	Negro man, 5 ft 8-9 ins, slender, 120 lbs, dark complexion.	Henderson Co KY	Knox Co IN	Martin Robinson	25 Aug 1853
74	White, Frances Ann	21	Dark mulatto woman, 5 ft 6 ins, 134 lbs, dark complexion.	Vincennes Knox Co IN	Knox Co IN	B F Thom	25 Aug 1853
74	McGreger, Joanna	17	Black mulatto woman, 5 ft 4 ins, 132 lbs, dark complexion.	Vincennes Knox Co IN	Knox Co IN	B F Thom	25 Aug 1853
75	White, Cornelia	7 mos	Dark mulatto babe, large fat hearty child.	Vincennes Knox Co IN	Knox Co IN		25 Aug 1853
75	Dubois, Albert	14	Mulatto boy 4 ft 8 ins, weighs 75 lbs, very light complexion.	Vincennes Knox Co IN	Knox Co IN	Lambert Burrvis Sen	25 Aug 1853
76	Dubois, Alice A	13	Heavy built, light complexion, freckles, yellow hair, 5 ft high.	Vincennes Knox Co IN	Knox Co IN	Lambert Burrvis	25 Aug 1853
76	Dubois, James	36	Mulatto man 5 ft 6 ins, 150 lbs; well built and intelligent.	Vincennes Knox Co IN	Knox Co IN	N B Barron	25 Aug 1853
77	Woods, William	23	Mulatto man 5 ft 9 3/4 ins, 150 lbs, light complexion.	IN	Knox Co IN	John Robinson	26 Aug 1853
77	Woods, Jemima	20	Mulatto woman 5 ft 4-5 ins, heavy built, light complexion.	Vincennes Knox Co IN	Knox Co IN	John Robinson	26 Aug 1853
78	Woods, Adaline	10 mos	Mulatto child, light built and complexion. Entitled to reside.	Vincennes Knox Co IN	Knox Co IN		26 Aug 1853

Knox County, Indiana

#	Name	Age	Description			Recorder	Date
78	Gill, Catherine	52	dark mulatto woman, 5 ft 3 ins, natural mark on lt arm 1 in long.	Frederick Co MD	Knox Co IN	Thomas J Beeler	27 Aug 1853
79	Toliver, George	10	Mulatto boy 4 ft 4 3/4 ins, trim built, dark complexion.	Vincennes Knox Co IN	Knox Co IN	Thos J Beeler	27 Aug 1853
79	White, Zachariah	24	Negro or colored man 5 ft 4 1/4 ins, 145 lbs, heavy, round face.	Daviess Co IN	Knox Co IN	N P Barron	27 Aug 1853
80	Hubbs, Mary Jan	19	Colored or negro woman, tall, slim, thick lips, dark complexion.	Knox Co IN	Knox Co IN	John Emison	27 Aug 1853
80	Landers, Cordelia	2	Mulatto child (dau of MJ Hobbs), slim, yellow or light complexion	Knox Co IN	Knox Co IN	John Emison	27 Aug 1853
81	Sanders, William	41	Negro man 5 ft 9 ins left arm lame, scars & cuts right hand.	Knox Co IN	Knox Co IN	M P Gee	27 Aug 1853
81	Sanders, Nancy	32	Negro woman 5 ft high, spare made, scar left leg, small pox scars	VA	Knox Co IN	M P Gee	27 Aug 1853
82	Sanders, Robert	13	Negro boy, heavy built and large of his age, dark complexion.	Knox Co IN	Knox Co IN	M P Gee	27 Aug 1853
82	Sanders, John	5	Negro boy 4 ft 5 ins, stout, heavy built, round face.	Knox Co IN	Knox Co IN	M P Gee	27 Aug 1853
83	Sanders, Sarah	8	Negro girl, slender built and bad health, small of her age, light	Knox Co IN	Knox Co IN	M P Gee	27 Aug 1853
83	Sanders, Martha	6	Negro girl, heavy built child rather light complexion.	Knox Co IN	Knox Co IN	M P Gee	27 Aug 1853
84	Sanders, Dora	5	Negro girl, light complexion, size common to children of her age.	Knox Co IN	Knox Co IN	M P Gee	27 Aug 1853
84	Sanders, Laura	3	Negro girl, rather light complexion.	Knox Co IN	Knox Co IN	M P Gee	27 Aug 1853

Knox County, Indiana

85	Sanders, Andrew	4	Negro boy, dark complexion, about make & size children of his age	Knox Co IN	Knox Co IN	M P Gee	27 Aug 1853
85	Sanders, William [Jr]	4 mos	Negro boy child, hearty, rather light complexion.	Knox Co IN	Knox Co IN	M P Gee	27 Aug 1853
86	Jackson, John	36	Mulatto man 6 ft 2 ins 165 lbs, well made.	Vincennes Knox Co IN.	Knox Co IN	N P Barron	27 Aug 1853
86	Jackson, Han[n]ah	13	Mulatto child, tall, slim, light complexion.	Vincennes Knox Co IN	Sullivan IN	N P Barron	27 Aug 1853
87	Jackson, George W	11	Mulatto boy heavy built light complexion, burn scar on back.	Vincennes Knox Co IN	Sullivan IN	N P Barron	27 Aug 1853
87	Jackson, Louisa	9	Mulatto girl, tolerably heavy built, light complexion.	Vincennes Knox Co IN	Sullivan IN	N P Barron	27 Aug 1853
88	Jackson, Elizabeth	7	Mulatto, rather slim built light complexion.	Vincennes Knox Co IN	Sullivan IN	N P Barron	27 Aug 1853
88	Jackson, Eliza	5	Mulatto girl of light complexion and stout built.	Vincennes Knox Co IN	Sullivan IN	N P Barron	27 Aug 1853
89	Jackson, Margaret	3	Mulatto girl, slender built, light complexion.	Vincennes Knox Co IN	Sullivan IN	N P Barron	27 Aug 1853
89	White, William	23	Negro man 5 ft 7 3/4 ins, 140 lbs; slim built.	MD	Knox Co IN	Elihu Stout	29 Aug 1853
90	McGregory, John Nelson	26	Mulatto man, 5 ft 6 ins, 140 lbs, yellow complexion	TN	Knox Co IN	Frank Branch	29 Aug 1853
90	Burch, Louisa	27	Dark mulatto 5 ft 6 1/2 ins, 148 lbs, dark complexion; large.	Daviess Co IN	Knox Co IN	N P Barron	29 Aug 1853
91	Burch, Abraham Hamilton	5	Mulatto boy, fine hearty, well made; son of Abraham-Louisa Burch.	Vincennes Knox Co IN	Knox Co IN	N P Barron	29 Aug 1853

#	Name	Age	Description	From	To	Registrant	Date
91	Burch, Mary	17	Mulatto, 5 ft high, 130 lbs, light complexion, hazel eyes.	Vincennes Knox Co IN	Knox Co IN	John Ewing	29 Aug 1853
92	Burch, George	11	Mulatto boy 4 ft high 90 lbs, dark complexion, slender built.	Vincennes Knox Co IN	Knox Co IN	John Ewing	29 Aug 1853
92	Burch, Henry	10	Mulatto boy, 3 1/2 ft high, heavy built; son of Abraham-Roda B.	Vincennes Knox Co IN	Knox Co IN	John Ewing	29 Aug 1853
93	Springs, James E.	19	Negro man 5 ft 8 ins, 138 lbs, slim built, cross eyed, scars.	Knox Co IN	Knox Co IN	James Thompson	29 Aug 1853
93	Parker, Delila	35	Negro woman 5 ft 4 ins, heavy built, 150 lbs, scar over left eye.	TN	Knox Co IN	John M Cook	29 Aug 1853
94	Lamount, Fanny Ann	21	Negro woman, tall slender, tolerably light, 110 lbs, 5 ft 5 ins.	Knox Co IN	Knox Co IN	John M Cook	29 Aug 1853
94	Taylor, Harriett	22	Negro woman 5 ft 3 1/2 ins, 166 lbs, large fleshy woman.	Vincennes Knox Co IN	Knox Co IN	Thomas J Beeler	29 Aug 1853
95	Davis, Rebecky Ann	24	Negro woman 5 ft 7 ins 165 lbs; light complexion, slender built.	White Co IN	Knox Co IN		30 Aug 1853
95	Hay, William Henry	4	Negro boy, slender made & built, son of Jessey & Frances Hay.	Knox Co IN	Knox Co IN		30 Aug 1853
96	Hay, Frances	22	5 ft 4 ins, weighs 135 lbs, well made & heavy built.	Knox Co IN	Knox Co IN	Robert Hodgens	30 Aug 1853
96	Hay, Albert	2	Negro boy, dark brown color, brown curley hair; 2 ft 7 ins high.	Knox Co IN	Knox Co IN	Robert Hodgen	30 Aug 1853
97	Hay, Peter L.	6 mos	Negro boy, son of Jesse & Frances Hay; entitled to reside in IN.	Knox Co IN	Knox Co IN	Robert Hodgin	30 Aug 1853
97	Springs, Eliza	12	Negro girl, dark color, 4 ft 4 ins, light built, 100 lbs.	Knox Co IN	Knox Co IN	Robert Hodgin	30 Aug 1853

Knox County, Indiana

	Name	Age	Description			Witness	Date
98	Purry, Elizabeth	9	Negro girl of dark color, thick lips, 4 ft 4 ins, scar on knee.	Knox Co IN	Knox Co IN	Robert Hodgen	30 Aug 1853
98	Purry, George	4	Negro boy of dark complexion, thick lips, 3 ft 3 ins, 50 lbs.	Knox Co IN	Knox Co IN	Robert Hodgens	30 Aug 1853
99	Purry, Charles	9	Negro boy 4 ft 3 ins, quite dark, blind in rt eye, thick lips	Knox Co IN	Knox Co IN	Robert Hodgen	30 Aug 1853
99	Springs, Isabell	17	Negro woman of dark color, 5 ft 3 ins, heavy built, 130 lbs.	Knox Co IN	Knox Co IN	Robert Hodgens	30 Aug 1853
100	Springs, Margaret	23	Negro woman 5 ft 5 ins, heavy built, 150 lbs, scar near rt eye.	Knox Co IN	Knox Co IN	Robert Hodgen	30 Aug 1853
100	Springs, William	41	Negro man 5 ft 8 ins, blind in both eyes.	Knox Co IN	Knox Co IN	Abraham Smith	30 Aug 1853
101	Richey, Aaron	69	Negro man 5 ft 5 ins, 160 lbs, dark complected & robust old man.	VA	Knox Co IN	Elihu Stout	31 Aug 1853
101	Richey, Archey	25	Negro man 5 ft 10 ins, 170 lbs, dark. Son Aaron-Sarah Richey.	Knox Co IN	Knox Co IN	A B McKee	31 Aug 1853
102	Richey, Indiana	25	Negro woman 6 ft high 120 lbs, dark complexion, slender built.	Knox Co IN	Knox Co IN	A B McKee	31 Aug 1853
102	Richey, Sarah	34	Negro woman 5 ft 6 ins 160 lbs, heavy; dau of Aaron-Sarah Richey.	Knox Co IN	Knox Co IN	A B McKee	31 Aug 1853
103	Smith, Emily	33	Negro woman, low & heavy built, dark complexion; scar on forehead	Knox Co IN	Knox Co IN	M P Gee	31 Aug 1853
103	Smith, Mary Elizabeth	10	Negro girl, low & heavy built; daug of Wm & Emily Smith; dark.	Knox Co IN	Knox Co IN	M P Gee	31 Aug 1853
104	Smith, Sarah Frances	--	Slim, slender rather light complexion. Dau Wm-Emily Smith.	Knox Co IN	Knox Co IN	M P Gee	31 Aug 1853

Knox County, Indiana

104	Rusk, Fanny	51	Negro woman, stout, heavy; dark complexion	VA	Knox Co IN	Mrs. Eliza L.M. Shaw	31 Aug 1853
105	Oaks, Henrietta	25	Low heavy built woman, rather dark complexion.	Knox Co IN	Knox Co IN	Mrs. Eliza L.M. Shaw	31 Aug 1853
106	Rusk, Andrew	20	Negro man 5 ft high, 136 lbs, dark complexion.	Knox Co IN	Knox Co IN	Mrs. Eliza L.M. Shaw	31 Aug 1853
106	Rusk, Abraham	18	Negro man, slim & slender built rather dark complexion.	Knox Co IN	Knox Co IN	Mrs. Eliza L.M. Shaw	31 Aug 1853
107	Rush, Sarah Ann	16	Negro girl, slim and slender built dark complexion.	Knox Co IN	Knox Co IN	Mrs. Eliza L.M. Shaw	31 Aug 1853
107	Rusk, Eliza Ann	10	Negro girl tolerably slim built dark complexion.	Knox Co IN	Knox Co IN	Mrs. Eliza L.M. Shaw	31 Aug 1853
108	Rusk, James Benjamin	4	A stout heavy built child of his age dark complexion.	Knox Co IN	Knox Co IN	Mrs. Eliza L.M. Shaw	31 Aug 1853
108	Graves, Samuel	19	Negro man 5 ft 6 ins, 149 lbs, stout, dark complexion.	Knox Co IN	Knox Co IN	Thos J Beeler	31 Aug 1853
109	Cottee, Jefferson	18	Mulatto boy 5 ft 8 3/4 ins, 150 lbs, yellow complexion.	Vincennes Knox Co IN	Knox Co IN	Andrew Gardner	31 Aug 1853
109	Cottee, John	16	Mulatto boy, light built and light complexion.	Vincennes Knox Co IN	Knox Co IN	Andrew Gardner	31 Aug 1853
110	Posey, Thomas	33	Negro man 5 ft 10 1/2 ins, well built, 178 lbs. Light complexion.	Vincennes Knox Co IN	Knox Co IN	W A Jones	1 Sept 1853
110	Posey, Hester	28	Mulatto woman, 5 ft high, 175 lbs, light complexion, fine looking	MS	Knox Co IN	W A Jones	1 Sept 1853
111	Posey or Watson, Jane	13	Mulatto girl 4 ft 70 lbs; dau of Hester Posey	MS	Knox Co IN	W A Jones	1 Sept 1853

Knox County, Indiana

111	Posey, Isedore	2	Mulatto girl, light complexion; dau Thomas & Hester Posey.	Vincennes Knox Co IN	Knox Co IN	W A Jones	1 Sept 1853
112	Posey, Mary	8	Mulatto girl, 3 ft 6 ins, 50 lbs. Dau of Thomas & Hester Posey	Vincennes Knox Co IN	Knox Co IN	W A Jones	1 Sept 1853
112	Posey, Thomas [Jr]	4	Mulatto boy, brown color, heavy built; son of Thomas-Hester Posey.	Vincennes Knox Co IN	Knox Co IN	W A Jones	1 Sept 1853
113	Posey, William	10	Mulatto boy 3 ft 8 ins, 63 lbs, light complexion. Son T&H Posey.	Vincennes Knox Co IN	Knox Co IN	W A Jones	1 Sept 1853
113	Lewis, Lucey	50	Negro woman, large fleshy, 175 lbs, 5 ft high, light complexion	KY	Knox Co IN	Elihu Stout	1 Sept 1853
114	Lewis, Margaret E.	21	Negro woman, dark color, 5 ft 4 ins; two scars on rt hand.	Knox Co IN	Knox Co IN	Elihu Stout	1 Sept 1853
114	Lewis, Edward	19	Negro man, dark color, 5 ft 10 ins, scar over right eye.	Knox Co IN	Knox Co IN	Elihu Stout	1 Sept 1853
115	Lewis, Mary Jane	19	Negro woman, dark color, 5 ft high, 4 fingers rt hand disfigured.	Knox Co IN	Knox Co IN	Elihu Stout	1 Sept 1853
115	Lewis, Ledia [Lydia]	16	Negro girl, dark color 5 ft 2 ins, scar right arm.	Knox Co IN	Knox Co IN	Elihu Stout	1 Sept 1853
116	Lewis, Daphana	14	Negro girl, dark color, 4 ft 10 ins high, scar back of neck.	Knox Co IN	Knox Co IN	Elihu Stout	1 Sept 1853
116	Lewis, Charlotte	12	Negro girl, dark brown color, 3 ft 8 ins, 50 lbs; had bad health.	Knox Co IN	Knox Co IN	Elihu Stout	1 Sept 1853
117	Lewis, Lucy	10	Negro girl, dark born color, 4 ft high, heavy, 80 lbs.	Knox Co IN	Knox Co IN	Elihu Stout	1 Sept 1853
117	Lewis, Maria	8	Negro girl, dark brown color, 3 ft 8 ins. Dau Benjamin-Lucy L.	Knox Co IN	Knox Co IN	Elihu Stout	1 Sept 1853

Knox County, Indiana

118	Lewis, Hannah	6	Negro girl, dark brown, 3 ft 8 ins, pigeon toed. Dau: Ben-Lucy L	Knox Co IN	Elihu Stout	1 Sept 1853
118	Davis, Joshua	19	Negro man, dark color, thick lips, scar upper lips; 170 lbs.	Knox Co IN	R G McClure	2 Sept 1853
119	Davis, John	31	Negro man 5 ft 10 ins, 160 lbs, heavy, dark color, thick lips.	Shawneetown IL	R G McClure	2 Sept 1853
119	Davis, Thomas	7	Negro boy, son of Becky Ann Davis; of dark brown color.	Lawrence Co IL	Robert G. McClure	2 Sept 1853
120	Davis, Louisa I.	--	Dau of Mary Ann Brady, of dark color, light built.	Lawrence Co IL	Robert G McClure	2 Sept 1853
120	Brady, Henry	61	Negro man 5 ft 9 ins, 138 lbs, of dark brown color.	Washington Co VA	M P Gee	2 Sept 1853
121	Brady, Jane	62	Light brown color, 5 ft high, weighs 120 lbs, Henry Brady's wife.	KY	M P Gee	2 Sept 1853
121	Richey, William	46	Negro man 5 ft 6 ins 160 lbs, stout heavy built, dark complexion.	Knox Co IN	Elihu Stout	3 Sept 1853
122	Richey, George	15	Negro boy, stout heavy built, dark complexion.	Knox Co IN	Elihu Stout	3 Sept 1853
122	Richey, Sarah C	7	Negro woman, slim built dark complexion.	Knox Co IN	Elihu Stout	3 Sept 1853
123	Richey, Daniel	9	Negro boy, rather heavy built stout & hearty, light complexion.	Knox Co IN	Elihu Stout	3 Sept 1853
123	Richey, Rollins	5	Negro boy, slender built, dark complexion.	Knox Co IN	Elihu Stout	3 Sept 1853
124	Richie, Lemiza	2	Negro girl, stout, heavy built, dark complexion.	Knox Co IN		3 Sept 1853

Knox County, Indiana

124	Silence, Mariam	53	Negro woman, stout built, dark complexion.	Fayette Co KY	Knox Co IN	Mrs Beeler	3 Sept 1853
125	Granville, William	18	Mulatto boy, tall, slender built, light complexion.	VA	Knox Co IN	Elihu Stout	3 Sept 1853
125	Richie, Frances	43	Negro woman, 5 ft 2 ins, 140 lbs, common size, Wm Richie's wife.	VA	Knox Co IN	Elihu Stout	3 Sept 1853
126	Hubbs, Eliza Ann	14	Negro girl tall & slim built, dark complexion.	Knox Co IN	Knox Co IN	Mrs. Beeler	3 Sept 1853
126	Hubbs, Benjamin	12	Negro boy, tolerably heavy built, dark complexion.	Knox Co IN	Knox Co IN	Mrs. Beeler	3 Sept 1853
127	Hubbs, Elizabeth	9	Negro girl, slim built, dark complexion.	Knox Co IN	Knox Co IN	Mrs. Beeler	3 Sept 1853
127	Hubbs, Judy	7	Negro girl, thick, heavy built, dark complexion.	Knox Co IN	Knox Co IN	Mrs. Beeler	3 Sept 1853
127	Hubbs, Robert	21	Negro man about 5 ft 7 ins, 155 lbs, dark complexion.	Knox Co IN	Knox Co IN	Mrs. Beeler	3 Sept 1853
128	Hubbs, Aaron	17	Negro boy, very heavy built, dark complexion.	Knox Co IN	Knox Co IN	Mrs. Beeler	3 Sept 1853
129	Gordon, Andrew	23	Negro man 5 ft 10 ins, 165-170 lbs, dark complexion	Knox Co IN	Knox Co IN	Archibald Simpson	3 Sept 1853
129	Gordon, Sarah	20	Negro woman, low heavy set, dark complexion.	Knox Co IN	Knox Co IN	Elihu Stout	3 Sept 1853
130	Gordon, Joseph	60	Negro man, 5 ft 6 1/2 ins, 160 lbs, right thigh broken near hip.	PA	Knox Co IN	Elihu Stout	3 Sept 1853
130	Gordon, Catherine	14	Negro girl, tall, slim built, dark complexion.	Knox Co IN	Knox Co IN	Elihu Stout	3 Sept 1853

Knox County, Indiana

131	Gordon, Martin	12	Negro boy, stout heavy built, rather light complexion.	Knox Co IN	Knox Co IN	Elihu Stout	3 Sept 1853
131	Gordon, Harrison	3	Negro boy, stout heavy built, hearty child.	Knox Co IN	Knox Co IN	Elihu Stout	3 Sept 1853
132	Gordon, Elizabeth	9	Negro girl, tolerably slim built, dark complexion	Knox Co IN	Knox Co IN	Elihu Stout	3 Sept 1853
132	Gordon, Hannah	7	Negro girl, low heavy set child, dark complexion.	Knox Co IN	Knox Co IN	Elihu Stout	3 Sept 1853
133	Gordon, Hannah	--	Negro woman, low heavy woman, dark complexion.	Knox Co IN	Knox Co IN	Elihu Stout	3 Sept 1853
133	Gordon, Albert	--	Negro boy, heavy stout built, left thumb off, very short nose.	Knox Co IN	Knox Co IN	Elihu Stout	3 Sept 1853
134	Gordon, William	16	Negro boy, tall, rather slim built, dark complexion.	Knox Co IN	Knox Co IN	Elihu Stout	3 Sept 1853
134	Butler, John	21	Negro man 5 ft 6 3/4 ins, 138 lbs, mole in left hand, dark compl.	Knox Co IN	Knox Co IN	N P Barron	3 Sept 1853
135	Richey, Abraham	37	Negro man 5 ft 7 3/4 ins, 160 lbs, . . . scar left leg, dark color.	VA	Knox Co IN	William E Cook	3 Sept 1853
135	Richea, Hannah	40	Negro woman 5 ft high, heavy built, light complexion.	Knox Co IN	Knox Co IN	William E Cook	3 Sept 1853
136	Richea, Daniel	16	Negro boy, tall slim built, red spot left thumb, dark complexion.	Knox Co IN	Knox Co IN	William E Cook	3 Sept 1853
136	Richea, Aaron	16	Negro boy, heavy built rather light complexion.	Knox Co IN	Knox Co IN	William E Cook	3 Sept 1853
137	Richea, William H	14	Negro boy tall, slender built, dark complexion.	Knox Co IN	Knox Co IN	Wm E Cook	3 Sept 1853

Knox County, Indiana

137	Richea, George W	11	Negro boy heavy built, dark yellow complexion.	Knox Co IN	Knox Co IN	Wm E Cook	3 Sept 1853
138	Richea, Charles E	9	Negro boy, rather tall, slender built, dark complexion.	Knox Co IN	Knox Co IN	Wm E Cook	3 Sept 1853
138	Richea, Sarah Elizabeth	8	Negro girl, tall & slender built, yellow complexion.	Knox Co IN	Knox Co IN	Wm E Cook	3 Sept 1853
139	Richey, Abraham	6	Negro boy, heavy built, yellow complexion.	Knox Co IN	Knox Co IN	W E Cook	3 Sept 1853
139	Richae, Eliza F. Isidore	2	Negro girl, tall & slim built, yellow complexion.	Knox Co IN	Knox Co IN	Wm E Cook	3 Sept 1853
140	Richea, John	--	Negro boy, fat fleshy child, yellow complexion [Infant]	Knox Co IN	Knox Co IN		3 Sept 1853
140	Newton, Jessey	52	Negro man 6 ft high 160 lbs scar top of head, dark complexion.	TN	Knox Co IN	Wm E Cook	3 Sept 1853
141	Newton, Percillia	43	Negro woman, tall, rather slim, dark complexion, scar near lip.	VA	Knox Co IN	Elihu Stout	3 Sept 1853
141	Newton, Mary Elizabeth	20	Negro woman tall & slender built, brown color.	Knox Co IN	Knox Co IN	Wm E Cook	3 Sept 1853
142	Newton, William H	18	Negro boy, tall slender built, dark complexion, scar on rt cheek.	Knox Co IN	Knox Co IN	Wm E Cook	3 Sept 1853
142	Newton, Sarah Elizabeth	16	Negro girl tolerably heavy built, dark complexion.	Knox Co IN	Knox Co IN	Wm E Cook	3 Sept 1853
143	Newton, Charles	12	Negro boy tall and spare made, dark complexion.	Knox Co IN	Knox Co IN	Wm E Cook	3 Sept 1853
143	Newton, Frances	8	Negro girl, heavy built & stout, dark complexion.	Knox Co IN	Knox Co IN	W E Cook	3 Sept 1853

Knox County, Indiana

144	Newton, Rose Ann	6	Negro girl, heavy built, light complexion.	Knox Co IN	Knox Co IN	Wm E Cook	3 Sept 1853
144	Cox, Patsy	26	Negro woman 5 ft 2-3 ins, 117 lbs, burn scar on lt arm, stammers.	Knox Co IN	Knox Co IN	J C Denny	3 Sept 1853
145	Hill, Francis	50	Negro man 5 ft 1 in, 117 lbs, low built, knife scar on rt cheek.	Lincoln Co NC	Knox Co IN	J C Denny	8 Sept 1853
145	Hill, Hester	40	Negro woman 5 ft high spare made mole on chin, 120 lbs.	Delaware	Knox Co IN	J C Denny	8 Sept 1853
146	Hill, Andy	13	4 ft high, 100 lbs, son of Francis & Hester Hill.	Terre Haute IN	Knox Co IN	J C Denny	8 Sept 1853
146	Hill, Moses Hansham	11	Negro boy 4 ft high, yellow color, son of Francis & Hester Hill.	Evansville IN	Knox Co IN	J C Denny	8 Sept 1853
147	Hill, Nancy	6	Negro girl, dark color, spare built; dau of Francis & Hester Hill	Vincennes Knox Co IN	Knox Co IN	J C Denny	8 Sept 1853
147	Hill, George	5	Negro boy dark color, spare & well made, son of Frances & Hester.	Vincennes Knox Co IN	Knox Co IN	J C Denny	8 Sept 1853
148	Cox, Elijah	49	Negro man 5 ft 8 ins high dark color, thick lips.	Shelby Co KY	Knox Co IN	J C Denny	8 Sept 1853
148	Cox, Jane	36	Negro woman 5 ft 3 ins 150 lbs, brown color, heavy built.	Knox Co IN	Knox Co IN	J C Denny	8 Sept 1853
149	Cox, Thomas	3	Negro boy dark brown color, son of Elijah & Jane Cox.	Knox Co IN	Knox Co IN	J C Denny	8 Sept 1853
150	Cox, Fanny Ann	15	Negro girl 5 ft high slender made 120 lbs brown color.	Knox Co IN	Knox Co IN	J C Denny	8 Sept 1853
150	Cox, Purlina	9	Negro girl 4 ft high 90 lbs tolerably heavy built, well made.	Knox Co IN	Knox Co IN	J C Denny	8 Sept 1853

Knox County, Indiana

151	Cox, Uriah	20	Negro boy 5 ft 9 ins 158 lbs, slender, pigeon toed, clumsey.	Knox Co IN	Knox Co IN	J C Denny	8 Sept 1853
151	Cox, Roseanna	19	Negro woman 5 ft high 130 lbs, heavy set & stout built.	Knox Co IN	Knox Co IN	J C Denny	8 Sept 1853
152	Louis, Frank	14	Mulatto boy 5 ft slim built light yellow complexion.	Vincennes Knox Co IN	Knox Co IN	Jacob Smith	12 Sept 1853
152	Louisan, [Louis]--	6 yrs	Mulatto boy stout heavy built light yellow complexion.	Vincennes Knox Co IN	Knox Co IN	N P Barron	12 Sept 1853
153	Carter, Dean Pruden	14 yrs.	Mulatto girl stout heavy built rather dark complexion.	Knox Co IN	Knox Co IN	Thomas J Beeler	13 Sept 1853
153	Carter, Arthur	12	Mulatto boy stout heavy built dark complexion.	Knox Co IN	Knox Co IN	Thomas J Beeler	13 Sept 1853
154	Carter, John Williams	9	Mulatto boy, rather light built, dark complexion.	Knox Co IN	Knox Co IN	Thomas J Beeler	13 Sept 1853
154	Carter, Delphi	7	Mulatto boy, slim, yellow complexion; 3 fingers rt hand crooked.	Carroll Co IN	Knox Co IN	Thomas J Beeler	13 Sept 1853
155	Malone, Emaline	20	Negro woman 5 ft 5 1/2 ins 150 lbs, rather light complexion.	Daviess Co IN	Knox Co IN	Jacob Smith	15 Sept 1853
155	Allen, Harrison	21	Negro man 5 ft 5 ins 130-40 lbs, dark complexion.	Knox Co IN	Knox Co IN	James C Denny	30 Sept 1853
156	Rollins, Andrew	17	Negro boy dark brown color 5 ft 5 ins, scar left leg below knee.	Knox Co IN	Knox Co IN	Andrew Parcell	29 Sept 1853
156	Allen, Prince	70	Negro man 5 ft 6 ins white head dark complexion, rt hand crippled	SC	Knox Co IN	James C. Denny	30 Sept 1853
157	Allen, Prince Jr.	14	Negro boy, slim built right light complexion.	Knox Co IN	Knox Co IN	James C Denny	30 Sept 1853

Knox County, Indiana

157	Allen, Charles	11	Negro boy slim built rather light complexion.	Knox Co IN	Knox Co IN	James C Denny	30 Sept 1853
158	Allen, James	9	Negro boy low heavy built rather light complexion.	Knox Co IN	Knox Co IN	James C Denny	30 Sept 1853
158	Ember, Eli	40	Negro man 5 ft 7 ins 165 lbs, stout, heavy, light complexion.	SC	Knox Co IN	James C Denny	12 Sept 1853
159	Ember, Sarah [nee: Butler]	30	Negro woman, stout 5 ft 4 ins, 140 lbs, light complexion.	LA	Knox Co IN	James C Denny	1 Oct 1853
159	Ember, Mary L	7	Negro girl slim built, light complexion; dau of Eli-Sarah Ember	Knox Co IN	Knox Co IN	James C Denny	1 Oct 1853
160	Ember, James Anderson	6	Negro boy, slim built, rather light complexion; son Eli-Sarah.	Knox Co IN	Knox Co IN	James C Denny	1 Oct 1853
160	Ember, Joseph	3	Negro boy, heavy built, light complexion. Son Eli-Sarah Ember.	Knox Co IN	Knox Co IN	James C Denny	1 Oct 1853
161	Ember, Mary	33	Negro woman, slim built 120 lbs, rather light complexion.	Knox Co IN	Knox Co IN	James C Denny	1 Oct 1853
161	Ember, Matthias	10	Negro boy, heavy built, small of age, light complexion.	Knox Co IN	Knox Co IN	James C Denny	1 Oct 1853
162	Ember, Mary Elizabeth	9	Negro girl heavy built light complexion dau: Chas. & Mary Ember.	Knox Co IN	Knox Co IN	James C Denny	1 Oct 1853
162	Ember, Ellen	7	Heavy built, small, light complexion; dau of Chas & Mary Ember.	Knox Co IN	Knox Co IN	James C Denny	1 Oct 1853
163	Ember, Josephine	2	Negro girl, weakly, sickly, crippled leg, light complexion.	Knox Co IN	Knox Co IN	James C Denny	1 Oct 1853
163	Newton, Peter	31	Negro man 5 ft 6 ins 160 lbs slender & small, light complexion.	Knox Co IN	Knox Co IN	Wesley Hollingsworth	7 Oct 1853

Knox County, Indiana

164	Rider, Hannah	51	Negro woman 5 ft 4 ins, 127 lbs, scars: eye, temple and lf arm.	Scott Co KY	Knox Co IN	Thos J Beeler	15 Oct 1853
164	Carnan, Lucy Ann	8	Mulatto girl, slim, bright; several body marks, light hair.	Louisville KY	Frankfort KY	Thos J Beeler	15 Oct 1853
165	Lane, W. C.	37	Mulatto man 5 ft 7 1/2 ins, 150 lbs, stout; blacksmith by trade.	Vincennes Knox Co IN	Knox Co IN	Mrs. A. Woblverton	29 Oct 1853
165	Butler, George	45	Negro man 5 ft 6 ins, dark complexion.	Knox Co IN	Knox Co IN	Samuel Emison	6 Dec 1853
167	Butler, Clarisa	46	Negro woman 5 ft 2 3/4 ins, rather light complexion.	Knox Co IN	Knox Co IN	Samuel Emison	6 Dec 1853
167	Butler, Abraham	18	Negro boy 5 ft 3 ins heavy built rather light complexion.	Knox Co IN	Knox Co IN	Samuel Emison	6 Dec 1853
168	Butler, Bradford	16	Negro boy 5 ft 2-3 ins high slender, dark complexion.	Knox Co IN	Knox Co IN	Samuel Emison	6 Dec 1853
168	Butler, James	13	Negro boy small slender built rather light complexion.	Knox Co IN	Knox Co IN	Samuel Emison	6 Dec 1853
169	Butler, Immanuel	7	Negro boy stout heavy built rather light complexion.	Knox Co IN	Knox Co IN	Samuel Emison	6 Dec 1853
169	Butler, Benjamin	10	Negro boy, heavy set well built, rather light complexion.	Knox Co IN	Knox Co IN	Samuel Emison	6 Dec 1853
170	Rollins, Daniel	423	Negro man 6 ft stout heavy built light complexion.	VA	Knox Co IN	A B McGee	23 Dec 1853
170	Robbins, Catherine	42	Mulatto woman, low heavy built, yellow complexion.	Lawrence Co IL	Knox Co IN	A B McKee	23 Dec 1853
171	Duncan, Jane Maria	21	Mulatto woman low heavy built very light complexion.	Lawrence Co IL	Knox Co IN	A B McKee	23 Dec 1853

Knox County, Indiana

171	Rollins, Mary Elizabeth	20	Mulatto woman 5 ft 6 ins light complexion, short mid finger left.	Knox Co IN	Knox Co IN	A B McKee	23 Dec 1853
172	Rollins, John	18	Mulatto boy 5 ft 6 ins heavy built rather light complexion.	Knox Co IN	Knox Co IN	A B McKee	23 Dec 1853
172	Rollins, James D	17	Mulatto boy tall slender built full lips light complexion.	Knox Co IN	Knox Co IN	A B McKee	23 Dec 1853
173	Rollins, Elias	15	Mulatto boy slim built light complexion.	Knox Co IN	Knox Co IN	A B McKee	23 Dec 1853
173	Rollins, Martha Ann	6	Mulatto girl slender built full eyes dark complexion.	Knox Co IN	Knox Co IN	A B McKee	23 Dec 1853
174	Rollins, George H	4	Mulatto boy heavy built full eyes bold look, light complexion.	Knox Co IN	Knox Co IN	A B McKee	23 Dec 1853
174	Rollins, Harriet Arvillia	11	Mulatto girl tall, slender built, full eyes, light complexion.	Knox Co IN	Knox Co IN	A B McKee	23 Dec 1853
175	Rollins, Paul	9	Mulatto boy, strait slender, pleasant continance, light complex.	Knox Co IN	Knox Co IN	A B McKee	23 Dec 1853
175	Rollins, Madora M	3	Mulatto girl, heavy built, very full eyes, light complexion.	Knox Co IN	Knox Co IN	A B McKee	23 Dec 1853
176	Rollins, Margaret Amelia	1	Mulatto child, light complexion.	Knox Co IN	Knox Co IN	A B McKee	23 Dec 1853
176	Rollins, Sarah C	13	Mulatto girl rather low heavy built full eyes, yellow complexion.	Knox Co IN	Knox Co IN	A B McKee	23 Dec 1853
177	Rollins, Frances Cornelia	12	Rather tall well made full eyes light complexion.	Knox Co IN	Knox Co IN	A B McKee	23 Dec 1853
177	Silence, Jacob	50	Negro man 6 ft 165 lbs, dark with copper complexion, gray headed.	VA	Knox Co IN	Elihu Stout	27 Feb 1854

Knox County, Indiana

178	Silence, Lydia	23	Negro woman tall slender built rather dark complexion.	Knox Co IN	Knox Co IN	Elihu Stout	27 Feb 1854
178	Silence, James Irvin	22	Negro man 5 ft 4-5 ins dark complexion slender built.	Knox Co IN	Knox Co IN	Elihu Stout	27 Feb 1854
179	Silence, John	16	Negro boy stout heavy built dark complexion inclined to brown.	Knox Co IN	Knox Co IN	Elihu Stout	27 Feb 1854
179	Silence, William	19	Negro man tall slender light complexion scar forehead ankle broke	Knox Co IN	Tippecanoe IN	Elihu Stout	27 Feb 1854
180	Silence, Frances	13	Negro girl slender built copper color or rather dark.	Knox Co IN	Knox Co IN	Elihu Stout	27 Feb 1854
180	Silence, Teresa	10	Negro girl slim slender built light complexion.	Knox Co IN	Knox Co IN	Elihu Stout	27 Feb 1854
181	Silence, Emanuel	4	Negro boy, heavy built copper or rather dark complexion.	Knox Co IN	Knox Co IN	Elihu Stout	27 Feb 1854
181	Thomas, Charlotte	3	Negro girl tolerably heavy built light complexion.	Knox Co IN	Knox Co IN	Elihu Stout	27 Feb 1854
182	Thomas, Sally	1 1/2	Negro girl slender built light complexion.	Knox Co IN	Knox Co IN	Elihu Stout	27 Feb 1854
182	Barbor, Archibald	25	Negro man 5 ft 10 ins 192 lbs, scars neck. Dark complexion.	Daviess Co IN	Knox Co IN	N P Barron	27 Feb 1854
183	Duncan, Robert	34	Negro man 5 ft 5 ins 150 lbs, scars on temple and right leg.	Vincennes Knox Co IN	Vincennes Knox Co IN	Elihu Stout	4 Mar 1854
183	Clark, John S.	20	Negro man 5 ft 10 3/4 ins 175 lbs, scars face, hand, ankle. Dark.	Vincennes Knox Co IN	Knox Co IN	Benj F Thom	15 June 1854
XXX	Carter, Charlotte	35	Mulatto woman 5 ft 3 ins 135 lbs and well built.	Jackson TN	Knox Co IN	R H Gould	19 June 1854

Knox County, Indiana

XXX	Carter, Jane	15	Mulatto girl, very good looking 120 lbs.	Jackson TN	Knox Co IN	Rachael McGill	19 June 1854
184	Purrier, Susan [Carter]	17	Mulatto 5 ft high 135 lbs, good looking woman.	Jackson TN	Knox Co IN	Rachael McGill	19 June 1854
184	Carter, Mitilda	10	Mulatto 4 ft high weights 63 lbs fine looking girl.	Jackson TN	Knox Co IN	Rachael McGill	19 June 1854
185	Davis, Margaret	27	Colored woman 5 ft 5 1/2 ins of copper color, slender built.	Vincennes Knox Co IN	Knox Co IN	Thomas J Beeler	10 July 1854
185	Davis, John Edward	6	Mulatto boy small, slender built, light complexion.	Vincennes Knox Co IN	Knox Co IN	Thos J Beeler	10 July 1854
186	Davis, Richard L.	18 mos	Mulatto boy heavy built child of his age.	Vincennes Knox Co IN	Knox Co IN	Thos J Beeler	10 July 1854
186	Davis, Sarah	30	Negro woman 5 ft 3 1/2 ins 148 lbs copper color round face.	Vincennes Knox Co IN	Knox Co IN	B P Wheeler	11 July 1854
187	Ember, William H	37	Negro man 5 ft 8 1/3 ins 145 lbs dark complexion scars on lt leg.	Knox Co IN	Knox Co IN	Wm E Cooke	28 July 1854
187	Lamount, George	52	Mulatto man 5 ft 9 1/2 ins 156 lbs light complexion scars knees.	Knox Co IN	Knox Co IN	Elihu Stout	2 Aug 1854
188	Lamount, Martha Jane	15	Mulatto woman tolerably spare built light complexion.	Knox Co IN	Knox Co IN	Elihu Stout	2 Aug 1854
188	Lamount, John Henry	14	Mulatto boy tolerably stout brown color dark complexion.	Knox Co IN	Knox Co IN	Elihu Stout	2 Aug 1854
189	Lamount, William Edward	10	Mulatto boy tolerably stout and heavy dark complexion.	Knox Co IN	Knox Co IN	Elihu Stout	2 Aug 1854
189	Lamount, George Washington	8	Mulatto boy, stout, light bright complexion.	Knox Co IN	Knox Co IN	Elihu Stout	2 Aug 1854

Knox County, Indiana

190	Lamount, James Franklin	5	Stout heavy built dark complexion or brown color.	Knox Co IN	Knox Co IN	Elihu Stout	2 Aug 1854
190	Lamount, Charles Emmanuel	3	Mulatto boy spare built tolerably light complexion.	Knox Co IN	Knox Co IN	Elihu Stout	2 Aug 1854
191	Booker, William	44	Negro man 5 ft 3 ins 138 lbs, dark complexion, some grey hairs.	SC	Knox Co IN	Wm E Cooke	10 Aug 1854
191	Booker, George W.	7	Negro boy heavy set, light complexion.	Knox Co IN	Knox Co IN	Wm E Cooke	10 Aug 1854
192	Booker, Emma Jane	6	Negro girl slim & slender made light complexion.	Knox Co IN	Knox Co IN	Wm E Cooke	10 Aug 1854
192	Purier(Lamount), Nancy	52	Mulatto woman, small, light complexion, hair almost straight.	Knox Co IN	Knox Co IN	Elihu Stout	15 Aug 1854
193	Purier, Jane	20	Mulatto woman, low very heavy built, light complexion, sandy hair	Knox Co IN	Knox Co IN	Elihu Stout	15 Aug 1854
103	Purier, Samuel	18	Mulatto man tall slim light complexion, injured toe left foot.	Knox Co IN	Knox Co IN	Elihu Stout	15 Aug 1854
194	Purier, Rachael	15	Mulatto girl, tall large dark complexion, mark near neck.	Knox Co IN	Knox Co IN	Elihu Stout	15 Aug 1854
194	Purier, Sarah	12	Mulatto girl, low heavy built, light complexion, straight hair.	Knox Co IN	Knox Co IN	Elihu Stout	15 Aug 1854
195	Purier, Eliza	10	Mulatto girl, spare built light complexion straight hair.	Knox Co IN	Knox Co IN	Elihu Stout	15 Aug 1854
195	Campbell, Harrison	9	Mulatto boy heavy built dark complexion, facial scars eye & cheek	Knox Co IN	Knox Co IN	Elihu Stout	15 Aug 1854
196	Johnson, Alice	20 mos	Negro girl dark complexion, dau of Cyrus Johnson.	Knox Co IN	Knox Co IN	Elihu Stout	15 Aug 1854

Knox County, Indiana

196	McGriffin, David	5 mos	Mulatto boy a light complected child.	Knox Co IN	Knox Co IN	Elihu Stout	15 Aug 1854
197	Satters, Julia Ann	36	Negro woman dark complexion 5 ft 6 ins scar on left wrist.	Knox Co IN	Knox Co IN	Samuel Emison	23 Sept 1984
197	McGraw, David	82	5 ft 10 ins high slim built light complexion.	VA	Knox Co IN	John D Gardener	26 Sept 1854
198	Graves, William	73	Negro man 5 ft 5 1/4 ins 152 lbs, dark complexion, thick lips.	Knox Co IN	Vincennes Knox Co IN	N P Barron	10 Apr 1855
198	Taylor, Henry	26	Negro man 5 ft 6 ins, scars on breast & forearms, rickets in back	Knox Co IN	Edinburg, Johnson Co IN	H L Cornoyer	1 Sept 1855
199	Knight, Aaron	48	About 5 ft 7 ins 159 lbs trim built, rather copper color.	MD	Vincennes Knox Co IN	John Mamey, S R Dunn	11 Aug 1856
199	Smith, William	25	Mulatto man 5 ft 7 ins 150-165 lbs, copper color.	Jefferson Co IN	Vincennes Knox Co IN	Obedeah B Wetzel	22 Sept 1856
200	Allen, Mary Jane	36	Negro woman tall slender dark complexion, scar left side mouth.	Knox Co IN	Knox Co IN	John Wise	24 Sept 1856
200	Lofton, Ellen	29	Negro woman heavy built dark complexion.	Daviess Co IN	Knox Co IN	Benj J Thorn	26 Mar 1857
201	Lofton, Nancy Jane	7	Negro girl heavy built rather light complexion.	Vigo Co IN	Knox Co IN	B F Thorn	26 Mar 1857
201	Lofton, Monroe P.	5	Negro boy heavy built of rather light complexion.	Vigo Co IN	Knox Co IN	Benj F Thorn	26 Mar 1857
202	Lofton, Alice Victoria	1	Negro girl infant, heavy built, complexion not very dark.	Vigo Co IN	Knox Co IN	B F Thorn	26 Mar 1857
202	Purier, James Thomas	24	Mulatto man 5 ft 10 1/2 ins 160 lbs yellow complexion.	Vincennes Knox Co IN	Vincennes Knox Co IN	John M Clark	28 Apr 1857

Knox County, Indiana

203	Vinager, Ann Margaret	28	Mulatto woman 5 ft 4 1/2 ins, 115 light complexion.	KY	Vincennes Knox Co IN	A L Bornoyer	14 Apr 1858
204	Hawkins, Jacob	66	Mulatto man light complexion 5 ft 6 ins 150 lbs.	SC	Daviess Co IN	Elihu Stout	12 May 1858
204	Baird, Martha J.	35	Negro woman dark complected 5 ft high 140 lbs.	Knox Co IN	Knox Co IN		12 June 1858
205	Baird, Wesley	35	Mulatto man light complected 5 ft 6 ins 150 lbs.	Knox Co IN	Knox Co IN		12 June 1858
205	Baird, Eveline	9	Mulatto girl light complected 60 lbs 4 ft high.	Knox Co IN	Knox Co IN		12 June 1858
206	Baird, John	7	Mulatto boy light complected weighs 45 lbs, 3 ft 7 ins high.	Knox Co IN	Knox Co IN		12 June 1858
206	Baird, Frances	5	Mulatto girl light complected weighs 50 lbs 3 ft high.	Knox Co IN	Knox Co IN		12 June 1858
207	Baird, James	3	Mulatto boy dark complected 3 ft high and weighs 35 lbs.	Knox Co IN	Knox Co IN		12 June 1858

REGISTER OF NEGROES AND MULATTOES IN MARTIN COUNTY, INDIANA

Names	Age	Description	Place of Birth	Residence	Names of Witnesses	Date Registered
Hart, Pleasant	--	A dark mulatto, about 5'9" tall, weighs 175 lbs.	NC	Rutherford Twp, Martin Co, IN	Aaron D. Vandeverve	Aug 6 1853
Wood, Jesse	57	A dark mulatto, about 5'9" tall, heavy set. Has scar on right shin a little below the knee.	VA	Martin Co, IN	Absolem Fields	Sep 8 1853
Reves, James, alias Baxter.	50	Negro about 5' 9 or 10" in height, weighs 135 lbs with a long scar on the back of the left hand.	Arlington, VA (raised in KY)	Martin Co, IN	Joseph A. Daugherty	Sep 8 1853
Reves, Keziah, alias Keziah Baxter.	--	A dark mulatto about 5' 6" in height and weighs 175 lbs.	[Unknown] Raised in KY.	Martin Co, IN	Joseph A. Daugherty Clement J. Horsey	Sep 8 1853
Reaves, Nathaniel	20	Man of color, black 5' 7"in height, rather slim made. A mark or scar from a cut on the forefinger of left hand.	Madison Co, KY	Martin Co, IN	Joseph A. Daugherty Clement J. Horsey	Sep 12 1853
Loggan, Milly	over 50	A black woman some 5' 3 or 4" high with a scar from a burn on the left wrist.	KY, near Crop Plain.	Martin Co, IN	Jackson Duglass	Sep 12 1853
Loggin, Isaiah	14	Rather dark mulatto with a scar from cut on the knuckle of the forefinger of the left hand.	TN	Martin Co, IN	Jackson Duglass	Sep 12 1853
Loggin, Millford	13	A mulatto, rather dark.	IN	Martin Co, IN	Jackson Duglass	Sep 12 1853
Loggin, Levi	10	A mulatto lad rather dark.	IN	Martin Co, IN	Jackson Duglass	Sep 12 1853
Harden, William H.	25	A lite mulatto, 5' 3" in height. Son of Free Parents.	East TN	Martin Co, IN	Henry Henson	Nov 5 1853

Martin County, Indiana

Name	Age	Description	Origin	Witness/Reference	Date
Harden, Wilson P.	17	A mulatto, 5' 3" in height. Son of Free Parents.	East TN	Henry Henson	Nov 5 1853
Irwin, George	28	A mulatto man, 5' 5" in height with a scar on the forehead at the edge of the hair. Son of Free parents.	Madison Co, KY	Aaron D. Vandevere	Nov 9 1853
Cary, William G.	26	A mulatto man about 6' in height with the end of the middle finger of the left hand cut off.	White Co, TN	Barack Gaddis / Lewis R. Rogers	None given
Baxter, Nancy	30	A black woman, 5' 2" in height.	Madison Co, KY	William N. Raney	Mar 25 1856
Means, Nancy	55	A black woman, 5' 3" in height.	Randolph Co, NC	John Dorset	June 18 1856
Rickman, Jarmin	33	A mulatto man 6' 1" in height with a scar on his right shin.	White Co, TN	Eli B. Etchison	Sep 7 1857
Bell, James M.	28	A mulatto man 5' 10" in height; heavy made; weighing about 190 lbs, upom whose face near the nose on the left side is a mole; the right side of the face and forehead scarred by burn.	Martin Co, IN	Thomas Halbert	Jan 13 1868
Rickman, Thomas J.	22	A dark mulatto about 5' 10" in height and weighs about 160 lbs at this time.	TN	E. B. Mason	Oct 16, 1860

Perry Twp, Martin Co, IN (for Rickman, Thomas J.)
Martin Co, IN (for all others above)

REGISTER OF NEGROES AND MULATTOES IN OHIO COUNTY, INDIANA

Names	Age	Description	Place of Birth	Residence	Names of Witnesses	Date Registered
Barkshire, Samuel	55	Mulatto, heavy set about 5 feet ten inches high, weight about 175 pounds.	Harrison Co, KY	Rising Sun, IN	Thomas H. Gilmore	July 19 1854
Barkshire, Frances	47	Dark brown cullor about 5 feet high, weighs about 140 pounds.	Augusta, GA	Rising Sun, IN	Thomas H. Gilmore Saml Barkshire	July 19 1854
Barkshire, Arthur	29	Dark brown cullour about 5 feet high, weighs about 145 pounds.	Boone Co, KY	Rising Sun, IN	Thomas H. Gilmore Saml Barkshire	July 19 1854
Barkshire, Garret	27	Dark brown cullour about 5 1/2 feet high, weighs about 145 pounds.	Boone Co, KY	Rising Sun, IN	Thomas H. Gilmore Saml Barkshire	July 19 1854
Barkshire, Matilda	25	Dark brown cullour about 4 feet high, weighs about 125 pounds.	Boone Co, KY	Rising Sun, IN	Thomas H. Gilmore Saml Barkshire	July 19 1854
Barkshire, Woodford	21	Dark brown or yellow complexion, about 6 feet high, weighs about 150 pounds.	Boone Co, KY	Rising Sun, IN	Thomas H. Gilmore Saml Barkshire	July 19 1854
Barkshire, Emily	22	Dark mulatto or brown cullour about 4 feet high, weighs about 125 pounds.	Boone Co, KY	Rising Sun, IN	Thomas H. Gilmore Saml Barkshire	July 19 1854
Barkshire, Minerva	19	Brown mulatto about 4 1/2 feet high, weighs about 125 pounds.	Boone Co, KY	Rising Sun, IN	Thomas H. Gilmore Saml Barkshire	July 19 1854
Barkshire, Fanny	30	Brown mulatto about 4 feet high, weighs about 140 pounds.	VA	Rising Sun, IN	Thomas H. Gilmore Saml Barkshire	July 19 1854
Eddington, Harriet	9	Brown mulatto about 3 feet high, weighs about 60 pounds.	Rising Sun, IN	Rising Sun, IN	Samuel Barkshire	July 19 1854
Eddington, Gustavus	15	Brown mulatto about 4 feet high, weighs about 110 pounds.	Rising Sun, IN	Rising Sun, IN	Saml Barkshire	July 19 1854

Name		Description		Location	Registrant	Date
McCloud, Marshall	5	Brown mulatto about 3 feet high, weighs about 60 pounds.	Hamilton Co, OH	Rising Sun, IN	Saml Barkshire	July 19 1854
Macie, Rhoda	88	Very dark brown or black complexion, about 5 feet 8 or 10 inches high, weeighs about 120 to 130 pounds.	VA	Ohio Co, IN	John Wallace	March 14 1855
Wright, Septha E.	35	Mulatto about 5 feet high, weighs about 160 lbs, heavy set man.	KY	Rising Sun, IN	Samuel Barkshire	March 3 1857
Wright, Gonzolda	35	Mulatto about 5 feet high, freckled face, weighs about 125 lbs.	Madison, IN	Rising Sun, IN	Samuel Barkshire	March 3 1857
Wright, Septha E. [Jr]	10	Mulatto about 4 feet high, weighs about 60 lbs.	Rising Sun, IN	Rising Sun, IN	Samuel Barkshire	March 3 1857
Lee, Hetta	50	Dark Brown colour, heavy set about 5 feet high weighs about 135 lbs.	VA	Rising Sun, IN	Saml Barkshire	March 3 1857
Lee, Aaron	22	Dark Brown complexion about 5 1/2 feet high weighs about 145 or 50 lbs.	IN	Rising Sun, IN	Saml Barkshire	March 3 1857
Lee, Joseph	21	Dark Brown complexion about 5 1/2 feet high weighs about 145 or 50 lbs.	IN	Rising Sun, IN	Saml Barkshire	March 3 1857
Lee, Polly Ann	17	Dark Brown complexion about 5 feet high weighs about 130 lbs.	IN	Rising Sun, IN	Saml Barkshire	March 3 1857
Lee, Isaiah	7	Dark mulatto about 3 1/2 feet high weighs 40 lbs.	IN	Rising Sun, IN	Saml Barkshire	March 3 1857
George, Violette	60	Dark or Black complexion about 5 feet high, weighs about 120 lbs.	VA	Rising Sun, IN	Saml Barkshire	March 3 1857
Moss, William	60	Dark Brown or mulatto some freckles on his face about 5 1/2 feet high weighs 150 lbs.	VA	Rising Sun, IN	Saml Barkshire	March 3 1857

REGISTER OF NEGROES AND MULATTOES IN ORANGE COUNTY, INDIANA

Names	Age	Description	Place of Birth	Residence	Names of Witnesses	Date Registered
Archie, Wm. L.	36	Rather dark mulatto, 5 ft and 3 ins. high, very curly hair, high forehead	Orange Co, NC	Orange Co, IN	Hiram Lindley (of Wm)	24 June 1853
Burnett, Thomas	46	Rather dark mulatto, 5 ft 10 ins; curly hair, rather prominent cheek bones; finger on left hand crooked forward caused by a cut.	Orange Co, NC	Orange Co, IN	Henry Miller	24 June 1853
Archie, Martha	32	Rather light negro woman about 4 ft. 9 1/4 in high	Pitsylvania Co, Va.	Orange Co, IN	William Morris	24 June 1853
Cosley, Lucy Ann	5	Quite light colored mulatto about 3 ft 6 1/2 ins. high	Franklin Co, MO	Orange Co, IN	William Morris	24 June 1853
Roberts, Elias	64	Mulatto, 5 ft 9 ins high, gray hair, heavy set, weight 185 or 190 lbs.	NC	Orange Co, IN	William G. Chambers	27 Aug 1853
Roberts, Nancy	54	Light mulatto, gray hair, heavy set, height 165 lbs, 5 ft 4 ins.	NC	Orange Co, IN	William G. Chambers	27 Aug 1853
Roberts, Zachariah	19	Mulatto 5 ft 11 ins, curly hair, well built	Orange Co, IN	Orange Co, IN	William G. Chambers	27 Aug 1853
Roberts, John	14	Mulatto 5 ft high, curly hair, large scar left arm above wrist	Orange Co, IN	Orange Co, IN	William G. Chambers	27 Aug 1853
Roberts, Eliza J.	7	Mulatto 3 ft 8 ins.- fair	Orange Co, IN	Orange Co, IN	William G. Chambers	27 Aug 1853
Thomas, Samina A.	15	Mulatto 4 ft 11 1/2 in high	Orange Co, IN	Orange Co, IN	William G. Chambers	27 Aug 1853
Thomas, Nancy	14	Dark mulatto 5 ft high	Orange Co, IN	Orange Co, IN	William G. Chambers	27 Aug 1853
Thomas, Elias W.	9	3 ft 8 in high, dark mulatto	Vigo Co, IN	Orange Co, IN	William G. Chambers	27 Aug 1853
Chavis, Banister	35	Light mulatto 5 ft 10 1/2 ins	NC	Orange Co, IN	William G. Chambers	27 Aug 1853
Chavis, Henry	10	Light mulatto 4 ft 4 1/2 ins	Orange Co, IN	Orange Co, IN	William G. Chambers	27 Aug 1853

Orange County, Indiana

Name	Age	Description	Origin	Residence	Witness	Date
Chavis, Nancy	9	Light mulatto 4 ft 1 1/2 ins	Orange Co, IN	Orange Co, IN	William G. Chambers	27 Aug 1853
Chavis, Rachel	5	Light mulatto 3 ft 6 ins high	Orange Co, IN	Orange Co, IN	William G. Chambers	27 Aug 1853
Chavis, Riley	4	Light mulatto 3 ft 3 1/2 ins	Orange Co, IN	Orange Co, IN	William G. Chambers	27 Aug 1853
Chavis, Thomas	2	Light mulatto 2 ft 7 ins high	Orange Co, IN	Orange Co, IN	William G. Chambers	27 Aug 1853
Chavis, Sarah	32	Mulatto 5 1.2 ft high	NC	Orange Co, IN	William G. Chambers	27 Aug 1853
Thomas, Mathew	45	5 ft 3 in high, quite dark	NC	Orange Co, IN	William G. Chambers	27 Aug 1853
Thomas, Mary	37	5 ft 4 1/2 in, light mulatto	Orange Co, IN	Orange Co, IN	William G. Chambers	27 Aug 1853
Thomas, Joseph	18	5 ft 5 in, dark mulatto	Orange Co, IN	Orange Co, IN	William G. Chambers	27 Aug 1853
Thomas, Mary A.	14	4 ft 11 in high, mulatto	Orange Co, IN	Orange Co, IN	William G. Chambers	27 Aug 1853
Thomas, Sarah A.	12	4 ft 7 in high, mulatto	Orange Co, IN	Orange Co, IN	William G. Chambers	27 Aug 1853
Thomas, Jeremiah	9	4 ft high, dark mulatto	Orange Co, IN	Orange Co, IN	William G. Chambers	27 Aug 1853
Thomas, William	7	3 ft 9 in high, dark mulatto	Orange Co, IN	Orange Co, IN	William G. Chambers	27 Aug 1853
Thomas, John H.	4	3 1/2 ft high, mulatto	Orange Co, IN	Orange Co, IN	William G. Chambers	27 Aug 1853
Thomas, Adaline S. E.	2	2 ft 8 1/2 in high, mulatto	Orange Co, IN	Orange Co, IN	William G. Chambers	27 Aug 1853
Husbands, Aisley	24	Full blooded negro 5 ft 1 in (Resident of Daviess Co, Indiana)	NC	Daviess Co, IN	J. Wilson	29 Aog 1853
Lingle, Dudley A.	27	About 5 ft 7 1/2 ins, full blooded negro, 2 scars on right wrist, underside of arm and a small piece off left ear	KY	Orange Co, IN	Newton Wright	30 Aug 1853
Lynch, Harmon	38	About 6 ft 2 ins high, mulatto, heavy beard, scar on top of left arm	NC	Orange Co, IN	Alfred McVey	1 Sept 1853
Roberts, Benjamin	17	About 5 ft 3 ins, bright mulatto	Indiana	Orange Co, IN	Henry Thompson	1 Sept 1853
Clemens, Francis	66	Very black negro 5 ft 4 1/2 in	Amherst Co, VA	Orange Co, IN	Josiah Hazlewood	1 Sept 1853

Orange County, Indiana

Name	Age	Description	Origin		Date
Clemens, Nancy Ann	45	Very dark complexion 5 ft 3 1/2 ins.	VA	Orange Co, IN	Josiah Hazlewood	1 Sept 1853
Clemens, Martha A.	21	Very dark complexion 5 ft 1 in.	Orange Co, IN	Josiah Hazlewood	1 Sept 1853
Clemens, Sarah J.	19	Very dark complexion 4 ft 9 ins.	Orange Co, IN	Josiah Hazlewood	1 Sept 1853
Clemens, Mary E.	14	Very dark complexion	Orange Co, IN	Josiah Hazlewood	1 Sept 1853
Clemens, Wm.	18	Very dark complexion	Orange Co, IN	Josiah Hazlewood	1 Sept 1853
Clemens, Maria	10	Very dark complexion	Orange Co, IN	Josiah Hazlewood	1 Sept 1853
Newby, Solomon	53	Dark mulatto, 5 ft -- ins.	NC	Orange Co, IN	Josiah Hazlewood	1 Sept 1853
Newby, Margaret	38	Dark mulatto, 5 ft 2 1/2 ins.	NC	Orange Co, IN	John Cotes	1 Sept 1853
Newby, Lucinda	22	Dark color 4 ft 4 1/2 ins.	NC	Orange Co, IN	John Cotes	1 Sept 1853
Newby, Emaline	16	Dark colored mulatto	NC	Orange Co, IN	John Cotes	1 Sept 1853
Newby, James	9	Very dark mulatto	Orange Co, IN	Orange Co, IN	John Cotes	1 Sept 1853
Newby, Geo. J.	3	Very dark mulatto	Orange Co, IN	Orange Co, IN	John Cotes	1 Sept 1853
Newby, Moses W.	1	Dark mulatto	Orange Co, IN	Orange Co, IN	Leanid Lindley	1 Sept 1853
Baxter, Amos	42	Dark mulatto 5 ft 6 1/2 in.	KY	Orange Co, IN	John Cotes	1 Sept 1853
Baxter, Allen C.	29	Dark mulatto 5 ft 4 1/2 in.	Orange Co, IN	Orange Co, IN	John Cotes	1 Sept 1853
Baxter, Sabl[i]ne	7 mos.	Light mulatto	Orange Co, IN	Orange Co, IN	Leanid Lindley	1 Sept 1853
Chandler, Samuel	55	Mulatto 6 ft 1 1/2 in. high.	NC		John Cotes	1 Sept 1853
Chandler, Martha	49	About 5 ft 8 1/2 ins. high, light mulatto	NC		John Cotes	1 Sept 1853
Chandler, Leanid	14	Very light mulatto	Orange Co, IN	Orange Co, IN	John Cotes	1 Sept 1853

Orange County, Indiana

Name	Age	Description	From	To	Witness	Date
Chandler, Sina J.	13	Light mulatto	Orange Co, IN	Orange Co, IN	John Cotes	1 Sept 1853
Chandler, David	14	Very light mulatto	Orange Co, IN	Orange Co, IN	John Cotes	1 Sept 1853
Chandler, Martha A.	8	Bright mulatto	Orange Co, IN	Orange Co, IN	John Cotes	1 Sept 1853
Chandler, Joyce A.	7	Bright mulatto	Orange Co, IN	Orange Co, IN	John Cotes	1 Sept 1853
Sweat, Nancy	29	Bright mulatto 5 ft 9 ins.	NC	Orange Co, IN	John Cotes	1 Sept 1853
Sweat, Mary Ann	9 mos.	Light mulatto	Orange Co, IN	Orange Co, IN	Oliver Lindley	1 Sept 1853
Weaver, Clemenda	6	Bright mulatto	Orange Co, IN	Orange Co, IN	John Cotes	1 Sept 1853
Roberts, Lucretia	65	Mulatto 5 ft 4 1/2 ins.	NC	Orange Co, IN	John Cotes	1 Sept 1853
Roberts, Umphrey	26	Dark mulatto 5 ft 10 1/2 ins	NC	Orange Co, IN	John Cotes	1 Sept 1853
Roberts, Lucretia (II)	6	Mulatto	Orange Co, IN	Orange Co, IN	John Cotes	1 Sept 1853
Roberts, Anna	24	Light mulatto, 5 ft 4 1/2 ins.	NC	Orange Co, IN	John Cotes	1 Sept 1853
Roberts, James	1	Light mulatto	Orange Co, IN	Orange Co, IN	James Danner	1 Sept 1853
Roberts, Sarah C.	8	Light mulatto	NC	Orange Co, IN	John Cotes	1 Sept 1853
Roberts, Archie	5	Light mulatto	NC	Orange Co, IN	John Cotes	1 Sept 1853
Roberts, Sarah C.	8	Light mulatto	NC	Orange Co, IN	John Cotes	1 Sept 1853
Dungill, Wright	26	Light mulatto, 6 ft high	NC	Orange Co, IN	John Cotes	1 Sept 1853
Dungill, Betsy Jane	19	Light mulatto, 5 ft high	Orange Co, IN	Orange Co, IN	John Cotes	1 Sept 1853
Roberts, James	25	Dark mulatto, 6 ft 1/2 inch high	NC	Orange Co, IN	James Danner	1 Sept 1853
Roberts, Unity	26	Mulatto, 5 ft 1 inch high	NC	Orange Co, IN	Albert Johnson	1 Sept 1853
Roberts, Martha M.	2	Mulatto	Orange Co, IN	Orange Co, IN	James Danner	1 Sept 1853
Clark, Henry	20	Mulatto	Orange Co, IN	Orange Co, IN	Jeremiah Wilson	5 Sept 1853

Orange County, Indiana

Name	Age	Description	Origin	Residence	Registered by	Date
Roberts, Wiley	50	About 5 ft 5 1/2 ins, light mullatto	NC	Orange Co, IN	J. S. Merritt	5 Sept 1853
Roberts, Mary	40	About 5 ft 5 high, light mullatto	NC	Orange Co, IN	J. S. Merritt	5 Sept 1853
Roberts, Jnoth P.	14	Light mulatto	Orange Co, IN	Orange Co, IN	J. S. Merritt	5 Sept 1853
Roberts, Allen	12	A light mulatto	Orange Co, IN	Orange Co, IN	Jonathan P. Chambers	5 Sept 1853
Roberts, Bryant	9	Light mulatto	Orange Co, IN	Orange Co, IN	Jonathan P. Chambers	5 Sept 1853
Roberts, Mary C.	7	Light mulatto	Orange Co, IN	Orange Co, IN	Jonathan P. Chambers	5 Sept 1853
Clark, Frederick	18	Light mulatto about 5 ft 5 high	Orange Co, IN	Orange Co, IN	John C. Albert	5 Sept 1853
Roberts, Sarah	60	Dark mulatto 5 ft 4 ins.	NC	Orange Co, IN	Hiram Braxton	7 Sept 1853
Guthrie, James	56	Full blooded African 6 ft high	NC	Orange Co, IN	Jnoth. L. Jones	7 Sept 1853
Clark, Lucy	50	Full blooded negro 5 ft 1/2 in.	NC	Orange Co, IN	Jeremiah Wilson	9 Sept 1853
Johnson, Lovina	31	Mulatto 5 ft 5 ins. high	NC	Orange Co, IN	Jeremiah Wilson	9 Sept 1853
Johnson, Andrew J.	13	Dark mulatto	Orange Co, IN	Orange Co, IN	Jeremiah Wilson	9 Sept 1853
Johnson, Catharine	11	Dark mulatto	Orange Co, IN	Orange Co, IN	Jeremiah Wilson	9 Sept 1853
Johnson, Sarah E.	9	Dark mulatto	Orange Co, IN	Orange Co, IN	Jeremiah Wilson	9 Sept 1853
Johnson, Wm. H.	7	Dark mulatto	Orange Co, IN	Orange Co, IN	Jeremiah Wilson	9 Sept 1853
Johnson, Jno. W.	5	Dark mulatto	Orange Co, IN	Orange Co, IN	Jeremiah Wilson	9 Sept 1853
Means, Fanny L.	17	Dark mulatto	Orange Co, IN	Orange Co, IN	Jer. Wilson	9 Sept 1853
Hawkins, Jer	60	Mulatto, heavy built, 5 ft. 5 ins.	VA	Orange Co, IN	Jer. Wilson	9 Sept 1853
Hattaway, John	30	Light mulatto 5 ft 10 ins.	Orange Co, IN	Orange Co, IN	Jer. Wilson	10 Sept 1853

Orange County, Indiana

Name	Age	Description	Origin	Residence	Recorder	Date
Scott, Alvin	37	Quite light mulatto 5 ft 5 1/2 ins.	NC	Orange Co, IN	Benjn M. Pritchard	10 Sept 1853
Scott, Elizabeth	16	Dark mulatto	NC	Orange Co, IN	Benjn M. Pritchard	10 Sept 1853
Scott, Sarah A.	10	Very light mulatto	Orange Co, IN	Orange Co, IN	Benjn M. Pritchard	10 Sept 1853
Scott, Berry	9	Light mulatto	Orange Co, IN	Orange Co, IN	Benjn M. Pritchard	10 Sept 1853
Scott, Ruel	5	Light mulatto	Orange Co, IN	Orange Co, IN	Benjn M. Pritchard	10 Sept 1853
Thomas, Jordan	37 1/2	About 3/4 negro blood, 5 ft 5 1/2 ins high	NC	Orange Co, IN	Simon Dixon	15 Sept 1853
Thomas, Candis	36 1/2	Light mulatto 5 ft 5 1/2.	NC	Orange Co, IN	Simon Dixon	15 Sept 1853
Thomas, Mary E.	13	Mulatto	Vigo Co, IN	Orange Co, IN	Jnoth P. Chambers	15 Sept 1853
Thomas, Benjamin T.	11	Dark mulatto	Vigo Co, IN	Orange Co, IN	Jnoth P. Chambers	15 Sept 1853
Thomas, Wm. A.	6 1/2	Dark mulatto	Vigo Co, IN	Orange Co, IN	Jnoth P. Chambers	15 Sept 1853
Scott, Alfred	24	Mulatto, almost white, very fair, 5 ft 5 in high	NC	Orange Co, IN	James Hallowell	17 Sept 1853
Scott, Martha J.	16 1/2	Mulatto, almost white, very fair, 5 ft 5 in high	VA	Orange Co, IN	James Hallowell	17 Sept 1853
Todd, Pearson	43	About 5 ft 8 1/2 in high, full blooded negro	KY	Orange Co, IN	Henry R. Williamson	19 Sept 1853
Todd, Malvina	32 1/2	Mulatto, about 5 ft 1 in high	Ky	Orange Co, IN	Henry R. Williamson	19 Sept 1853
Todd, Morris B.	--	Near full blooded African		Orange Co, IN	Henry R. Williamson	19 Sept 1853
Todd, Amanda J.	9 1/2	Mulatto	Orange Co, IN	Orange Co, IN	Henry R. Williamson	19 Sept 1853
Todd, Wm. P. Q.	8	Mulatto	Orange Co, IN	Orange Co, IN	Henry R. Williamson	19 Sept 1853
Todd, Hiram H.	6	Mulatto	Orange Co, IN	Orange Co, IN	Henry R. Williamson	19 Sept 1853
Todd, John E.	3 1/2	Mulatto	Orange Co, IN	Orange Co, IN	Henry R. Williamson	19 Sept 1853

Orange County, Indiana

Name	Age	Description	Birthplace	Residence	Witness	Date
Walker, Charles	68 1/2	Negro 5 ft 7 1/2 in high	VA	Orange Co, IN	Elizabeth Taylor	19 Sept 1853
Walker, Jane	68	Negro 5 ft 6 in high	KY	Orange Co, IN	Elizabeth Taylor	19 Sept 1853
Taylor, Hiram	16	Mulatto	--	Orange Co, IN	Elizabeth Taylor	19 Sept 1853
Bonds, Penelope	50	Negro five feet high	NC	Orange Co, IN	Davey Clendenin	23 Sept 1853
Bonds, Jno W.	24 1/2	Mulatto 5 ft 4 ins. high	SC	Orange Co, IN	Davey Clendenin	23 Sept 1853
Bonds, Monroe	14	Mullatto	Orange Co, IN	Orange Co, IN	Davey Clendenin	23 Sept 1853
Butler, Thomas	86 1/2	5 ft 7 1/2 high, full blooded Negro	MD	Orange Co, IN	Arthur J. Simpson	4 Oct 1853
Lynch, Martha	39	5 ft 1 in high, mulatto with European blood	NC	Orange Co, IN	Arthur J. Simpson	8 Oct 1853
Lynch, Mila	18	Dark color with Indian blood	NC	Orange Co, IN	Vincent Moore	8 Oct 1853
Husbands, Laura	21	5 ft 2 1/2 ins, almost full blooded negro, part Indiana	NC	Orange Co, IN	Arthur J. Simpson	8 Oct 1853
Scott, Martin Sr.	75	Mulatto, half white blood, about 5 ft 8 3/4 in high, scar on left breast.	NC	Orange Co, IN	Cornelius White	4 Nov 1853
Scott, Joseph	37	Mulatto, 3/4 white blood, about 5 ft 5 in high, mole on neck in front.	NC	Orange Co, IN	Cornelius White	4 Nov 1853
Scott, Isaac	52	About half white blood 5 ft 10 ins.	NC	Orange Co, IN	Aaron Andrew	10 Nov 1853
Roberts, Giliann	14 1/2	Mulatto of slender form	NC	Orange Co, IN	Benjn. M. Pritchard	17 Nov 1853
Roberts, Jno. L.	28	About 5 ft 11 ins, mulatto	NC	Howard Co, IN	Benjn. M. Pritchard	17 Nov 1853
Burnett, Enoch	18	Light mulatto	NC	Orange Co, IN	Josiah Hazlewood	17 Nov 1853
Roberts, Wm. R.	22	Light mulatto 5 ft 10 1/2 ins	Orange Co, IN	Orange Co, IN	Charles McVey	11 March 1854
Scott, John M.	12	Light mulatto rather slender	Orange Co, IN	Orange Co, IN	William Hill	2 Aug 1854

Orange County, Indiana

Scott, Daniel I.	10	Light mulatto	Orange Co, IN	Orange Co, IN	William Hill	2 Aug 1854
Scott, Jemima	46	Light mulatto high cheek bones 5 ft	NC	Orange Co, IN	Oliver Lindsey	3 Aug 1854
Scott, Joseph K.	21	Mulatto 5 ft 8 1/4 in high	NC	Orange Co, IN	Oliver Lindsey	3 Aug 1854
Scott, Elizabeth	20	Mulatto 5 ft 2 3/4 in high	NC	Orange Co, IN	Oliver Lindsey	3 Aug 1854
Scott, Zachariah L.	18	Mulatto	Orange Co, IN	Orange Co, IN	Oliver Lindsey	3 Aug 1854
Scott, Sanders J.	16	Dark mulatto slender made	Orange Co, IN	Orange Co, IN	Oliver Lindsey	3 Aug 1854
Scott, Needham L.	14	Light mulatto	Orange Co, IN	Orange Co, IN	Oliver Lindsey	3 Aug 1854
Scott, Doctor F.	7	Light mulatto	Orange Co, IN	Orange Co, IN	Oliver Lindsey	3 Aug 1854
Scott, Mary A.	3	Mulatto spine disease	Orange Co, IN	Orange Co, IN	Oliver Lindsey	3 Aug 1854
Wright, Edmund	57	Full blooded African	Franklin Co, NC	Orange Co, IN	Jesse Field	Nov 1856
Hart, John O.	20 1/2	Light mulatto 5 ft 11 inches	Granville Co, NC	Orange Co, IN	James Butler	17 Nov 1856
Goins, Sinajane	19	A mulatto 5 feet and 5 ins, small scar on the upper lip and left cheek.	Washington Co, IN	Orange Co, IN	Elias Lindley	10 June 1861

REGISTER OF NEGROES AND MULATTOES IN SWITZERLAND COUNTY, INDIANA

Names	Age	Description	Place of Birth	Residence	Names of Witnesses	Date Registered
Nidah [Nivey], Isaac [See note on last entry]	34	Dark mulatto, five feet ten inches high, and weigh about 180 pounds.	Giles Co, VA	Switzerland Co, IN	James H. Titus	25 July 1853
Mackney, James William	24	A jet black man, five feet eight inches high, weighs about 165 pounds; has 2 scars on his left hand, one across the forefinger and one across the thumb.	Shanandoah Co, VA	Switzerland Co, IN	James Coles	15 Sept 1853
Andrews, George	41	Dark mulatto, five feet six inches high with a scar on his upper lip, scar on his left cheek and a scar on his breast.	Gallatin Co, KY	Switzerland Co, IN	James H. Titus	16 Dec 1853
Andrews, James William	9	Dark mulatto with a scar on his chin.	Gallatin Co, KY	Switzerland Co, IN	James H. Titus	16 Dec 1853
Andrews, Eliza Ann	7	Dark mulatto, has no scars or perceivables.	Gallatin Co, KY	Switzerland Co, IN	James H. Titus	16 Dec 1853
Andrews, Laura	4	Dark mulatto.	Switzerland Co, IN	Switzerland Co, IN	James H. Titus	16 Dec 1853
Andrews, Sarah	1 1/2 yrs	Dark mulatto child.	Switzerland Co, IN	Switzerland Co, IN	James H. Titus	16 Dec 1853
Andrews, Antica	28	Daark mulatto, five feet high.	Gallatin Co, KY	Switzerland Co, IN	James H. Titus	16 Dec 1853
Blanton, William	50	Black (jet) six feet high & lame in both legs, said lameness caused by rheumatism.	Gallatin Co, KY	Switzerland Co, IN	Ira M. Malin	28 Dec 1853
Blanton, Vina	About 60	Jet black person, about 5 feet high, no marks on her person.	Galllatin Co, KY	Switzerland Co, IN	Ira M. Malin	28 Dec 1853

Switzerland County, Indiana

Nivey, John (Not entered but listed on separate sheet in book)	7	Born July 26, 1846, light color.	Not stated	Not stated	Not stated	Not stated
Nivey, James (Not entered but listed on separate sheet in book)	5	Born January 1, 1848, light color.	Not stated	Not stated	Not stated	Not stated
Nivey, Milla Ann (Not entered but listed on separate sheet in book)	4	Born April 15, 1849, light color.	Not stated	Not stated	Not stated	Not stated
Nivey, Margaret Jane (Not entered but listed on separate sheet in book)	2	Born September 17, 1850, light color.	Not stated	Not stated	Not stated	Not stated
Nivey, Elizabeth Frances (Not entered but listed on separate sheet in book)	1	Born March 4, 1852, light color.	Not stated	Not stated	Not stated	Not stated
Nivey, Isaac [Jr.] (Not entered but listed on separate sheet in book)	3 wks	Born July 6, 1853, light color.	Not stated	Not stated	Not stated	Not stated
Nivey, Elizabeth (Not entered but listed on separate sheet in book)	26	Born June 20, 1827, his wife [Husband is believed to be "Isaac Nidah" #1]	Not stated	Not stated	Not stated	Not stated

REGISTER OF NEGROES AND MULATTOES IN WASHINGTON COUNTY, INDIANA

Names	Age	Description	Place of Birth	Residence	Names of Witnesses	Date Registered
Strawder, Rhoda	53	Female mulatto, 5 ft 8 1/4" tall	Newberry District, SC	Washington Co, IN	Henry Albertson William Weston	17 Sept 1853
Miller, James Trevan	17	Male mulatto, 5 ft 9 3/4"	Newberry District, SC	Washington Co, IN	Henry Albertson William Weston	17 Sept 1853
White, Denson	48	Negro about 6 ft, blind in right eye & the little finger of his left hand off.	Perquimans Co, NC	Washington Co, IN	Thomas N. Jordon Alexander Attkisson	19 Sept 1853
Newby, Thompson	48	Negro 5 ft 5" height	Perquimans Co, NC Born: 4 Apr 1805	Washington Co, IN	Thomas N. Jordon Alexander Attkisson	22 Sept 1853
Newby, Penniah	45	Negress about 5 ft 2 inches height	Perquimans Co, NC Born: 4 Apr 1808	Washington Co, IN	Christopher Denny Thomas N. Jordon	22 Sept 1853
Newby, Robert	19	Negro about 5 ft 6 inches height. Son of Thompson and Penniah Newby.	Washington Co, IN Born: 29 Jan 1834	Washington Co, IN	Allen Brown	26 Sept 1853
Newby, Alexander	17	Negro tall and slim, rather light. Son of Thompson and Penniah Newby.	Washington Co, IN Born: 27 Jan 1836	Washington Co, IN	Allen Brown	26 Sept 1853
Newby, Priscilla Ellen	14	Negress, rather slim made. Daughter of Thompson and Penniah Newby.	Washington Co, IN Born: 6 Nov 1839	Washington Co, IN	Allen Brown	26 Sept 1853
Newby, Martha	9 1/2	Negress, thick & heavy set. Daughter of Thompson and Penniah Newby.	Washington Co, IN Born: 12 Apr 1844	Washington Co, IN	Allen Brown	26 Sept 1853
Newby, William George	7	Negro, small for his age, rather thick set. Son of Thompson and Penniah Newby.	Washington Co, IN Born: 10 Oct 1846	Washington Co, IN	Allen Brown	26 Sept 1853

Washington County, Indiana

Name	Age	Description	Origin	Residence	Witness	Date
Newby, Joseph Henry	3 1/2	Negro small for his age, rather light color. Son of Thompson and Penniah Newby.	Washington Co, IN Born: 16 Mar 1850	Washington Co, IN	None stated	26 Sept 1853
Newby, Amanda	1 1/4	Negress. Daughter of Thompson and Penniah Newby.	Washington Co, IN Born: 18 Jun 1852	Washington Co, IN	Allen Brown	26 Sept 1853
White, Nathan	22	Negro 5 ft 4 3/4 ins & is lacking in intelligence.	Washington Co, IN	Washington Co, IN	Elisha Denny	17 Oct 1853
Potter, Richmond	46	Mulatto male, 5 ft 7 1/2 " light complexion.	Salisbury, NC	Washington Co, IN	Joseph Trueblood	28 Oct 1853
Potter, Clarkey	36	Negress about 5 ft 5 or 6 inches, bright complexion.	Perquimans Co, NC	Washington Co, IN	Joseph Trueblood	28 Oct 1853
Potter, George W.	16	Mullatto male, tall of his age, light complexion.	Washington Co, IN	Washington Co, IN	Joseph Trueblood	28 Oct 1853
Potter, Joseph	13	Mulatto male, tall of his age, light complexion.	Washington Co, IN	Washington Co, IN	Joseph Trueblood	28 Oct 1853
Potter, John H.	11	Mulatto male, tall of his age, rather light complexion.	Washington Co, IN	Washington Co, IN	Joseph Trueblood	28 Oct 1853
Jordan, Isaac	55	Negro 5 ft 7", stout made very black.	Pasquotank Co, NC	Washington Co, IN	Wm. N. Trueblood	5 Nov 1853
Jordan, Charlotte	52	Mulatto female, low of stature, bright complexion.	Northampton Co, NC	Washington Co, IN	Wm. N. Trueblood	5 Nov 1853
Jordan, Charles Emery	10	Negro boy, light complexion, not tall for his age.	Washington Co, IN	Washington Co, IN	Wm. N. Trueblood	5 Nov 1853
Parker, George W.	35	Negro, five feet 7 inches, light complexion.	Not stated	Washington Co, IN	Wm. N. Trueblood	5 Nov 1853
Parker, Eliza Jane	24	Negress, light complexion.	Not stated	Washington Co, IN	Wm. N. Trueblood	5 Nov 1853

Washington County, Indiana

Name	Age	Description	Origin	Resident	Date
Parker, Marietta	4	Negress, black complexion.	Washington Co, IN	Wm. N. Trueblood Washington Co, IN	5 Nov 1853
Parker, Louise Jane	1 1/2 yrs	Negress, dark complexion.	Washington Co, IN	Wm. N. Trueblood Washington Co, IN	5 Nov 1853
Parker, George S.	1 mo.	Negro, dark complexion.	Washington Co, IN	Wm. N. Trueblood Washington Co, IN	5 Nov 1853
Christy, Israel	38	Negro, about 5 ft 8 or 9" in height, dark.	Newberry District, SC	Samuel McClanahan Washington Co, IN	26 Dec 1853
Christy, Lucinda	35	Negress, a dark color.	Clark Co, IN	Samuel McClanahan Washington Co, IN	26 Dec 1853
Christy, Jesse	16	Negro, dark color.	Washington Co, IN	Samuel McClanahan Washington Co, IN	26 Dec 1853
Christy, Eliza Jane	13	Negress of dark color.	Washington Co, IN	Samuel McClanahan Washington Co, IN	26 Dec 1853
Christy, Levin	8	Negro of dark color.	Washington Co, IN	Samuel McClanahan Washington Co, IN	26 Dec 1853
White, Jeremiah	28 or 29	Mulatto, 5 ft 6 1/2", light color.	Green Co, KY	Wm. Lewelling Washington Co, IN	31 Dec 1853
White, Rachel	28 or 29	Colored female of dark color.	Washington Co, IN	Wm. Lewelling Washington Co, IN	31 Dec 1853
White, Malinda	14	Colored female of a light color.	Washington Co, IN	Wm. Lewelling Washington Co, IN	31 Dec 1853
Parker, James Henry	11	Dark mulatto, well grown of his age.	Washington Co, IN	Wm. Lewelling Washington Co, IN	31 Dec 1853
Cloud, Peter	42	Mulatto male, 5 ft 8 1/2" stout made.	Orange Co, NC	John L. Merraugh Washington Co, IN	3 Jan 1854

Washington County, Indiana

Name	Age	Description	Origin	Residence	Owner/Witness	Date
Cloud, Roseanne	27	Light mulatto female about 5 ft 3 1/2 inches in height & stout made.	Henry Co, KY	Washington Co, IN	John L. Merraugh	3 Jan 1854
Cloud, David	10	Mulatto boy well grown of his age, slender made, light complexion.	Washington Co, IN	Washington Co, IN	Wm. J. Johnson	3 Jan 1854
Cloud, John Henry	10 mos.	Mulatto child, light complexion.	Washington Co, IN	Washington Co, IN	James J. Briscoe	3 Jan 1854
Christy, Sophia	40	Negress about 5 ft 6", dark complexion.	Perquimans Co, NC	Washington Co, IN	John W. Reyman	15 Jan 1854
Christy, Elias	19	Negro of dark complexion & well grown of his age.	Washington Co, IN	Washington Co, IN	John W. Reyman	15 Jan 1854
Christy, Sarah E.	14	Negress, dark complexion, well grown of her age.	Washington Co, IN	Washington Co, IN	John W. Reyman	15 Jan 1854
Christy, Elvira	12	Negress of dark complexion, well grown of her age.	Washington Co, IN	Washington Co, IN	John W. Reyman	15 Jan 1854
Christy, Eliza Ann	8	Negress of dark complexion, well grown of her age.	Washington Co, IN	Washington Co, IN	John W. Reyman	15 Jan 1854
Christy, Albert Asbury	6	Negro boy of dark complexion & well grown of his age.	Washington Co, IN	Washington Co, IN	John W. Reyman	15 Jan 1854
Christy, Levitha Mabel	4	Negro child of dark complexion, etc.	Washington Co, IN	Washington Co, IN	John W. Reyman	15 Jan 1854
Blan[d], G. V. R.	29	Mulatto, 5 ft 8" well made, dark straight hair & light complexion.	Nelson Co, KY	Washington Co, IN	Townsend Cutshaw	27 Feb 1854
Lee, Esther	30	Colored female, low of stature, dark complexion tho' not entirely black, black curly hair.	Charlestown, Clark Co, IN	Washington Co, IN	David G. Caubill	20 Mar 1854
Richardson, Mahala	19	Mulatto female, 5 ft 1" high, light complexion black wavy hair.	Sumner Co, TN	Washington Co, IN	Jason B. Blackington	21 Mar 1854

Washington County, Indiana

Name	Age	Description	Birthplace	Residence	Reference	Date
Cloud, Mary Eliza	9 mos.	Mulatto female child, light complexion.	Washington Co, IN (born 19 Feb 1855)	Washington Co, IN	Dr. Joshua Trueblood	1 Nov 1855
Demar, Elizabeth	36	Mulatto female of ordinary stature, 5 ft 7 1/4" with black wavy hair.	Not stated	Washington Co, IN	Alex Attkisson	31 Mar 1856
White, Robert A.	21	Dark mulatto somewhat heavy set kinky hair and measures 5 ft 3" and 1/2.	Washington Co, IN	Washington Co, IN	Alexander Attkisson	10 Dec 1856
Blan[d], Austin	21	Light mulatto male, somewhat heavy set, strait hair, eyes dark but not black and measures with boots on five feet & nine inches in height.	Louisville, KY	Washington Co, IN	Wm. Donathan	6 Jan 1857
DeMarrs, Sina D.	25-30	Dark mulatto somewhat heavy set hair long & kinky or wirey and measures 5 ft 2 1/2".	Lexington, KY	Washington Co, IN	Alex Attkisson	30 Jan 1857
Christie, Sampson	--	Negro male 5 ft 7 1/2", light built with a scar running nearly transversely across his right cheek once of a deep negro coulour.	Newberry DIstrict, SC	Washington Co, IN	Alex Attkisson	15 Apr 1857
Christie, Augustus R.	14	Negro boy 5 ft 2 1/2" light built & rather light coulour.	Jackson Co, IN	Washington Co, IN	None given	15 Apr 1857
Christie, Theodore	13	Negro boy 4 ft 7 1/4", ordinary built light coulour.	Washington Co, IN	Washington Co, IN	None given	15 Apr 1857
Christie, Betsy	28	Negro woman 5 ft 6 1/2" light coulour.	Clark Co, IN	Washington Co, IN	None given	15 Apr 1857
Christie, Walter	8	Negro boy 4 ft 3/4" slender, deep negro coulour.	Washington Co, IN	Washington Co, IN	None given	29 Apr 1857
Christie, Georgia V.	9	Negro girl 4 ft 4" slender & dark of coulour.	Washington Co, IN	Washington Co, IN	None given	29 Apr 1857

Washington County, Indiana

Name	Age	Description	Place	Destination	Witnesses	Date
White, Mary Elizabeth	19	Negro girl 5 ft 3 1/2" light black colour.	Salem, IN	Washington Co, IN	None given	2 Nov 1857
Roberts, James	17	Negro boy 5 ft 7 1/2", slender form deep black color, kinky hair.	Salem, IN	Washington Co, IN	None given	7 Apr 1858
Bland, George	25	Negro man 5 ft 11 1/2" dark complexion & kinky hair.	Louisville, KY	Washington Co, IN	America Anderson	1 Jun 1858
Goodwin, Willis	23	Negro man 5 ft 9" slender black colour, has thick kinky hair & a scar on the inner side of the right knee a little below the cap.	Salem, IN	St Lewis, MO	None given	14 Jan 1859
Goins, John A.	24	Bright mulatto man, 5 ft 8 ins in height, black and nearly straight hair, has three scars, one nearly in the center of the forehead between and slightly above the eyebrows, one on the bridge of the nose & one on the thigh & is built light.	Jackson Co, IN	Washington Co, IN	None given	2 Feb 1860
Goins, Elisha	21	Bright mulatto man, six feet one and 3/4 inches in height, black and nearly strait hair has several scars about his hands and one on the left side of the chin nearly one inch in length and is strait and well made.	Jackson Co, IN	Washington Co, IN	Benj. F. Harmon Zach. Goins	2 Feb 1860
Maybery, William A.	26	Bright mulatto man, five feet ten and a half inches in height, his skin somewhat frecklier, has a scar a little to the right side of the forehead extending into the hair, hair kinky.	Not stated	Washington Co, IN	John L. Menaugh Alfred Pringle Samuel Mayberry	6 Mar 1860

Washington County, Indiana

Name	Age	Description	Place	Witness	Date
Weaver, Harvey	20	Light complected negro man, five feet eight inches in height of somewhat slender built, kinky hair but inclining to strait, two small scars on the back of the left hand, one near the thumb & one near the wrist.	Washington Co, IN	Zachariah S. Garriott, Engr.	25 May 1860
Anderson, America	54	Light complected negro woman, five feet nine inches in height, of large body and well built, a scar on the upper lip, kinky hair and very black.	Nelson Co, KY	Draten [Drayton] Christy	20 Aug 1860
Gillimn, Jacob	16	Light coloured negro boy, five feet five inches in height, well built and has black nearly straight.	Orange Co, IN	America Anderson	20 Aug 1860
Bland, Susan	22	Negro woman, the mother of three children, of a light colour about five feet three and a half inches in height, has a mole in the palm of the left hand & a slight scar over the right eye.	Salem IN	Joseph F. Cutshaw	7 May 1861
Bland, Sarah Frances	23	A very bright mulatto woman, the mother of four children, five feet one and three fourths inches high.	KY	Daniel Voyles	7 May 1861
Evans, Matilda	51	Negro woman with two daughters 15 & 16 years of age, a light colour, has a mole in the palm of the left hand & is five feet & five inches high an rather heavy set.	KY	Moses Foster	7 May 1861
Jackson, John Henry (data on loose paper in book)	19	Colored male, well grown, tall and of light color.	Scott Co, IN	Jordon Pritchard	Not stated

Washington County, Indiana

Jackson, Mary (data on loose paper in book)	17	Colored female, tall, rather bushy hair, light color.	Scott Co, IN	Washington Co, IN	Jordon Pritchard	Not Stated
Jackson, Martha (data on loose paper in book)	16	Light, thick made.	Scott Co, IN	Washington Co, IN	Jordon Pritchard	Not stated
Jackson, Henrietta (data on loose paper in book)	60	Light color, stout made, about 5 ft 5 in.	Bourbon Co, KY	Washington Co, IN	Jordon Pritchard	Not stated
Jackson, Thomas McKee (data on loose paper in book)	14	Light, well grown.	Scott Co, IN	Washington Co, IN	Jordon Pritchard	Not stated

INDEX

A

Adams,
  John, 27
Allen,
  Charles, 141
  Harrison, 140
  James, 141
  James H., 88
  Mary Jane, 147
  Prince, 140
  Prince Jr., 140
Allums,
  Andrew, 88
  Asbury, 88
  Elizabeth, 88
  Osbery, 88
Anderson,
  America, 169
  John, 10
  William I., 88
Andrews,
  Antica, 161
  Eliza Ann, 161
  George, 161
  James William, 161
  Laura, 161
  Sarah, 161
Anthony,
  Catherine Elvira, 81
  Charlotte, 110
  David, 110
  Elijah, 81
  Elijah [Jr], 81
  Hannah, 81
  Hannah [Jr], 81
  Jepther, 81
  Maria Jane, 81
  Melisha, 81
  Nancy, 81, 110
  Nelly Miss, 81
  Noah, 81
  Oliver, 81
  Ophelia, 81
  Sarah Ann, 81
  William, 110
Archie,
  Martha, 153
  William L., 153
Artus,
  Eliza Jane, 55
  Hardy, 57
  Phoebe, 55
Ashby,
  Mary Jr., 55
  Mary Sr., 55
  Richard, 55

B

Bailey,
  Edward, 19
  Sarah, 19
  Silena, 19
Baird,
  Eveline, 148
  Frances, 148
  James, 148
  John, 148
  Martha J., 148
  Wesley, 148
Baker,
  James, 34
  Milly, 85
Baldwin,
  Anna, 10
  Gabriel, 10
Banks,
  Britton, 47
Barbor,
  Archibald, 144
Barker,
  Benjamin F., 38
Barkley,
  James, 37
Barkshire,
  Arthur, 151
  Emily, 151
  Fanny, 151
  Frances, 151
  Garret, 151
  Matilda, 151
  Minerva, 151
  Samuel, 151
  Woodford, 151
Bass,
  Alexander, 47
Baxter,
  Allen C., 155
  Amos, 155
  James [Reves], 149
  John, 28
  Keziah [Reves], 149
  Nancy, 150
  Sabine, 155
Beatty,
  Henry Clinton, 89
  John H. I., 89
  Lydia Ann, 89
Bell,
  Charlie, 81
  David, 80
  Delania, 80
  James M., 150
  John, 81
  Lewis, 80
  Martin, 80
  Nathaniel, 80, 87
Bellier,
  Elizabeth, 120
  John Henry, 120
  Josephine, 120
  Prosper, 120
Bentley,
  Rebecca, 27
Bird,
  Edward, 39
  Eliza Ann, 83
  George Jefferson, 83
  Lucinda E. R., 39
  Mary Ellen, 83
  Peter, 32
  Sarah E., 39
Bishop,
  Amy Hetty Ann, 80
  Mariah, 78
  Mitchell, 78
  Sarah Jane, 80
  Stanford, 80
  Willis Ceraloo, 80
Blackburn,
  Frances, 89
  Mary J., 36
  Robert, 89
Blackwell,
  Juliet A., 38
Bland,
  Austin, 167
  G. V. R., 166
  George, 168
  Sarah Frances, 169

INDEX

Susan, 169
Blanks,
　Christy Ann, 4
　Eli, 4
　Elizabeth, 4
　John, 3
　Willis, 4
Blanton,
　Vina, 161
　William, 161
Blockwell,
　Franklin A., 30
Bolden,
　Daniel, 5
Bolin,
　Anna Elizabeth, 15
Bonds,
　Jno. W., 159
　John, 30
　Monroe, 159
　Penelope, 159
Booker,
　Emma Jane, 146
　George W., 146
　William, 146
Boon,
　Sylvia, 69
Boone,
　Lucinda, 70
Borday,
　John Henry, 89
Boulain,
　Woodward, 89
Boung,
　Thomas, 89
Boyd,
　Peterson, 12
　William R., 12
Brady,
　Henry, 135
　Jane, 135
Brandon,
　Lemuel, 113
Brannon,
　Delelia, 82
　Henry, 82
Braxson,
　Washington, 38
Brayboy,
　Stephen, 47
Brent,
　Carrie A. B., 28
　Julia Ann, 28
　Robert Armstrong, 28
　William D., 28
Brewer,
　Edward, 121
　George, 121
　Mary Ann, 121

Samuel, 121
Briggs,
　Isaac H., 45
Broady,
　John, 89
Brooks,
　Lewis, 127
　Milley, 127
Brown,
　Ann E., 33
　Frances A., 33
　John E. P., 33
　Lew, 89
　Lewis J., 33
　Lucy, 18
　Martha A., 33
　Thomas J., 32
Brunswick,
　George Washington, 120
　Hannah M., 120
　Hester Anne, 119
　James, 118
　Mary, 118
　Nancy Ann, 120
　Ophelia, 119
　Rachael, 119
　Theodore, 120
　Thomas, 119
Brust,
　Danderfield, 11
Bull,
　John, 90
　Joseph S., 90
Bunch,
　Adam, 10
　Charlotte, 20
　Mary A. E., 19
　Nancy, 10
Bunday,
　Henry, 90
Burch,
　Abraham Hamilton, 130
　George, 131
　Henry, 131
　Louisa, 130
　Mary, 131
Burgess,
　Eliza, 128
　Thomas, 128
　Thomas E. W., 128
Burke,
　Cook, 90
Burnett,
　Enoch, 159
　Thomas, 153
Butler,
　Abraham, 142
　Albert, 28
　Benjamin, 142

Bradford, 142
Clarisa, 142
George, 142
Immanuel, 142
James, 142
John, 137
Thomas, 159

C

Campbell,
　Cora E., 28
　Harrison, 146
　Marianna, 25
　Morgan, 29
　Nancy, 29
Carnan,
　Lucy Ann, 142
Carpenter,
　Sarah, 30
　William, 11
Carsey,
　Alexander, 107
　Dennis, 107
　Eliza Jane, 111
　Ephraim, 107
　Ephram, 114
　George, 113
　Hulbert, 113
　Mariah Jane, 113
　Sally, 107
　Stephen, 107
　Willis, 111
Carter,
　Alexander, 90
　Ann M., 44
　Arthur, 140
　Augustus, 127
　Charlotte, 144
　Dean Pruden, 140
　Delphi, 140
　Edward, 40
　Elizabeth L., 125
　Hannibal, 31
　James, 14
　James E., 14
　Jane, 127, 145
　John Williams, 140
　Joseph, 127
　Leonard, 25
　Melinda, 125
　Melissa F., 21
　Mitilda, 145
　Morgan, 90
　Nathaniel, 21
　Peter, 90
　Preston, 44
　Richard, 117

INDEX

Susan, 21
Cary,
  William G., 150
Caster,
  Laura Bell, 36
Causby,
  Susan, 90
  William, 90
Cay,
  Thomas H., 33
Chandler,
  David, 156
  Joyce A., 156
  Leanid, 155
  Martha, 155
  Martha A., 156
  Samuel, 155
  Sina J., 156
Chaplain,
  Charles, 91
  Eason J., 91
  Gabrella, 91
  Mary Catherine, 91
Chavis,
  Banister, 153
  Henry, 153
  Nancy, 154
  Rachel, 154
  Riley, 154
  Sarah, 154
  Thomas, 154
Cheeves,
  John, 59
Cheevis,
  James, 52
  John, 52
  Sarah J., 52
  Saylisa, 64
Christie,
  Augustus R., 167
  Betsy, 167
  Georgia V., 167
  Sampson, 167
  Theodore, 167
  Walter, 167
Christy,
  Albert Asbury, 166
  Elias, 166
  Eliza Ann, 166
  Eliza Jane, 165
  Elvira, 166
  Israel, 165
  Jesse, 165
  John Franklin, 79
  Levin, 165
  Levitha Mabel, 166
  Lucinda, 165
  Mariah Ann, 79
  Sarah E., 166

Sophia, 166
  William, 79
Clair,
  Otha James, 23
Clark,
  Eliza, 120
  Frances, 121
  Frederick, 157
  Henry, 156
  James, 35
  John S., 144
  Lovina Mariah, 121
  Lucy, 157
  Mary, 121
  Milia, 121
  Queen Victoria, 121
  Samuel, 120
  William W.G.W., 121
Clay,
  Eliza B., 35
  Florence B., 35
  Harriet A., 35
  Henrietta, 35
  Henry, 35
  Henry Harrison, 91
  Mary Ann, 35
  William, 91
Claybrook,
  John, 91
Clemens,
  Francis, 154
  Maria, 155
  Martha A., 155
  Mary E., 155
  Nancy Ann, 155
  Sarah J., 155
  William, 155
Clifton,
  John, 43
Clinton,
  Hueston, 66
Cloud,
  David, 166
  John Henry, 166
  Mary Eliza, 167
  Peter, 165
  Roseanne, 166
Clouston,
  Ann M., 36
  Joseph W., 36
Coates,
  James, 67
Coffin,
  Daniel H., 31
  Isabella, 37
  Rebecca A., 37
Cole,
  Henry, 51
  Thomas, 54

Cook,
  Cecilia, 20
  Thomas, 11
Cooper,
  Samuel, 11
Cordron,
  Thomas, 32
Cosby,
  John, 91
Cosley,
  Lucy Ann, 153
Cottee,
  Antone, 121
  Gabriel, 121
  Jefferson, 133
  John, 133
Cousins,
  Cynthiana, 73
  George, 73
  Joseph A., 46, 74
  Mary J., 42
  Thomas, 74
  Wlliam, 74
Cox,
  Elijah, 139
  Fanny Ann, 139
  Isiah, 118
  Jane, 139
  Patsy, 139
  Purlina, 139
  Roseanna, 140
  Thomas, 139
  Uriah, 140
Cozens,
  Elizabeth, 84
  Frances Marion, 84
  George Marshall, 84
  James, 82
  John, 84
  Mary Ann, 83
  Sarah Isabella, 84
  Tabitha, 83
Crider,
  Benjamin, 91
  John Wesley, 92
  Lucinda, 92
Curzy,
  Dolly, 5
  Edward, 5
  Eliza, 5
  John, 5

D

Davidson,
  John, 71
Davis,
  Adaline, 34

INDEX

Eliza Jane, 34
Jesse, 34
John, 34, 135
John Edward, 145
Joshua, 135
Louisa I., 135
Margaret, 145
Martin, 34
Davis,
  Mary, 34
  Rebecky Ann, 131
  Richard L., 145
  Sarah, 145
  Thomas, 135
  William, 34
Day,
  Elizabeth, 119
  Jesse, 119
  Margaret, 119, 121
  Mary, 119
  Wilson, 119
Deal,
  Parthenia, 19
Dean,
  Sandy, 92
Demar,
  Elizabeth, 167
DeMarrs,
  Sina D., 167
DeMars,
  Margaret B., 44
  Sina, 44
Demines,
  John, 37
Dennis,
  Enoch Wagoner, 108
  James Walter, 108
  John William, 107
  Margaret, 114
  Margaret Ann, 108
  Mary Eliza, 108
  Peter, 107
  Robert Maxwell
    Johnson, 108
  Sarah Elizabeth, 107
Dericoat,
  Absolom, 92
Devol,
  Anna Bell, 43
  Martha J., 43
  Pleasant, 43
Ditto,
  Edward, 92
Dixon,
  Samuel, 77
Dockery,
  Cain, 86
  Hannah, 86
Donaldson,

Dary, 47
Dove,
  Mary J., 40
  William A., 40
Dubois,
  Albert, 128
  Alice A., 128
  James, 128
Dudley,
  Alice Ann, 85
  Henry, 84
  Lawney, 82
  Malinda Jane, 84
  Martha Ann, 84
  Melissa, 84
  Nicey, 82
  Sally, 82
  Sarah, 84
  William, 84
Duncan,
  Jane Maria, 14
  Patsy Ann, 24
  Robert, 144
  Solomon, 10
Dungill,
  Betsy Jane, 15
  Wright, 156
Dunlop,
  Jane, 112
  Martha, 112
  Nancy, 112
  Peter, 112
  William, 112
Dye,
  Acquilla Anna, 108
  Daniel, 108
  James William, 108
  Nancy Jane, 108

E

Eddington,
  Gustavus, 151
  Harriet, 151
Edington,
  Gustavus I., 48
Edwards,
  Grace, 116
  William, 17
  Wm. W., 4, 41
Ellington,
  Nelson, 92
Ember,
  Eli, 141
  Ellen, 141
  James Anderson, 141
  Joseph, 141
  Josephine, 141

  Mary, 141
  Mary Elizabeth, 141
  Mary L., 141
  Matthias, 141
  Sarah [nee: Butler],
    141
  Tobitha, 117
  William H., 145
Embers,
  Charles H., 125
  Mariam A., 125
  Sarah H., 124
  Thomas C., 125
  William P. Q., 124
Ergum,
  Anthony, 32
Eustis,
  Hugh, 18
Evans,
  Matilda, 169
  William L., 62
  William T., 92
  Zebidee, 111

F

Fant,
  Willis, 47
Farmer,
  Charles, 118
  Dianna, 118
  Edith, 118
  London, 118
  Nancy Jane, 118
Ferguson,
  Tabitha, 53
Findley,
  Caroline, 37
  Elias, 33
  Elias T., 28
  Emily, 36
  James W., 33
  Mary Jane, 34
Finley,
  Alexander D., 24
  Almyra, 70
  Andrew J., 43
  Bell, 71
  Caroline, 69
  Catherine, 15, 26
  Charles H. W., 24
  Claridge U. A., 24
  Cornelia A., 28
  Dicey, 70
  Eliza Ann, 70, 71
  George, 12
  Hardin, 17, 25
  Harriet Ellen, 69

INDEX

Hellena, 24
Isaac, 26, 68
James, 26, 43
James S., 43
James W., 24
Jasper, 44
John, 12, 15, 73
Julia, 44
Julia Ann, 26
Lewis, 70
Lucinda J., 24
Martha, 24
Martin, 17
Mary, 24
Mary A., 35
Mary Ann, 43
Mary C., 26
Mary J., 24
Mary Margaret, 69
May C., 44
Milley, 69
Nancy, 34
Nathaniel, 70, 72
Newton, 45
Oilsey, 69
Othello, 24
Paul, 46
Peter, 32
Preston, 24
Randolph T., 24
Rebecca, 70
Richard R., 23
Solon, 69
Susannah, 23
Thomas J., 24
Virginia, 44
Wesley, 36
William H., 24
William Preston, 71
Fisher,
  Alice, 36
  Margaret, 45
  May, 45
  Nelson, 45
  William, 45
Flinn,
  Anna, 18
  Edmonia D., 40
  James, 18
  Louisa, 18
  Martha, 40
  Mary Ellen, 18
  Samuel, 18
  Samuel S., 18
  Zion, 18
Ford,
  James, 29
Foree,
  Eliza J., 28

Forson,
  John R., 92
Foster,
  John, 19
Fowles,
  John C. N., 34
Franklin,
  Benjamin, 15
  Jane, 38
Free,
  Lydia, 75
Freeman,
  Archibald, 47
  Crankey, 13
  Henry, 16
  James H., 16
  Jane, 16
  John H., 17
  John S., 16
  Mary L., 16
  Sarah Jane, 16
French,
  Gideon, 92
  Strawder, 93
  William, 93
Fuller,
  John, 26, 31
Fulton,
  James, 19
  Patty, 19

G

Galbreath,
  Dianah, 3
  Edmund, 3
Gardner,
  Harriet Jane, 93
  Isaac, 93
George,
  Eliza, 35
  Frances, 35
  Violette, 152
Gering,
  William, 93
Gibson,
  Susan, 29
Gill,
  Catherine, 129
Gillimn,
  Jacob, 169
Glascoe,
  Charles Green, 57
  Clarissa Emeline, 57
  Harriet, 56
  Mary, 65
  Townsend, 56
Goen,

  Adam A., 39
  Elizabeth, 39
  Jesse, 39
  John, 39
Goens,
  Harriet, 38
  Isabella, 43
Goings,
  Anderson, 16
  George, 86
  John, 86
  Nancy, 85, 86
  Napoleon, 65
  Phebe, 86
Goins,
  Claiborne, 44
  Elisha, 168
  Henry, 22
  John A., 168
  Sinajane, 160
Goodwin,
  Willis, 168
Gordon,
  Albert, 137
  Andrew, 136
  Catherine, 136
  Elizabeth, 137
  Hannah, 137
  Hannah [II], 137
  Harrison, 137
  Joseph, 136
  Martin, 137
  Sarah, 136
  William, 137
Gould,
  Anthony, 127
Graham,
  Lucy Ann, 63
  Martha A., 65
  Morris R. W., 63
  Washington, 63
  William, 46
Granville,
  William, 136
Graves,
  Samuel, 133
  William, 147
Gray,
  Eliza, 42
Green,
  Charles Lewis, 60
  Samuel, 62
Greenlee,
  Emanuel G., 26
  George G., 12
  Harriet M., 12
  Mary, 12
  Mary E., 12
  Sarah J., 12

INDEX

Susan E., 12
William J., 12
William P. Q., 12
Greer,
 Allen, 50
 Ann, 50
 Charles, 64
 Elizabeth, 67
 Harriet Caroline, 50
 Henry, 50
 John, 64
 Kasiah, 64
 Martha, 50
 Mary Jane, 67
 Mary Lizer, 50
 William M., 65
 Willis, 50
 Zilpy, 50
Grey,
 Granderson, 93
Griffin,
 Isaac, 93
 Kenoway, 13
Guthrie,
 James, 157

H

Haden,
 George W., 26
Hagen,
 Rachael, 35
Halton,
 Charles, 93
Hamby,
 Harrison, 67
Hamlet,
 Ann Eldora, 94
 Anna, 93
 George, 94
Hancock,
 John, 37
Handy,
 William H., 25
Harden,
 William H., 149
 Wilson P., 150
Hardgrave,
 Charles David
  Vandamore, 94
 Peter, 94
Hardiman,
 Martha, 56
Harding,
 Edward, 41
 Eliza, 41
 Joseph, 41
 Sarah, 41

Sullivan G., 41
Virginia I. H., 41
William, 41
Harper,
 Alexander, 20
 Barbara A., 20
 Benjamin, 13
 Elizabeth, 14
 Grigg, 110
 Henry, 20, 32
 James, 14
 Jane, 111
 John, 14
 John W., 40
 Lucinda, 39
 Martha A., 20
 Middleton, 20
 Nancy Ann, 42
 Patsey, 39
 Rebecca, 20
 Riley, 109
 Sally, 20
 Sarah A., 40
 Sylvania, 40
 Thomas, 109
 William, 20
Harris,
 Ann Marie, 94
 Beverly, 11
 Chapman, 94
 Chapman M., 94
 Charles Walker, 94
 Clarietta, 11
 Daniel, 94
 Elizabeth, 61
 Elwiza, 95
 Enoch, 11
 George Henry, 95
 Gertrude, 95
 Henry, 5, 95
 Josephine, 61
 Lutitia, 61
 Mahala, 11
 Mary Elizabeth, 95
 Maston, 95
 Nancy A., 61
 Patsey Ann, 95
 Paulina, 11
 Phoebe, 30
 Richard, 11
 Theodore, 95
 Thomas, 11
 Virginia, 11
 Virginia A., 95
 William, 61
 William Henry, 30
Hart,
 John O., 160
 Pleasant, 149

Hatcher,
 George W. Griffith, 8
 John, 8
 Sophia, 8
Hattaway,
 John, 157
Hawkins,
 Jacob, 148
 Jer, 157
 Joseph, 18
 Nancy, 27
 Philip, 29
Hay,
 Albert, 131
 Frances, 131
 Jesse, 117
 Peter L., 131
 William Henry, 131
Hayden,
 George W., 26
Hays,
 Elva C., 27
 James, 47
 Sarah Frances, 27
 Shadrick, 27
Heard,
 Jonathan, 29
Henderson,
 Harrison, 112
 Leonidus M., 37
 Samuel, 37
 Shadrick, 26
 Taburn, 52
Henry,
 Thomas I., 114
Hill,
 Abraham, 3
 Abraham Augustus, 6
 Agrippa, 113
 Ananis, 110
 Andrew Jackson, 6
 Andy, 139
 Bluford A., 111
 Catharine, 6
 Francis, 139
 George, 139
 Hester, 139
 Jefferson, 114
 Lewis, 113
 Mary Ann, 115
 Mary Eveline, 6
 Moses Hansham, 139
 Nancy, 139
 Susan Henrietta, 6
Hillgem,
 Osborne, 26
Hilyard,
 James K. 43
Holley,

INDEX

Nancy, 49
Rode, 48
Sanford, 49
Sarah, 49
Hollon,
  Jack, 44
  Joseph, 37
Holmes,
  John, 55
  Rachel, 60
Holton,
  Joseph, 96
Hood,
  Ephraim, 115
  Fanny, 116
  Hannibal, 116
  James H., 115
  John, 111
  Josiah, 48
  Lucinda J., 15
  Mary, 116
  Robert, 11
  Rosanna, 27
  William, 25, 115
Hord,
  Mary Ann, 34
Howard,
  Charles, 122
  Elizabeth M., 122
  John, 122
  Mary, 122
  Nancy Jane, 124
  Rosana, 122
  Thomas, 122
  Thomas Frederick, 30
  William, 122
Hubbard,
  Jeremiah, 96
Hubbs,
  Aaron, 136
  Benjamin, 136
  Eliza Ann, 136
  Elizabeth, 136
  Judy, 136
  Mary Ann, 129
  Robert, 136
Hueston,
  Joseph, 60
Hullman,
  Jasper, 110
Hunt,
  Mary Elizabeth, 57
  Sarah, 50
  William Calvin, 57
Hursh,
  Moses B., 18
Hurst,
  Anna Belle, 12
Husbands,

Aisley, 154
Laura, 159
Huttals,
  Elijah F., 96

I

Irwin,
  George, 150

J

Jackson
  Amelia, 33
  Andrew, 33
  Andrew Leroy, 33
  Eliza, 130
  Elizabeth, 130
  George W., 130
  Hannah, 130
  Henrietta, 170
  Henry, 96
  John, 130
  John Henry, 169
  Louisa, 130
  Margaret, 130
  Martha, 170
  Mary, 170
  Missy, 26
  Sarah M., 33
  Thomas, 170
Jacobs,
  Charles, 96
  James, 36
  Sarah C., 36
Jamison,
  Mary Ann, 21
Jenkins,
  Ann, 19
Jenks,
  Ellen, 27
Johnson,
  Alice, 146
  Andrew J., 157
  Catharine, 157
  Cecilia, 21
  Charlotte, 23
  David, 96
  George W., 23
  James, 96
  Jane, 96
  Jno. W., 157
  Judah, 114
  Louiza, 7
  Lovina, 157
  Mary, 23, 114

Mary A., 41
Richard, 9
Sarah E., 157
Sarah Esther, 115
Thomas L., 114
William H., 157
Jones,
  Ann Eliza Jane, 63
  Cornelia, 63
  Elizabeth, 60
  Enoch, 1, 57
  Hester Ann, 96
  Irvin, 1
  John, 63
  Lucinda, 2
  Lucy Ann, 1
  Martha J., 40
  Mary H., 2
  Minerva Ann, 63
  Octavia, 63
  Oliver, 2
  Pamela, 63
  Thomas, 2
  William Riley, 1
  Willis, 2
  Wm. R. Jr., 2
Jordan,
  Charles Emery, 164
  Charlotte, 164
  Isaac, 164
Justice,
  Henry, 35

K

Keller,
  Ephraim, 35
  John, 11
  William R., 35
King,
  Alexander, 51
  Araminta, 58
  Eliza Jane, 58
  Emiline, 114
  James Henry, 59
  Jane, 115
  Lucy Ann, 58
  Mary Amanda, 59
  Nancy Louisa, 58
  Spencer, 114
  Spencer Beverly, 114
  Washington, 43
Knight,
  Aaron, 124, 147
  Alevia, 124
  George, 119
  Miriam, 125
  Relivis, 124

INDEX

Knowland,
  Samuel, 125

L

Lamb,
  Hiram, 84
Lamount,
  Charles Emmanuel, 146
  Fanny Ann, 131
  George, 145
  George Washington, 145
  James Franklin, 146
  John Henry, 145
  Martha Jane, 145
  William Edward, 145
Landers,
  Cordelia, 129
Lane,
  W. C., 142
Lee,
  Aaron, 152
  Ellen, 109
  Esther, 166
  Hetta, 152
  Isaiah, 152
  James, 67
  John Wesley, 62
  Joseph, 152
  Margaret Jane, 43
  Polly Ann, 152
  William, 116
Leevy,
  Alexander, 4
Lewis,
  Charlotte, 134
  Daphana, 134
  Edward, 134
  Hannah, 135
  Ledia, 134
  Lucey, 134
  Lucy, 134
  Margaret E., 134
  Maria, 134
  Mary Jane, 134
  William, 38, 118
Like,
  Jacob, 51
Lingle,
  Dudley A., 154
Links,
  James E., 13
Lochler,
  John, 26
Locklayer,
  Amanda, 9
  Amanda J., 39
  James, 9
  Lukey, 9
  Thomas, 9
  Victoria, 9
Lockler,
  Alice, 26
Lofton,
  Alice Victoria, 147
  Ellen, 147
  Monroe P., 147
  Nancy Jane, 147
Loggan,
  Milly, 149
Loggin,
  Isaiah, 149
  Levi, 149
  Millford, 149
Long,
  John Wesley, 63
  Martha Ann J., 62
  Noah, 62
  Sarah J., 62
  Seption, 62
  Solomon, 63
Lott,
  Cyrus Baptist, 97
  Henry, 97
  John [II], 97
  John [I], 97
Louis,
  Frank, 140
  Louisan, 140
Lowery,
  Sampson, 26
Lucas,
  Angeline, 20
  Ellen, 20
  Elmina, 20
  Harriet, 20
  James, 20
  Julia Ann, 57
  Milton, 20
  Parmelia, 20
  Pleasant, 20
  Rebecca, 20
  Sarah Ann, 22
Lyles,
  Alfred, 55
  Angeline, 54
  Anna, 56
  Arra Jane, 65
  Arthelea, 54
  Barbara J., 55
  Casindany, 64
  Clapanty[Cleopatra], 53
  Drucilla, 54
  Eleanor, 55
  Isaac, 54
  Isabella, 58
  Jacob, 54
  James William, 66
  Jefferson, 60
  Jethro, 63
  Joel, 53
  John Thomas, 55
  Jonathan, 54
  Joseph, 53
  Joshua, 53
  Joshua Jr., 54
  Louisa, 55
  Mahala, 54
  Malinda, 61, 64
  Mary Ann, 55
  Mary Elizabeth, 56
  Mary Ellen, 53
  Mildred, 53
  Orvilla, 65
  Peggy Ann, 54
  Rachel E., 66
  Tabitha Elizabeth, 58
  William Henry, 55
  William M., 64
  Wilson, 65
Lynch,
  Harmon, 154
  Martha, 159
  Mila, 159

M

McCallister,
  Elizabeth, 59
  James, 59
  Rebecca, 59
  William Henry, 60
McCan,
  Peter, 51
McCloud,
  Marshall, 152
McCoppin,
  Marshall, 109
  Sarah, 109
McDaniel,
  Duncan, 62
  Emily Ann, 60
  Henderson Green, 63
  Jane C., 64
  Margaret, 63
  Thomas, 62
McGill,
  Arabella, 126
  Arthur, 125
  George A., 126
  Isiah, 126
  Jernene, 126
  Leaver C., 125

INDEX

Mary C., 126
Rachel, 126
McGilpin,
  Lucinda, 118
  Yorich, 118
McGraw,
  David, 147
McGreger,
  Joanna, 128
McGregory,
  John Nelson, 130
McGriffin,
  David, 147
McIntosh,
  Anna, 21
  Elizabeth, 21
  Husson, 21
  Janie, 21
  Mary F., 21
  William, 21
Macie,
  Rhoda, 152
Mackney,
  James William, 161
Madden,
  Daniel, 11
Malary,
  Elisha B., 65
  James W., 65
  Maria, 65
Mallard,
  Jeremiah, 67
Malone,
  Emaline, 140
Manly,
  Burkett, 22
  Charles, 22
  Elizabeth, 22
  James, 22
  John, 22
  Medora, 22
  Sarah, 22
  Sylvia, 22
  Thomas, 22
  William, 22
Martin,
  Ann E., 97
  Sarah Ellen, 97
  Thomas Jefferson, 97
Mason,
  Peter Hampton, 97
Massey,
  Susan, 15
Massie,
  Everett, 13
  George, 14
  Hiram D., 14
  Maria, 13
  Mary L., 13

Mayberry,
  John Alexander, 97
  William A., 168
Mayhoe,
  Drury, 9, 42
  Minerva, 42
  Nancy, 42
  William, 42
Means,
  Fanny L., 157
Medad,
  Edward, 19
  Emma, 16
Menows,
  Frances, 10
Merrill,
  Harry, 38
  Sarah, 38
Miles,
  Susan, 54
  Virginia, 53
Miller,
  Ann Mariah, 98
  Gabriel, 98
  James Trevan, 163
  Mariah, 98
  Sarah Ellen, 98
  Susan, 98
  Walter P., 18
Milton,
  Alexander, 31
  Cynthia Ann, 30
  Martha A., 17
Mitchell,
  Alvin, 77
  Burgess, 77
  Francis, 82
  Harrison, 82
  Hiram, 83
  John, 77
  Laura Ann, 82
  Martin, 98
  Mary Maranda, 83
  Milton, 85
  Priscilla, 6
  Samuel, 87
  Sarah, 82
  Serena, 85
  William, 83
Mitchem,
  Amelia M., 33
  Beverly L., 34
  Catherine, 10
  Charity E., 29
  Charles, 4, 45
  Clara C., 4, 42
  Daniel, 30
  Dedda A., 42
  Delphy, 41

  Edward, 45
  Ellen, 42
  Florence, 38
  Frances, 37
  Jacob, 28
  James N., 30
  Jane E., 10
  John D., 38
  Josephine, 45
  Lucinda Jane, 39
  Malinda, 33
  Mary Ann, 39
  Mary Susan, 38
  Moses, 30
  Richard H. L., 34
  Sarah Jane, 41
  Thomas A., 38
  Thompson, 32
  Wilson, 31
  Winney, 34
  Zachariah, 29
Mitchum,
  Aaron, 27
  Abraham, 18
  Allison, 26
  Amelia Ann, 27
  Amelia R., 27
  Andrew, 68
  Aquila R., 23
  Bright, 68
  Catharine, 71, 72
  Cyrus, 73
  David, 72
  Dumont, 71
  Edward, 27
  Elizabeth, 13
  Emanuel, 68
  George, 70
  George T., 23
  Hannah, 13
  Harriet, 18
  Harrison, 13
  Henry, 15
  Isiah, 71
  James H., 74
  John, 71
  John Dumont, 72
  John S., 23
  Johnson, 12
  Jonathan, 68
  Joseph, 68
  Joseph H. H., 23
  Julie Ann, 69
  Lewis, 12
  Loyd, 68
  Lucinda, 71
  Martha, 69
  Matilda, 13, 22
  Middleton, 71

INDEX

Mitchell, 71
Molly, 70
Monian, 68
Rhoda, 74
Si, 22
Thomas, 68
Virgin Mary, 69
Washington, 11
William A., 22
Mooreland,
  Edward, 64
  Peter Wright, 64
  William, 64
Morgan,
  James Wesley, 48
  Joseph, 48
  Matthew, 47
  Nancy, 48
  Sophonia Ann, 48
Morris,
  Batch, 82
  Elizabeth, 50
  George P., 128
  James F., 32
  Louisa V., 32
  Mary Elizabeth, 50
  Polly, 83
  William D., 32
  William W., 32
Moss,
  Elizabeth Jane, 75
  John Watson, 75
  Lydia, 75
  Lydia Ellen Lavina, 75
  Nathan, 75
  Thurzey C., 75
  William, 152
  William Henry, 75
Mukes,
  Fanny, 25
  George, 25
  Isaac, 17
  John, 25
  Reuben, 25
Muncey,
  Enos, 31
Munick,
  Anthony, 13
  James, 13

N

Nash,
  Alexander, 54
  John Calvin, 55
  Margaret, 54
Nelson,
  Leroy, 17
Nettles,
  Andrew J., 98
  Raimus, 98
Newby,
  Alexander, 163
  Alfred, 78
  Amanda, 164
  Bishop Parks, 79
  Caroline, 79
  Catherine Elvina, 78
  David, 77
  Edmund, 77
  Elizabeth Mariah, 79
  Emaline, 155
  Geo. J., 155
  Henry, 78(2)
  Isaiah, 78
  Isaiah Harrison, 86
  James, 77, 116, 155
  Jemima, 6
  John, 6
  Joseph Henry, 164
  Levi, 77
  Louisa Emeline, 86
  Lucinda, 155
  Margaret, 155
  Margaret Ellen, 86
  Martha, 163
  Martha Ann, 77
  Mary Ann Elvira, 86
  Mathew, 79
  Moses W., 155
  Nancy Jane, 78
  Penina, 6
  Penniah, 163
  Priscilla Ellen, 163
  Robert, 163
  Sarah Isabel, 86
  Solomon, 155
  Sophia, 79
  Thomas Edward, 79
  Thompson, 78, 163
  William George, 163
  Willis, 79
  Zilpha, 78
Newsom,
  Emily, 111
Newton,
  Charles, 138
  Frances, 138
  Jessey, 138
  Mary Elizabeth, 138
  Nathaniel, 117
  Percilia, 123
  Percilla, 138
  Peter, 141
  Rose Ann, 139
  Sarah Elizabeth, 138
  William H., 138
Nivey,
  Elizabeth, 162
  Elizabeth Frances, 162
  Isaac, 161
  Isaac [Jr], 162
  James, 162
  John, 162
  Margaret Jane, 162
  Milla Ann, 162
Nolcox,
  Elizabeth G., 58
  John Weston, 58
  Louisa, 58
  Mary Jane, 58
  Nancy Sue, 58
  Weston, 58
Nolton,
  Edward, 98
Noon,
  Calvin, 99
Norman,
  Augustus, 109
  Nancy, 109
  Willie, 109

O

Oaks,
  Henietta, 133
Oliver,
  Benjamin, 59
  Jacob, 59
  Lewis, 59
  Lucy, 59
  Mary Ann, 59
  Nancy Jane, 59
  Sarah, 59
Osborn,
  Thomas, 7
Oswell,
  Wright, 69
Overstreet,
  David, 99
  Edward, 99
  Gracey Ann, 99
  Mary Jane, 99
  Samuel, 99
  William [II], 99
  William [I], 99
Owen,
  William, 99
Oxendine,
  Daniel, 1
  Priscilla Jane, 8
  Sarah L., 8
  Senith, 8

INDEX

P

Parham,
  Algeria, 31
  Alzera, 45
  George H., 31
  James, 4, 31, 45
  James B., 45
  James F., 45
  Joseph A., 45
  Victoria E., 45
Parker,
  Delila, 131
  Eliza Jane, 164
  Elizabeth Jane, 85
  Flora, 85
  George S., 165
  George W., 164
  Isaac, 85
  Isaac Jr., 85
  James Henry, 165
  Louise Jane, 165
  Marietta, 165
  Mary Ann, 85
  Moses, 77
  Priscilla, 85
  Thompson, 85
  Wright, 85
Parks,
  Amy, 78
Parsons,
  James W., 29
Patridge,
  Nancy Ann, 83
  Richard, 85
Patten,
  Mary Jane, 52
  Sally, 52
Payne,
  Oliver, 31
  William Henry, 31
Pell,
  Alexander, 16
  Ann Wasuba, 12
  Mary Frances, 12
Penn,
  Nancy, 83
  Sally, 83
  William, 83
Perkins,
  Louisa, 126
  Sarah E., 125
  Thomas E., 125
Perry,
  Gilly Ann, 62
  Nelson, 62
Pettiford,
  Drury, 110

Phillips,
  Cynthia, 111
  Elzora, 111
  Emily, 111
  Henry, 110
  Jesse, 113
  Joseph, 113
  Rosa, 110
  Silvester, 113
  Stephen, 113
  Wesly, 113
Pierson,
  Ann, 76
  Charles, 76
  Daniel, 75
  Jane, 76(2)
  Lewis, 76
Porter,
  Ann, 19
  Laderia Ann, 36
  Mary Jane, 27
Posey,
  Hester, 133
  Isedore, 134
  Jane, 133
  Mary, 134
  Thomas, 133
  Thomas [Jr], 134
  William, 134
Potter,
  Clarkey, 164
  George W., 164
  John H., 164
  Joseph, 164
  Richmond, 164
Price,
  James, 38
Purier,
  Charles, 118
  David, 120
  Eliza, 146
  Francis, 119
  Francis Jr., 119, 120
  George, 120
  Henry, 118
  James, 117
  James Thomas, 147
  Jane, 146
  Rachel, 146
  Samuel, 146
  Sarah, 146
  Sylvia, 117
  Tousant, 117
  Tousant Jr., 119
Purier (Lamount),
  Nancy, 146
Purrier,
  Susan [Carter], 145
Purry,

  Charles, 132
  Elizabeth, 132
  George, 132

R

Reaves,
  Nathaniel, 149
Reed,
  Francis, 32
Reese,
  George, 32
Rendand,
  Frances, 35
Reves,
  James, alias Baxter, 149
  Keziah, alias Baxter, 149
Rhea,
  Morris, 53
Richae,
  Eliza F. Isidore, 138
Richard,
  William, 41
Richards,
  Hannah, 40
  James, 19
  Jonnetta, 40
  Susan, 40
Richardson,
  Mahala, 166
Richea,
  Aaron, 137
  Abraham, 138
  Charles E., 138
  Daniel, 137
  George W., 138
  Hannah, 137
  John, 138
  Sarah Elizabeth, 138
  William H., 137
Richey,
  Aaron, 132
  Abraham, 137
  Archey, 132
  Daniel, 135
  George, 135
  Indiana, 132
  Lemiza, 135
  Rollins, 135
  Sarah, 132
  Sarah C., 135
  William, 135
Richie,
  Frances, 136
Rickman,
  Anna Belle, 15

INDEX

Edward, 25
Eliza, 15
Hezikiah, 15
Jarmin, 150
Shadrach, 15
Thomas J., 150
William E., 15
Rider,
  Hannah, 142
Rielor,
  Barbar, 42
Roach,
  James, 12
Robbins,
  Catherine, 142
Roberts,
  Abraham [II], 100
  Abraham [I], 99
  Allen, 157
  Anna, 156
  Archie, 156
  Benjamin, 154
  Bryant, 157
  Elias, 64, 153
  Elisha, 100
  Eliza J., 153
  Elmira, 65
  Enoch, 100
  Giliann, 159
  James, 156, 168
  James [Jr], 156
  Jno. L., 159
  Jnoth P., 157
  John, 153
  Joseph, 65
  Juletta, 65
  Lucretia, 156
  Martha M., 156
  Mary, 157
  Mary C., 157
  Mary Jane, 65
  Nancy, 153
  Sarah, 64, 157
  Sarah C., 156
  Susan, 64
  Timothy [II], 100
  Timothy [I], 100
  Unity, 156
  Wiley, 157
  William R., 159
  Zachariah, 153
Robertson,
  Harriet, 28
  Irenia, 13
Robinson,
  Calvin, 62
  James R., 100
  Paris T., 29
Robison,

Alice J., 30
Rollins,
  Andrew, 140
  Daniel, 142
  Elias, 143
  Frances Cornelia, 143
  George H., 143
  Harriet Arvilla, 143
  James D., 143
  John, 143
  Madora M., 143
  Margaret Amelia, 143
  Martha Ann, 143
  Mary Elizabeth, 143
  Paul, 143
  Sarah C., 143
  William, 16, 19
  William I., 117
Rolls,
  Rachel, 68
Ross,
  Eli, 23
  Jerome, 23
  John, 19
  Mary, 27
  Peter, 22, 23
  Solomon, 23
  Thomas, 27
Runnells,
  Richard, 10
  Washington R., 10
Runnolds,
  Caroline, 17
  Cecelia, 17
  Evaline, 17
  Frances, 17
  Zachariah J., 17
Rusk,
  Abraham, 133
  Andrew, 133
  Eliza Ann, 133
  Fanny, 133
  Harriet, 53
  James Benjamin, 133
  Morris, 53
  Robert, 53
  Sarah Ann, 133
  Sarah E., 53
Russel,
  Emeline, 51
  James M., 52
  Solomon, 52, 55
  Wooddy, 52
Russell,
  James, 10
  Levi T. 46
  Louisa A., 10
  Maria, 100

S

Sanders,
  Andrew, 130
  Belle W., 24
  Dora, 129
  Elija, 23
  John, 129
  Laura, 129
  Martha, 129
  Nancy, 129
  Robert, 129
  Sarah, 129
  Victoria, 24
  William, 129
  William [Jr], 130
Satters,
  Julia Ann, 147
Scott,
  Alfred, 158
  Alvin, 158
  Berry, 158
  Daniel I., 160
  Darling, 17
  Doctor F., 160
  Elizabeth, 158, 160
  George, 17
  Isaac, 159
  Jemima, 160
  John, 26
  John M., 159
  Joseph, 159
  Joseph K., 160
  Martha J., 158
  Martin Sr., 159
  Needham L., 160
  Philip, 47
  Ruel, 158
  Sanders J., 160
  Sarah H., 158
  Zachariah L., 160
Shafer,
  John C., 100
Shaw,
  Sarah Jane, 32
Short,
  Henry, 48. 49
  Jane, 49
Sibley,
  Henry, 48
Silence,
  Emanuel, 144
  Frances, 144
  Jacob, 143
  James Irvin, 144
  John, 144
  Lydia, 144
  Mariam, 136

INDEX

Teresa, 144
William, 144
Simeril,
  Mary F., 27
Simmons,
  Betsy Ann, 7
  Caroline, 7
  James, 7
  James B., 101
  John T., 101
  Lawson, 8
  Margaret, 7
  Mary Ann, 7
  Meredith, 8
  Rebecca Frances, 101
  Sarah Jane, 7
  Susan, 7
  Thomas S., 101
  Wm. Lawson, 7
Simonton,
  Catherine, 15
  Charles Fielding, 15
  Elizabeth, 15
Simrall,
  David, 29
  Sally, 29
Sims,
  Charles, 123
  Charlotte, 123
  Cornelius, 122
  Daniel, 18, 35
  Eleanor, 123
  Elizabeth, 122
  George W., 123
  Mary Ann, 35
  Priscilla Jane, 123
  Sarah, 123
  Thomas J., 123
  William, 123
Smith,
  Benjamin, 48
  Emily, 132
  Martha A., 45
  Mary Elizabeth, 132
  Sarah Frances, 132
  William, 147
Solters,
  Eneas Augusta, 123
  Indiana, 123
  Tobias, 123
Soven,
  James Henry, 53
Soyde,
  Jacob Wesley, 82
  Susan Amanda, 82
Spencer,
  Charles, 11
Springs,
  Eliza, 131

Henry I., 117
Isabell, 132
James E., 131
Judea, 117
Margaret, 132
William, 132
Stafford,
  Martha E., 115
  Polly, 101
  Richard, 115
  Stepney, 101
Stapp,
  Amerierd, 101
  Amstead, 101
  Horace, 101
  Washington, 101
Stephenson,
  Charles, 67
  Ellen, 67
  Jacob, 57
  James Wesley, 57
  Robert, 67
Stewart,
  Catherine, 17
  Celetina, 17
  Elijah, 51
  Elizabeth, 16
  Elizabeth Ann, 57
  Henry H., 126
  Joel, 51
  Keziah, 126
  Levina, 16
  Lucy, 51
  Maezina, 18
  Martha Jane, 18
  Mary Ellen, 16
  Mary Louisa, 51
  Mathew, 56, 126
  Nancy Ann, 57
  Rhoda Ann, 126
  Solomon, 51
  Susan, 57
  Thomas, 16
  Turther, 16
  Uriah, 16
  William H., 126
  William Henry, 51
  Yorich G., 126
Stonestreet,
  Benjamin, 102
  Emily Jane, 102
  Margaret, 102
  Martha, 102
  Mary, 102(2)
  Mary Ann, 102
  Nancy, 102
Strawder,
  Rhoda, 163
Stubblefield,

Samuel, 19
Sweat,
  Mary Ann, 156
  Nancy, 156

T

Taylor,
  Ann Eliza, 102
  Charles W., 102
  Charles William, 103
  Elizabeth, 103
  Harriett, 131
  Henry, 147
  Hiram, 159
  John, 37, 103
  Jonathan, 24
  Kingburry, 103
  Rebecca J., 37
  Sarah Ann, 103
  William M., 103
  William M. [II], 103
Terrell,
  William, 13
Terrill,
  Benjamin L., 14
  Elijah, 14
  Josephine C., 14
  Lewis, 14
  Nancy Ann, 14
  Patsy, 14
  Paul H., 14
Thergood,
  Barbra, 10
  Henry, 10
  Henry [Jr], 10
  Mary Catharine, 10
  Rebecca Jane, 10
  Zachariah, 10
Thomas,
  Abraham, 124
  Adaline S. E., 154
  Benjamin, 30
  Benjamin T., 158
  Candis, 158
  Charlotte, 144
  Edward, 117
  Elias W., 153
  Eliza, 124
  Elizabeth, 25
  Harriet, 25
  Isabella, 25
  Jeremiah, 154
  John H., 154
  Jordan, 158
  Joseph, 24, 154
  Joseph [Jr], 25
  Laura, 124

INDEX

Mary, 154
Mary A., 154
Mary E., 158
Mathew, 154
Nancy, 153
Sally, 144
Samina A., 153
Sarah A., 154
Sarah Louise, 124
William, 124, 154
William A., 158
Thomason,
  Charles, 103
Thompson,
  Frank, 11
Thornton,
  Austin, 104
  Henry, 104
Tivis,
  Nelson, 6
Todd,
  Amanda J., 158
  Elizabeth, 104
  Hiram H., 158
  John E., 158
  Malvina, 158
  Mary Eliza, 104
  Morris B., 158
  Pearson, 158
  Thomas Jefferson, 104
  William H., 104
  William P. Q., 158
Tolbert,
  Elias, 31
  Eliza J., 31
Toliver,
  George, 129
Tolliver,
  George, 28
Townsell,
  Lucinda, 25
Townsend,
  Job, 40
Truitt,
  Absolom, 12
Turman,
  Clarissa, 3
  Harry, 3
  Henry, 5
  James, 4
  Samuel, 5
Turner,
  George Washington, 127
  Hester, 127
  Rachel, 127
  Redford E., 9
  Sarah Louisa, 127
  Synthia P. Ann, 127

Theodore, 127
Washington Louis, 127
Tyree,
  Joseph Henry, 104
  Moses, 104

V

Valentine,
  Andrew, 109
  Caroline, 112
  James, 112
  Jesse, 112
  Martha, 112
  Samuel, 112
Vanderburg,
  Mary S., 13
  Sarah H., 13
Vickery,
  Addis, 115
  Allen, 115
  Emily, 104
  James, 109
  Mary Ann, 105
  Oliver, 115
  Rhoda, 109
Vinager,
  Ann Margaret, 148

W

Wadkins,
  John W., 41
  William, 41
Walden,
  Berry, 60
  Green Jackson, 56
  Henry D., 56
  James Warren, 56
  John W., 60
  Lucy, 56
  Lydia Ann, 56
Waldon,
  Henry, 52
Walker,
  Abraham, 123
  Charles, 159
  Christiana, 124
  Jane, 159
  Lyman T., 124
Wallace,
  Elias, 112
  Isaiah, 115
Waller,
  J. W., 121

James, 122
John W., 122
Keziah, 122
Lydia, 122
Ward,
  John, 37
  Mary Jane, 38
Washington,
  Cecilia A., 21
  Elizabeth, 21
  Emma U., 21
  George, 25
Waters,
  Ellen, 82
  William, 82
Watson,
  Cornelius, 15
  Jane, 133
  Joseph S., 16
  Martha J., 40
  Nancy L., 16
  Willis, 73
Weaver,
  Arthur, 42
  Clemenda, 156
  Daniel W., 42
  Emaline, 39
  Harvey, 169
  Richard, 31
  Silas, 26
  Temperance, 42
Webb,
  Eliza, 13
  Robert, 13
Welch,
  Eli, 72
  Nancy Jane, 72
Wetherington,
  Casandra, 21
  Joshua, 21
  Mary Ann, 21
Wheeler,
  Ephraim, 4
White,
  Alexander, 14
  Carolina, 125
  Cornelia, 128
  Denson, 163
  Frances Ann, 128
  Henry H., 36
  James B., 49
  Jane, 14
  Jeremiah, 165
  Joanna E., 125
  John W., 14
  Malinda, 165
  Mary Elizabeth, 168
  Michael, 14
  Nathan, 164

INDEX

Rachel, 165
Robert A., 167
William, 110, 130
Zachariah, 129
Whiteman,
  Sarah A., 9
  Susan, 9
  Thomas H., 9
Whitfield,
  Harmon, 117
Wicker,
  Amos, 105
Wiggins,
  A. Eliza, 66
  Harrison, 66
  John, 66(2)
  Joseph, 66
  Matilda, 66
  Samuel, 66
  Sophia, 66
  Thomas, 66
  William, 66
Williams,
  Amy, 28
  Jesse, 47
  Samuel, 105
  Tabitha, 52
  William, 105
Willis,
  Charles A., 23
  Eliza, 23
  Evaline, 22
  George, 22
  Mary A., 22
  Thomas W., 22
Wilson,
  Andrew M., 105
  Elijah, 51
  Frederick L., 30
  John, 44
  John M., 30
  Maria, 19
  Mary Ellen, 30
  Thomas, 19
Wimbley,
  Anderson, 52
  Firite, 52
Wimbly,
  David, 61
  Drury, 61
  Elizabeth Ann, 61
  Finetta, 61
  Frances, 60
  George, 61
  Jasper Newton, 60
  John Weston, 61
  Mary Ann, 61
  Nancy Ellen, 61
  Octavia, 60
  Robert, 62
  Sarah, 56, 61
  Virginia, 60
  William M., 61
Winn,
  Andrew, 105
  Minerva, 105
Winson,
  Elizabeth, 9
  Malileta C., 36
  Mary Jane, 9
  Peter, 9
  William Henry, 36
Winters,
  George, 9
  Maria, 9
Wood,
  Andrew, 44
  Curtis [II], 105
  Curtis [I], 105
  Frederick D., 44
  Jesse, 149
  Mary Jane, 44
  Vernon, 105
Woodall,
  William H., 36
Woodfork,
  Elizabeth, 105
  Gabriel, 105
Woods,
  Adaline, 128
  Jemima, 128
  William, 128
Worthington,
  Indiana, 40
Wright,
  Delphine, 41
  Edmund, 160
  Gonzolda, 152
  Septha E., 152
  Septha [Jr], 152

Y

York,
  Joshua, 48
Young,
  Robert, 67

www.ingramcontent.com/pod-product-compliance
Lightning Source LLC
Chambersburg PA
CBHW080550230426
43663CB00015B/2777